W9-AEW-143

Power, Protest, and the Public Schools

Power, Protest, and the Public Schools

Jewish and African American Struggles in New York City

MELISSA F. WEINER

RUTGERS UNIVERSITY PRESS

NEW BRUNSWICK, NEW JERSEY, AND LONDON

LIBRARY OF CONGRESS CATALOGING-IN-PUBLICATION DATA

Weiner, Melissa F.
  Power, protest, and the public schools : Jewish and African American struggles in
  New York City / Melissa F. Weiner.
    p.   cm.
  Includes bibliographical references and index.
  ISBN 978–0–8135–4772–5 (hardcover : alk. paper)
  1. African Americans—Education—New York (State)—New York. 2. African
  Americans—New York (State)—New York—Social conditions. 3. Jews—
  Education—New York (State)—New York. 4. Jews—New York (State)—New
  York—Social conditions. 5. Public schools—New York (State)—New
  York. 6. Discrimination in education—New York (State)—New
  York. 7. Racism in education—New York (State)—New York. 8. New York
  (N.Y.)—Race relations. 9. New York (N.Y.)—Social conditions. I. Title.
  LC2803.N5W45 2010
  371.829'9607307471—dc22

                                                            2009036233

A British Cataloging-in-Publication record for this book is available
from the British Library.

Visit our Web site: http://rutgerspress.rutgers.edu

Manufactured in the United States of America

To Hillary
For everything

CONTENTS

ACKNOWLEDGMENTS

Countless people have aided me in completing this project. To thank by name everyone who offered me intellectual, moral, and emotional support during these years would be impossible. Below are those who have had the most impact on me. For those unnamed, know that if I knew you between 2002 and 2009, you are appreciated.

I could not have completed this project without the aid of the librarians and archivists at New York City's Municipal Archives, the Schomburg Center for Research in Black Culture, the American Jewish Historical Society, the Jewish Theological Seminary, the YIVO Institute for Jewish Research, Radcliff College's Schlesinger Library, and the Library of Congress, especially Kenneth Cobb, Leonora Gidlund, Julie Koven, Lyn Slome, Elaine Kastel, Karla Goldman, and James Rosenbloom. I owe a special debt of gratitude to David Ment, the New York City Board of Education's archivist, who provided essential information about, and allowed me unfettered access to, the then-unorganized collection.

Academic mentors provided me with both the skills and support necessary to complete this project. Doug Hartmann, Ronald Aminzade, Penny Edgell, and Rose Brewer at the University of Minnesota fostered the development of my methodological skills and theoretical tools necessary to begin my career as a professional sociologist. Their continued support sustained my pursuit of this project as a book. Jonathan Zimmerman's generosity with his time and feedback, reading every word of my manuscript, pushed me to critically examine my assertions and include vital historical information to generate the most historically incisive and complete manuscript possible. Monte Bute enthusiastically talked me through chapter organization, the writing, research, and thinking processes, and conceptual and theoretical arguments. The arsenal of books he recommended to me facilitated the development of a better, and more historically and theoretically grounded, project. Anna Linders's astute observations and probing questions of theoretical issues enhanced the book's attention to sociological details.

My colleagues at Quinnipiac University provided support, advice, and encouragement during the seminal years of this writing. Lynne Hodgson

welcomed me with open arms into the Sociology Department and did everything possible to ensure my academic and personal security at QU. I could not
have been luckier to be hired alongside Cynthia Duarte, with whom, as a race
scholar, I could discuss my research, and who was my closest friend during these
years. Her emotional support was, and continues to be, immeasurable. The next
year, Hillary Haldane quickly became equally integral to my success. Her humor,
integrity, and keen academic insight got me through the darkest days and her
generosity of spirit helped me celebrate the brightest. I am also deeply indebted
to Lori Sudderth, Gloria Holmes, Marilyn Ford, Keith Kerr, Penny Leisring, Alan
Bruce, Kanicka Ingram, Patrick Frazier, and Hans Bergmann, who all provided
me with both the intellectual and emotional support necessary to complete this
project. Dean Bergmann and the College of Arts and Sciences provided generous
summer stipends to complete this manuscript and funds to attend conferences,
where I presented papers based on these findings and received essential feedback and support from the above-mentioned colleagues.

I am deeply grateful for my wonderful students at Quinnipiac University,
who, across courses and disciplines, through in-class conversations and probing
questions, forced me to think about the concepts addressed in this project in
new and different ways. They truly enhanced the final result. I have the honor of
acting as a faculty advisor to the Black Student Union, and these amazing young
men and women, every day, remind me and make me appreciate why I do what
I do. In this capacity, they have upheld my intense interest in this project and in
social justice issues. Their emotional strength has sustained my own. They are
truly my heroes. I would especially like to thank Anastacia Tucker, Carla Brown,
Shana Bennett, Ashley Hobby, Kerry Ellington, Simone Parker, and Olamide
Oduyingbo for their encouragement and inspiration. For the last two years, I
have had the privilege of mentoring Kwegyirba Croffie, who has been integral
to my happiness at QU. Her unwavering support and her astounding and inspi-
rational energy and involvement on campus enhance my own performance as
I try to live up to the title "mentor." Additional students who continue to act
as beacons of possibility from near and far include Mallory Grimste, Jennifer
Buckmeyer, and Jared Zeidman.

The adundant emotional support I received from friends and family was
essential to this book's completion. I am deeply grateful to my grad school
friends, Ana Prata, Trina Smith, Joyce Bell, and Pam Wald, who continue to
offer a friendly ear, eye, or shoulder. Stan Hill's generosity, humor, and ability
to always teach me something new make him one of my favorite people to be
around, whether I need a dose of, or break from, reality. NHCers, especially
Jeanie Andrews, Robyn Brown, Dave Delgrego, and Andrea Weinberger, have
proven themselves as people I can count on for just about anything. Friends
made in Minnesota, Kristin Young, Brett Pawielski, and Sabine Meyer, continue
to make their presence felt.

My family, though very small, has been tremendously supportive from afar as I pursued this project's completion, both during and after graduate school. My grandparents, Irene and Joseph Fuchs, left an indelible imprint on my character and educational career. The values they instilled in me, for education, a commitment to social justice, and a generosity of spirit made me who I am and this research project what it is. The Chalkin family, Hillary, Dennis, Max, and Charlie, graciously opened their home to me as I completed my data collection. Dennis, without hesitation, generously offered to shoot the cover photo and deserves every ounce of credit for the idea. My aunt, Anne Fuchs-Chesney, stood in for my mother at all the important moments. Her presence and support have been more powerful than I could have ever imagined. My "little" brother, David Weiner, has played an increasingly important role in my life, offering everything from encouragement to a good laugh to a ribbing about the Yankee–Red Sox rivalry. I am also grateful for the support of my father, Bruce Weiner.

Neither this book, nor my entire personal or professional trajectory, would have been possible without the love and support of Hillary Kelbick. Words simply cannot capture my gratitude. For nearly twenty years, Hillary has been like a mother to me. Without her unwavering support this book would not exist. It is also fitting that a book devoted primarily to strong female activists, most of whom were mothers, is dedicated to Hillary, one of the strongest and most ideologically invested mothers and women I have ever met.

Finally, my editor, Beth Kressel, earnestly aided every aspect of the book-writing process and offered incisive comments and feedback that made it a clearer, better book. I am deeply indebted to her time and care in making this project what it is.

Power, Protest, and the Public Schools

Introduction

Unlocking the Golden Door and
Unpacking the Great School Myth

"They are our children, not yours!" a Jewish mother shouted in Yiddish at members of New York City's (NYC) Board of Education who refused to improve the overcrowded, and vocationally oriented schools in their neighborhoods even though thousands of Jews had been working toward this effort for years. Forty years later, in 1957, Harlem mothers, known as the Harlem 9, fed up with the segregated, crumbling, overcrowded, and vocationally oriented schools in their neighborhoods, stood in the mayor's chambers demanding to know, "How long are we expected to sit back patiently and sacrifice the future of our children?"[1]

In 1937, Jewish educators and Zionist student groups attempting to institutionalize Hebrew courses in the public schools argued, "Jewish children are filled with a just pride when they see Hebrew on a par today with the outstanding languages of mankind." Over twenty years later, in 1959, African American parents demanded that schools institutionalize courses in African American history, emphasizing their contributions to the nation's narrative, to instill "character, pride, and dignity" in their children.[2]

Popular accounts of Jewish immigrants climbing the social ladder usually describe the key role of public schools in helping these youngsters earn a higher social position than their parents. But city schools did not grant Jewish students special opportunities. In fact, politicians and school administrators marginalized Jewish and African American students similarly at different points in NYC's history. They denied both groups important educational resources that appeared in schools with mostly native-born white students. The Board of Education implemented vocational and subpar curricula and repeatedly refused to address its constituents' very real concerns about the quality of their children's education. Mainstream white society perceived Jews in the early twentieth century, like African Americans during the post-migration 1950s and 1960s, as a racially inferior group less deserving of the public resources granted to other citizens.

1

The following chapters map out exactly how NYC's public schools inhibited social advancement for Jews and African Americans at different time periods; how activists, particularly parents and children, responded to inequality; and what changes, if any, resulted from their activism. Although the response by politicians and school administrators was surely disheartening for those who sought immediate and tangible results, this activism had long-term benefits that would underlie future activism. Jewish and African American protests against school inequality helped each group form a more cohesive identity and gave them the experience they would need to organize effective protests to combat other social inequalities.

Scholars generally apply two different theoretical models to describe Jewish and African American experiences in the United States. Race theories, applied almost exclusively to African Americans, emphasize the role of inequality and constraint in hindering full assimilation into American society. Ethnicity theories, applied to both white ethnics and new immigrants, emphasize movement toward assimilation and similar efforts to meld Old World cultures with American traditions. In reality, race as a social process, a system of power relationships, and structurally embedded meanings, defined the lives of both Jews and African Americans. Comparing their experiences, rather than analyzing them separately, allows for a more nuanced understanding of the way the schools shape racial meanings, patrol the boundaries of whiteness, and undergird a system of oppression.[3]

As shown in subsequent chapters, identity and education are far more complicated than any one theory applied to a particular group. Jews, in fact, did not climb the social hierarchy because of a particular zeal for education and ready assimilation into mainstream society as conventional wisdom indicates. In the first decades of the twentieth century, society racialized Jewish children in ways similar to African American youth, which deprived them of badly needed resources. Educational administrators often described Jewish children as delinquents with high drop-out rates whose limitations were rooted in a history of oppression and poverty. Society's racialization of Jewish immigrants, it turns out, was extremely similar to that of African Americans. Public schools played an important role in enforcing this assumed inferiority.

Both minority groups tried to combat this perception of their racial inferiority through changes to the school curriculum that highlighted each groups' achievements and unique histories. To gain equal recognition of marginalized identities, Jews, between 1929 and 1948, sought Hebrew language courses while African Americans attempted to replace discriminatory texts with those that accurately depicted African American history during the tumultuous years after World War II (1946) until the passage of the Civil Rights Act (1964). During these early protests for multicultural curriculum, activists' narratives reveal how they believed their Jewish and African American identities complemented their American one. These historical predecessors of contemporary culture wars contested the structure and form of education disseminated to Jewish and African American children as the schools struggled to ensure cultural hegemony.[4]

Largely absent from the historical record, these protests and the board's reactions testify to the complicated role the schools played in marginalizing racial minorities, and how students and their parents responded. In addition to combating racism, Jewish and African American protestors sought to affirm their respective status as American citizens deserving of equal access to education. Protestors recognized that schools, as one of the first public institutions in children's lives, mold their citizenship and identity. They realized that improving their children's education would help them achieve social mobility and success throughout life. A change in school curricula and the attitudes of administrators, they hoped, would help remove racial stigma and instead emphasize their similarities to other American youth. Examining protests against resource inequality provides further insight into how Jews and African Americans used schools as "trenches" of contested terrain to demand equality and rearticulate their identities in the face of severe oppression.[5] Asserting their claims as citizens, they sought to equalize resources in their children's schools through rich academic coursework rather than remedial studies, qualified teachers, and repairs to dilapidated school buildings. Scholars such as Lawrence Blum, Will Kymlicka, Tariq Modood, and Iris Young suggest that struggles over resources are really about basic citizenship rights and principles of democracy. The lack of access to school-based resources reveals the board's (and by proxy, the State's) perceptions of these groups as unequal citizens. Neither Jews nor African Americans, many of whom migrated to NYC from overseas and the South to enter these schools, were willing to accept these inequalities. Comparing Jews' efforts to remove the Gary Plan (1914–1917) and the Harlem 9's efforts to improve the segregated and inferior conditions in their children's schools (1956–1960) reveals the ways in which schools hindered these groups' access to citizenship rights.

Documenting Discontent

These stories of protest can only be told by paying specific attention to activists' actions and statements, particularly as they understood them. To do this, chapter 1 briefly reviews Jewish and African American histories to facilitate later embedding of Jewish and African American voices, sentiments and opinions and responses from the Board of Education in their particular social, cultural, and historical context. These histories reveal that neither Jews nor African Americans were considered full and equal citizens of the nation or NYC during these protest episodes. Secondary sources provide deep insight into the social and living conditions of these groups during these eras to paint a detailed picture of contemporary demographic and cultural aspects of each population living in NYC. I then zero in on each group's perceptions of and experiences with education, both historically and in NYC.

Setting the stage for protest descriptions, these histories place the stories, identities, and cultures of these disenfranchised groups at center stage, rather than appearing as silent and passive subjects.[6] Together with their actions and the responses of the schools to them, these voices, which appear prominently in chapters 2 through 5, issue a resounding challenge to the many myths of the public schools as well as those perpetuated by scholars who continue to view different racial groups through different theoretical lenses.

Race, Resources, and Riots

Jews' and African Americans' struggles to improve resources, described in chapter 2, ultimately mobilized hundreds of thousands of community members. Citywide strikes and boycotts challenged segregated and dual school systems for racialized minorities. Most activists rose from the poorest, least enfranchised communities of the city to challenge the mayor, the city's highest authority. Activists mobilized tactics rooted in their groups' historical and contemporary labor and civil rights struggles. Jews, in their efforts to remove the Gary Plan, contested vocational, religious, and military training and requested new schools, academic curriculum, and parental input into school administration. The Harlem 9 demanded an end to de facto segregated schools and the establishment of higher quality curriculum, buildings, and teachers in their neighborhoods' schools as well as community-based parental control over education. In each case, the Board of Education resisted even acknowledging that a problem existed and often reframed activists' arguments to suggest that unequal education was best for these groups. This stabilized the racial hierarchy to retrench resource inequalities and racial identities.

"'Citizen' and 'Citizenship' are powerful words. They speak of respect, of rights, of dignity" (Fraser & Gordon 1994: 90; Glenn 2002). Like any identity, citizenship, and belonging to the American community, is not static. Although (most) Jews and African Americans were both residents of the United States and members of a voting public in New York, this does not mean that they were perceived as equally valued compared to other members of society. That they had to fight for these rights reveals that the state did not consider them of equal worth to other citizens. The Board of Education selectively granted privileges to some groups and denied them to others. Without equal citizenship rights, these groups were kept outside the school's Golden Door and inhibited from achieving social and economic success in America. Chapter 3 documents and explicates the narratives Jews and African Americans used to gain access to these rights and resources. I find that demands for high educational quality sought to improve the situation of the group during eras when both Jews and African Americans existed at or near the bottom of NYC's racial and economic hierarchy. To do this, each group used a politics of semblance emphasizing voter/taxpayer rights, the role of the schools in educating *all* of the city's children equally, and community-controlled education. Of critical import are activists' similar efforts and language to access social, political, and economic opportunity and mobility.

Curriculum, Culture, and Contestation

"Multiculturalism" has become a buzzword in educational circles in the last fifteen years. However, these efforts are not new. Chapter 4 describes Jews' and African Americans' efforts to include Hebrew (1929–1948) and African American history (1946–1964), respectively, to challenge the hegemonic whiteness of the curricular canon. These early efforts to challenge dominant social ideologies are important precursors to today's critical multicultural movement, which has the dual goals of allowing for upward mobility and preserving cultural heritage and identity.[7]

During these efforts, Jews and African Americans worked to remove demeaning images from the curriculum and replace them with equal and accurate accounts of each groups' history. They supplemented this information with opportunities to participate in contemporary struggles that allowed for the convergence of their past and present histories. This critical multicultural education provided Jewish and African American children with practical and culturally rooted knowledge to promote upward mobility.

Comparing these different curricular efforts reveals similarities in material development and dissemination, teacher training, and efforts to institutionalize this curriculum in NYC's public schools through approval by different segments of the educational bureaucracy. Board reaction to these efforts was also comparable. All of these efforts resulted in only small symbolic changes to, rather than full inclusion in, the curriculum. Significant changes to the curriculum would have signaled a structural shift in the perceptions of each group by the Board of Education and other members of the educational establishment. When unsuccessful, Jews and African Americans increasingly relied on extra-academic institutions to achieve these goals and ensure that their children had access to the language, history, and culture of their ancestors.

The content of books and material that students encounter in schools is critical to maintaining and perpetuating racial identities and power relations. However, transformative knowledge and curriculum holds the potential to perpetuate group culture and rearticulate disparaged identities by challenging racialized identities. Chapter 5 features an in-depth examination of activists' narratives and course materials. In addition to demanding a place at the American curricular table, these groups believed that their contributions were vast and varied. Resembling traditional multicultural efforts, Jews and

African Americans highlighted their contributions to world history, Western civilization, and U.S. history. However, these efforts moved beyond traditional multiculturalism, which argues that all groups are equal, to a more critical form that places groups' achievements at the center of history and allows for participation in contemporary movements to recognize liberatory goals. Both Jews and African Americans highlighted the uniqueness of their cultures and disseminated materials designed to allow their children to subvert the dominant racial hierarchy and promote socioeconomic mobility. However, the board rejected these materials and only legitimized the most benign forms. Unable to open the Golden Door, parents built new institutions outside of the schools to provide their children with transformative culturally based knowledge.

Multicultural Social Movements and Reified Racialization

Protests explored in this book represent substantial efforts by two different racial groups to exert change in the schools based on their perceptions of being denied citizenship-based resources. Chapter 6 details the ways in which race, racial differences, the nonnegotiability of racial identities and the resulting discrimination structured the problems experienced and challenged by each group, as well as the opportunities, constraints, and resolutions for each group in each case. I argue that both social movements theories and multiculturalism literatures must consider embedded racial ideologies to fully capture the complex ways in which race affects access to critical social resources, such as quality education. This empirically substantiates the work of Calhoun (1993) and Tilly (2002), who argue that "new" social movements related to group identities are not solely contemporary phenomena. I build on these theories to explicitly describe the ways in which *racial* group identities are central to participation in, and are shaped during, social movements. This chapter introduces new terminology, *critical multicultural social movements*, to describe the role of existing power relationships, race, racial identities, and group cultures in shaping activists' opportunities, resources, and constraints using examples from previous chapters.

Racial identities not only changed during each movement but were critical to the development of later social movements and each group's political and economic success. These new identities reveal the transformative nature of social movements for collective identity development and the importance of examining school-based identity movements to document processes of identity formation. Given the similarities between these two racial groups described in the sociological literature using very different theories of group identity formation, I suggest reconsidering this theoretical binary to generate new and more inclusive theories.

In addition to addressing important identity-based concerns, chapter 6 explicates the role of the public schools, historically and today, in shaping racial identities, inequalities, and power relations. Drawing on both previously described cases and theories highlighting the place of schools within a larger racialized social system, I discuss the important implications of the belief in education to promote upward mobility among disadvantaged groups with the realities of persistent educational inequality, even in the face of concerted efforts to achieve equal treatment. Rooting this discussion in historical conceptions of racial differences reveals the extent to which the schools are invested in maintaining the privileged status of whiteness.

Aftermath: Diverging Racial Histories Post–Ocean Hill–Brownsville

When most people think about Jewish and African American conflict in NYC's public schools, they think not of the cases described in this book but of the Brownsville–Ocean Hill conflict and the ensuing teacher strikes, charges of anti-Semitism, and Black Panther marches (cf. Podair 2005). During this prolonged experiment, rather than each group challenging the schools independently, as occurred in the cases appearing here, Jews and African Americans faced off against each other. In 1968, NYC's long-simmering racial tension boiled over in Brownsville–Ocean Hill. Frustrated and angry about generations of educational inequality and the lack of African American control in the schools, the African American community demanded and received a key to the Golden Door, community control. Once inside, African Americans dismissed white teachers, many of whom were Jewish. By this point, American society viewed Jews similar to other whites. To African Americans, Jews, who were overrepresented in the educational establishment, represented the dominant white majority. Chapter 7 highlights the educational and social developments that have occurred since these historical cases. These are used to provide insight into both Jews' and African Americans' contemporary educational and racial statuses, Jewish and African American relations today, and the future of education for minority groups.

Central to the diverging histories of Jews and African Americans in America is the transformational aspect of whiteness in allowing Jews access to educational opportunities. Unable to find jobs during the Depression due to anti-Semitism, Jews stayed in schools through high school and attended college. By the 1970s, Jews, as whites, could use the public schools to achieve upward mobility. Many argue that Jews, like other European groups, particularly Italians, became white during and after World War II. During the war, rabbis served as military chaplains in every unit, signaling the army's acceptance of Judaism as an official American religion. Jews served valiantly alongside other European Americans against a common enemy, resulting in the development of an American identity divorced from previous national or ethnic affiliations. Many Americans expressed revulsion with the Holocaust and sympathized with Jewish victims, resulting in a global decline in anti-Semitism. After the war, like other European Americans, Jews gained access to a wide variety of veterans' benefits that allowed them to attend college and purchase homes in suburbs (those without restrictive covenants), thereby moving physically, occupationally, and socioeconomically away from racialized city neighborhoods and social positions. As Jews became part of the establishment, particularly in NYC, they perceived racial difference through a liberal lens. This ideology placed responsibility for success on group prowess and ambition rather than recognizing that structural inequalities, even with the passage of the Civil Rights, Voting Rights, and Fair Housing Acts, continued to hinder African Americans' opportunities. During the war, a critical juncture when racial equality for all groups could have been realized, the U.S. armed forces kept African Americans segregated and sectioned off from their fellow soldiers, and civilian Americans, and therefore consideration as equal citizens. For African Americans, this era saw the growth of an oppositional consciousness in the face of persistent educational inequality. Jews' unwavering belief that African American success would only come with their willingness to integrate and conform to American society, combined with African Americans' increased demands for autonomy, resulted in a clash of cultures during the Ocean Hill–Brownsville conflict of 1968–1971.

Because of these different experiences, both in the schools and in American society generally, Jews and African Americans maintained different ideas regarding equal treatment in the public schools. As whites, Jews no longer had to worry about racism blocking their children's access to high-quality education. Believing in an open American society, Jews argued that simply improving conditions within the public schools, rather than completely changing their structure, would allow African Americans to succeed educationally. Not recognizing the deeply rooted structures of racial inequality that privileged Jews while oppressing African Americans, Jews could not understand African Americans' desires to operate the schools autonomously rather than assimilate. But African Americans could never fully assimilate into a society intent on maintaining racial differences. Instead, African Americans sought community control of teacher hiring, classroom practices, and curriculum.

African Americans wanted more than just the key to the Golden Door, they wanted the power to completely remodel the insides of the building to promote equal treatment. Furnishings included autonomy in developing curriculum and policies to empower African American children through culturally based knowledge and learning styles. The practice of collective advancement over individualism challenged American ideologies of individualism and meritocracy. African Americans sought curriculum and resource-related changes that explicitly addressed institutional racism that had, for generations, kept them outside the door. African American educators believed these two important changes would allow future generations to rise above institutional racism and promote social, political, and economic success. The curriculum and practices found in these schools appeared in both African American cases described in this book. Freedom Schools opened and transformative knowledge became central to the schools' curriculum and structure as Rhody McCoy reconstructed African American education in NYC from the ground up. Jews' deep faith in racial liberalism left them unable to see the logic for curriculum and teaching styles rooted within the African American community. Facing a Board of Education reluctant to completely hand over the keys, much less allow for change, the experiment would not last long. After only three short years, the Jewish-dominated teachers union and board demanded back the keys. The door was again shut to African Americans.

This ideological split entrenched differences between groups that had, for generations, collaborated to counter social inequality. By 1971, the end of the Ocean Hill–Brownsville experiment, New Yorkers recognized Jews as white. Increasingly, Jews fled the city and left African Americans to fend for themselves in a city crippled by budget shortfalls. As social services dried up, neighborhoods crumbled, and the Bronx burned in the latter half of the 1970s, Jews viewed African Americans from afar as their own children attended the nation's best schools in the suburbs of Westchester and Nassau counties. Dropout rates skyrocketed among African American children attending overcrowded and crumbling schools built nearly a hundred years earlier. And today, NYC's African American children remain mired in the same low-quality public education they experienced during the Depression. However, the Brownsville–Ocean Hill experiment offers important insights into an alternative key to the Golden Door. Though still racialized, NYC's African American community gained sufficient power to force open the door and promote quality self-sustaining education within their community.

Contemporary Implications of a Historically Locked Door

The failure to acknowledge the similarities in educational prejudice faced at different time periods by both Jews and African Americans is itself an injustice. It obscures the role of America's schools—even in supposedly enlightened places such as New York City compared to the Jim Crow South—in promoting racism and denying educational resources based on prejudice. Policymakers could more effectively tackle resource inequality in today's schools by recognizing that even minority groups mythologized as the benefactors of public education, actually had to fight their local schools. The conclusion engages these findings to raise questions regarding the educational futures of contemporary immigrant and minority groups.

Schools continue to be championed as benevolent institutions providing marginalized and disenfranchised social groups with equal access to opportunities for social mobility and equality. This belies the reality that American public schools are simply one institution within a larger political system. When that political system is structured by racism, as Eduardo Bonilla-Silva (1997, 2006) and Joe Feagin (2005) describe, it becomes nearly impossible for the schools, run by administrators subscribing to society's dominant ideology, to do anything but replicate existing social inequality. American public schools—like so many public institutions—have played a central role in enforcing racial inequalities and ascribing racial identities.[8]

Recognizing this, minority parents have, throughout American history, challenged these inequalities to no avail. Although educational historians have examined how various social groups have succeeded or not in America's schools, no one has explicitly compared the activism against school inequality by two different racial groups. Doing so reveals how school administrators, regardless of students' race, reinforce the racial hierarchy and status quo.

1

New York City's Racial
and Educational Terrain

Many sociologists and historians would have us believe that Jews' and African Americans' experiences in America, and in American public schools in particular, could not have been more different. The usual tales depict Jews as hardworking, intellectually gifted immigrants who used innate abilities to rise through the ranks of America's racial and class hierarchies. On the other hand, African Americans are often looked at with contempt by the public and politicians, or with pity by sociologists, as a group that, unlike Jews, did little to improve their social, political, and economic situation or as agency-less individuals trapped in a racist system.[1] These beliefs and stories obscure similarities in both groups' social, political, and economic standings and their experiences in America, particularly in New York City. Their narratives—particularly their racial identities—diverge most clearly after World War II, at a point in American history when society offered Jews the opportunity to join mainstream America but did not extend the same offer to African Americans.

The story of racial diversity in New York City (NYC) begins many centuries earlier, in the early 1600s when racially, ethnically, and religiously diverse peoples arrived seeking social, political, and economic freedoms. In 1621, when the Dutch West India Company appropriated Manhattan for twenty-four dollars in beads and trinkets, slaves, indentured servants, middle-class merchants, elite explorers, and foreign royalty mixed in the streets. But they did not do so equally. Racial privilege, reinforced by wealth and land-owning and voting rights, maintained this hierarchy for centuries.[2]

Race in NYC, where Jews and African Americans have coexisted since Jews arrived in 1654, has always been contentious. Whites have always treated both groups as racial outsiders. But their processes of racialization differed considerably. Throughout their history in NYC, these groups jostled for position on an ever-changing racial terrain. While similarities between Jews and African

Americans resulted in similar experiences at many points in their histories, African Americans' history as an enslaved population in America proved the most important factor in their continued educational inequality.

Before the Great Migrations

In colonial NYC, with Native Americans considered the group with the lowest racial status, whites endowed free African Americans with more rights than Jews, who were unwelcome in Manhattan. The Dutch West India Company only allowed Jews to settle on the island if they promised not to become a burden to the colony (this became known as the Stuyvesant Compact). Free African Americans could vote, bear arms, and own property. Jews "were prohibited from owning land, exercising the vote, holding public office, worshiping in public and possessing firearms" (Foote 2004: 43). Nor could Jews live inside city walls. But life for African Americans was far from ideal. Slavery existed in NYC at the highest rates north of the Mason-Dixon line until 1827. Whites subjected African American slaves and freemen to residential segregation, financially based voting restrictions, exploitation, and fear of being stolen South under the Fugitive Slave Law. National debates about slavery, rather than enhancing African Americans' freedoms, found New Yorkers institutionalizing their inferior status.[3]

The Civil War affected Jews and African Americans in important ways. The war that freed the slaves heightened white supremacy and racist ideologies in NYC. On the grounds of their "whiteness," European immigrants demanded jobs, high-quality housing, schools, and full citizenship rights. By the war's end, immigrants, most of whom were Irish, had violently pushed African Americans out of the city during the infamous Draft Riots and exposed largely hidden racist ideologies. On the other hand, recent German Jewish arrivals used skills brought from Europe to become upwardly mobile merchants catering to the expanding Midwestern frontier (Cohen 1984; Goren 1970; Grinstein 1947; Sarna 1997). They began distribution, wholesale, clothing and manufacturing companies, many of which, such as Macy's, Sears, and Saks Fifth Avenue, still exist. German Jews maintained their social exclusivity, but their relatively small numbers and accommodation to American styles, values, and ideologies allowed them a measure of security.[4]

Following the Civil War, African Americans increased their presence in the city's business and industrial sectors but remained politically disenfranchised until the 1870 ratification of the Fifteenth Amendment. Though not considered white, Jews never faced this restriction in NYC. In the post–Civil War era, with whiteness established as the prerequisite for full citizenship, society's treatment of African Americans became the measuring stick to which immigrants compared their own status, asserting their rights, as whites, to well-paying jobs in industry and construction. As Jews assimilated, African Americans faced increasing exclusion. The racial hierarchy had flipped. But Jewish and African American similarities in NYC persisted, particularly as each community experienced dramatic population gains from immigrants who came to New York seeking a better life in the decades during and after the turn of the twentieth century. They met with similar reactions from previously settled Jews and African Americans and provoked similar racist responses from the city's political establishment and populace.

New York City Beckons: The Great Migrations

Jews arriving from the Pale resembled African American migrants from the South in terms of their historical experiences with violent oppression, occupational options, and limited educational opportunities. Poor and uneducated, Jews and African Americans arrived in NYC with outdated agrarian and primitive industrial skills that consigned them to low-wage jobs while cultural differences heightened discrimination against each group. Seeking economic success and social freedom for their children, Jews and African Americans held education in the highest regard but it often eluded their grasp.

Rural, Impoverished, Uneducated Jews in the Pale

During the fifty-year period between 1870 and 1920, two million Jews, one third of Eastern Europe's Jewish population, fled Russia's Pale of Settlements (present-day Poland, Lithuania, Belorussia, and Ukraine) and arrived on the shores of Manhattan. Barred from Russian schools and facing increased persecution, mandatory conscription, and deadly pogroms following the assassination of Alexander II in 1881, Jewish immigrants came to America seeking social and religious freedom (Kosak 2004; Nathans 2004).[5]

Jews in the Pale lived in extreme poverty. In rural areas, three to five families with up to thirty people crowded into dirty two- to three-room huts. Rough land inhibited grazing animals and yielded only "Jewish fruits" (Rischin 1978: 29)—beets, carrots, cabbage, onions, cucumbers, garlic, and horseradish. Scarce and expensive meat meant most Jews lived on bread, water, and vegetables. The Pale's cities, like other cities throughout Europe, confined Jews to walled-off ghettoes with gates that only opened during daylight hours. These conditions, combined with the community's isolation from medicine's significant advances of the early 1900s, resulted in high rates of disease, malnutrition, and death (Rubinow 1907).

In the Pale, most Jews worked as artisans, "cobblers, tailors, blacksmiths, tanners, hatmakers, carpenters, tinsmiths, harness makers, butchers, bakers, watchmakers, jewelers, and furriers" (Rischin 1978: 25–26). Despite laws to the contrary, Jews established small factories and worked as independent artisans producing high-quality products with outdated technology in nonmechanized factories. Women in the Pale did not attend school but worked and retained responsibility for managing the family's finances and businesses, from which they gained considerable knowledge of commerce, artisanship, and arithmetic (Rubinow 1907). Though Jewish men and women brought these skills to America, the market's saturation with similarly skilled immigrants and high costs of self-employment left most unable to capitalize on these experiences. Only factory workers entering the low-wage garment industry transferred their skills from the Pale to America.

Increasing unemployment and persecution in the Pale altered young working-class Jews' cultural terrain. Intrigued with Marxist socialism, they converted the Pale into a hotbed of revolutionary action and ushered in a new era in Eastern European Jewish history. Suddenly, young Jews refused to submit to tyranny and exercised revolutionary movements in coordinated strikes to improve working conditions and wages. These movements "stoked the fires of Jewish nationalism" (Rischin 1978: 46). As politics and pogroms forced them from the Pale, Jews brought their ideologies and networks to NYC's Lower East Side.

For most of their history in Eastern Europe, Jews' only route to education was via Torah study, as legal and extralegal quotas excluded them from state schools and universities and restricted them to religious education (Dubnow 1916; Rubinow 1907). For most Jewish boys, school meant only religious lessons until age thirteen. Learning Russian and math were forbidden. After their bar mitzvah, most entered the trades as apprentices to their father or uncles. Laws forbidding them from being tradesmen or master craftsmen in the Pale, or moving outside it for work, severely restricted their economic potential. And Jewish girls, forbidden from attending religious schools, learned only enough Yiddish at home to read and write a letter. Not until reaching America could Jewish boys and girls acquire a secular education.

Rural, Impoverished, Uneducated African Americans in the South

Prior to two large waves of migration, nearly 90 percent of African Americans lived impoverished existences in the rural South (Crew 1987; Meier & Rudwick 1976; Scheiner 1965; Trotter 1991). Tied to the land through the sharecropping system and laws prohibiting them from most jobs, African American families found themselves deeper and deeper in debt every year. Flooding, and a crop-destroying boll weevil infestation in 1915, compounded low wages, and decimated the Southern economy. Without cotton to pick, African American unemployment rose. Many sought refuge in Southern cities, where jobs continued to elude them. During these eras of economic duress, whites increasingly relied on lynching to reimpose the social order, and this heightened African Americans' instincts to leave the South permanently.

Pushed out of the South and pulled north by social, political, and economic freedoms, including higher wages, a shorter workday, and more job opportunities in the war-related industries, hundreds of thousands of African Americans moved North during each world war. There, they found less political and legal segregation and more freedom than ever before. And for the first time in American history, African American children were freed from the cotton fields and could attend school for the entire academic year.

During each migration, although those who left had more education than those who stayed, higher levels of educational attainment in the North meant migrants had less education than African Americans already living in the North (Reid 1927). This meant that, like recent Jewish transplants from the Pale, they were least qualified for most jobs and found themselves in the city's lowest-skilled and paid jobs. Many African Americans thus worked alongside Jews in garment industries.

Whites explicitly and consistently denied African Americans the education necessary for equal citizenship and full inclusion in American society. Yet African Americans have always fought for education to remove their "badge of slavery." With literacy punishable by death during slavery, African Americans risked their lives to learn to read and write. As the only group in America ever banned from education by federal policy, former slaves and their descendents continually demanded that local, state, and federal authorities provide them with education to access the status, benefits, and privileges of citizenship.[6]

Following a brief respite in the history of unequal education during Reconstruction, when the Freedmen's Bureau opened hundreds of schools across the South for former slaves, whites consistently denied education to African American children. Whites' racist projects politically and educationally disenfranchised African Americans by blocking their votes and redistributing funds to white schools, thereby strengthening the connection between education, citizenship, and whiteness. Poorly funded public schools emphasized vocational training to encourage African Americans to accept low wages and replicate their servant-class status. The sharecropping system's reliance on African American debt peonage guaranteed children's labor in the fields rather than regular school attendance. This segregated system ensured African Americans' stagnation on the lowest rungs of the social and racial ladder and their second-class citizenship status. Confronted with these inequalities, African Americans raised money, built schools, and hired teachers. Though poor, these schools fostered a strong sense of community. Teachers nurtured African American children and provided them with safe spaces to learn, express their ideas, and develop the tools necessary to survive and succeed in a white world.[7]

Moving North, African Americans perceived education as the key to upward mobility and the way out of segregated, economically depressed industries. But they encountered educational racism resembling that in the South. Writing of Northern schools in 1935, W.E.B. Du Bois stated that "Negroes are admitted and tolerated, but they are not educated; they are crucified" (331). Never content with inferior education, African American parents asserted their children's educational rights, often seeking new schools and resource equalization within a segregated framework rather than integration (Dougherty 2004; Douglas 2005).

The Promised Land? After the Great Migrations

Faced with similar problems, Jews and African Americans left the Pale and the American South for NYC. The great migrations of each group dramatically increased their representation in the city's population, resulting in similar effects on their communities' social, political, and economic conditions. Increased anti-Semitism and racism found Jews and African Americans encountering similar constraints as economically marginalized political outsiders. But within these population centers, Jews and African Americans developed and maintained insular networks, institutions, and cultural traditions to contend with discrimination. These cultures became essential tools in Jews' and African Americans' attempts to secure educational equality for their children as the city clamped down on their potential for success.

Demographic Shifts and Social Conditions

If the term "underclass" had existed in the early twentieth century, scholars and politicians would have applied it to Jews. However, the contemporary common perception of Jews as a "model minority" obscures the complex structural inequalities and their position in the class and racial hierarchy of America. The first decades of the twentieth century found Jews both economically deprived and socially isolated. Not only were they a large (and expanding) segment of the population, but differences in language and dress made them highly visible. At the turn of the century, with African Americans representing a negligible percentage of NYC's total population, Jews now resided with African Americans on the bottom of the racial ladder. This would be the case until the mid-twentieth century, when Jews became white and African Americans' status diminished.

By 1920, NYC held the largest concentration of Jews of any city worldwide. Their population tripled from 510,000 in 1901 to 1.5 million in 1915, when they comprised nearly 28 percent of the city's population. Comparatively, in 1910, only 91,709 African Americans lived in NYC, where they were poor but "invisible." In crowded tenement districts on Manhattan's Lower East Side and Harlem, and in Flatbush and Brownsville in Brooklyn, highly concentrated Jewish populations contended with dirt, disease, and high unemployment, juvenile delinquency, and dropout rates. Low pay ($400 a year when the city average was $600) forced many families to either employ children at home after school or remove children from school to work in sweatshops alongside their parents. Many Jewish families took in boarders to pay the rent and received charity from the Hebrew Immigrant Aid Society (HIAS). In other words, in 1910, the "Lower East Side tenement was every bit as dismaying as the Negro slum" (Greer 1972: 133).[8]

These social conditions made crime, particularly juvenile delinquency, "endemic to the Lower East Side" (Rischin 1986: 90). Jewish criminals, including members of the notorious Murder Inc., made headlines nationwide (Cohen 1999). In 1909, approximately 3,000 Jewish children were brought before the Juvenile Court (Rischin 1986). A police commissioner went so far as to argue that 50 percent of all delinquents were Jewish (Greer 1972; Steinberg 1989). He was wrong, but his statement reveals how many New Yorkers, and Americans nationwide, perceived Jews. As the Depression set in, so too did nativism and anti-Semitism (Wenger 2003). The Ku Klux Klan, Father Charles Coughlin, and Henry Ford's *Dearborn Independent* blamed the nation's economic woes on the Jews. America listened. Employers refused to hire Jews, resulting in higher unemployment for Jews than for other European whites. Psychologists worried that extensive anti-Semitism would produce an inferiority complex among young American Jews, an argument also mobilized regarding African American children (Diner 2003).

As the "Negro Mecca," "Negro Heaven," "City of Refuge," "the Promised Land," and a "Negro Metropolis" (Brandt 1996; Johnson 1991; McKay 1940; Podair 2003; Scheiner 1965), NYC, and Harlem in particular, was the ultimate destination for African Americans hoping to improve their and their children's occupational and educational opportunities. In the early twentieth century, the African American population expanded from 17,580 in 1860 to 91,709 by 1910 with new arrivals from the Atlantic South prior to the turn of the century, and from the West Indies after 1900. Yet this was still only 2 percent of Manhattan's population. African Americans competed fiercely with Germans, Italians, and Irish immigrants for low-wage jobs. Other African Americans took advantage of segregated middle-class industries to create a vibrant professional class. By the Depression, the African American population had exploded to 458,444 in 1940 and continued to expand to 747,608 in 1950 and 1,087,931 (14 percent of the city's population) by 1960 (Glazer & Moynihan 1963). Of these, many spent more than 40 percent of their income on rent, took in boarders, and held rent parties to pay bills, much like Jews had a half-century earlier.

Postwar changes in the economy created housing and employment crises and entrenched the urban economic ghetto. In 1945, NYC was the "premier industrial city," with more than 40 percent of the working population employed in the industrial sector. But in the ten years after World War II, the economy shifted from blue- to white-collar. The 1949 Federal Housing Act allowed the government to financially assist private land developers rebuilding "blighted and destroyed areas." This kernel of legislature allowed urban renewal to destroy both neighborhoods and industries employing African Americans, leaving them unemployed and homeless at rates far higher than whites. Displaced residents poured into Bedford-Stuyvesant, Harlem, and the South Bronx, compounding concentrated poverty. Exacerbating these problems, white flight, facilitated by government policies for white veterans, diminished the property tax base and public funding for essential services. By the 1950s, African American neighborhoods existed as internal colonial outposts, policed by members of the racist state, with its citizens confined to second-class public services and infrastructure to maintain structural inequality.[9]

Nevertheless, African Americans, like Jews during the 1920s, made important gains in the postwar era. African American women nearly doubled their representation in professional, clerical, and managerial fields (from 4 to 7 percent) while increased union membership allowed African Americans' salaries to begin to catch up to whites (Glazer & Moynihan 1963). Antidiscrimination laws allowed many to acquire secure and well-paying jobs in the government sector. But for most, little had changed and NYC's African American residents remained mired in poverty and socially, economically and educationally disenfranchised.

Aggravating Jews' and African Americans' economic duress, whites politically disenfranchised both groups. Although whites lifted most restrictions against Jews' ability to vote and hold local office by the Civil War, African Americans, even in NYC, could not vote until 1873. Nationally, poll taxes, literacy requirements, and grandfather clauses kept African Americans disenfranchised well into the twentieth century. Neither Jews' nor African Americans' large populations during the 1910s–1930s and 1940s–1960s, respectively, translated into political clout. In NYC, Jews and African Americans, though large in number, voted disproportionately less than other groups, were uncommitted to a particular political party, and lacked sufficient representation in city, state, and federal government to promote improvements for their communities.[10]

Cultural Institutions and Calamities

Arriving in NYC for similar reasons, and experiencing similarly large population influxes, Jewish and African American communities now had the numbers and communal institutions necessary to confront racial inequalities. Both groups used community-embedded cultural resources to provide for newcomers. At the same time, Jewish and African American elites expressed increasing concern about negative reprisals due to immigration. These new waves of highly visible low-income migrants, with different styles of dress and speech, far outweighed each community's middle classes and alarmed white New Yorkers, who enacted and engaged in social policies and practices that enforced these groups' difference from the larger population. The African American and Jewish middle-class, though small, lost their tentative position of power as sentiment turned sharply against these groups. NYC's Jews felt anti-Semitism's peak between 1910 and World War II. Social clubs expelled their German Jewish cofounders while boards of major industries, particularly financial and industrial corporations, resorts, and hotels barred Jews and colleges imposed quotas. Jews experienced the sharpest reversal in status compared to African Americans as whites stopped considering German Jews as "almost white," revealing the perpetual contestability of racial status.

African Americans faced increasing competition over low-wage jobs and overcrowding as new immigrants pushed into their neighborhoods and pushed African Americans out. Social supports in African American communities simply could not keep up with the demand for aid generated by increasing concentrated poverty. This poverty, visible to European immigrants in adjacent neighborhoods, and often subject to media scrutiny, provided whites with all the evidence they needed to perceive African Americans as different and inferior to themselves, in contrast to other Europeans who, by the 1950s, had begun experiencing economic mobility.

To reverse this pattern, both Jews and African Americans engaged and expanded upon existing organizations to promote upward mobility and cultural assimilation. In doing so, they strengthened and heightened collective group identities. Jewish fraternal orders, mutual benefit societies, burial associations, orphanages, hospitals, and schools, legacies of the Stuyvesant Compact, struggled to clothe, feed, and shelter recent immigrants. The very existence of such institutions testifies to the economic duress under which Jews found themselves through much of NYC's history. While few Jews went to NYC's public almshouses, most received some form of aid from the city's dozens of Jewish charities (Grinstein 1947).

Wealthy, mostly German, Jews created educational facilities, synagogue centers, and philanthropies to preserve Jewish culture, Americanize "traditional" Russian Jews, unify NYC's Jewish community, and protect it from an anti-Semitic grip that exacerbated social and economic disenfranchisement (Brumberg 1986; Dushkin 1918; Goren 1970; Gorelick 1981; Moore 1981; Prell 1999; Rischin 1978). But they did so condescendingly (Rischin 1986). For example, the Jewish Educational Alliance forbade Yiddish, deprecated Russian Jews' culture, admonishing them to embrace American styles. Most Russian Jews resisted these efforts, sent their children to Old World–style *cheders* and participated in *landsmanshaftn*, hometown organizations (Howe 1976; Rischin 1978; Soyer 1997). Although not planning on returning to Russia, as other immigrants often did, these Jews contented themselves with maintaining their cultures while assimilating just enough to promote their children's success in America (Kosak 2000; Prell 1999).

Lacking a wealthy population base and religious organizations with substantial budgets, African Americans had more difficulty addressing poverty than did Jews. Not that they did not try. Churches, fraternal organizations, informal networks, and established organizations, such as the National Urban League, greeted each wave of African American migrants (Johnson 1991; Reid 1927; Scheiner 1965). They also conducted employment campaigns to place workers in white-owned businesses, promote tenants' rights, improve wages, and provide benefits for the poor. While achieving some successes, they were ultimately limited by American society's racist system.

Collective Consciousness and Cultures

Fostered by community-based organizations and daily interaction between new migrants and long-established residents of segregated neighborhoods, Jews and African Americans developed strong communal cultures and collective consciousnesses. *Yiddishkeit*, the "New Negro" of the Harlem Renaissance, Zionist, and Pan-African nationalist movements integrated historical and contemporary experiences in America and abroad. Together, these new interpretations of American inequality and networks of interaction laid the groundwork for movements seeking social, political, and economic equality.

Within the Jewish community, cultures deeply rooted in oppositional consciousnesses and religious traditions developed through centuries of repeated expulsion and ghettoization. In America, everything changed. A backdrop of secularism, Americanization campaigns, and multiple ethnic groups highlighted Jews' unique cultures. Although they adapted their ethnic and religious cultures, they retained their oppositional outlook. *Landsmanshaftn* and other Jewish voluntary organizations reinforced communal solidarity and cultural norms (Soyer 1997). *Yiddishkeit*, which embraced European Jewish culture and folk traditions, flourished in Jewish neighborhoods and appeared in Jewish magazines, newspapers, theater, and musical venues (Howe 1976; Rischin 1978). Jewish popular culture complicated race relations as Jews both appeared in blackface minstrel shows and condemned discrimination against African Americans in multiple media (Diner 1998; 2003).

Brought by Eastern European Jews from the Pale, Zionism surfaced in America in the 1880s (Blau 1976). However, Jews' daily struggles for economic survival in America made Zionism an important, but ethereal, ideology until after the turn of the century. Theodore Herzl's *Der Judenstaat*, published in 1897, breathed new life into the movement by appealing to Americanizing Jews. Despite raising questions of Jewish loyalty to America while supporting a sovereign Jewish state, Zionism gained popularity in the 1920s and 1930s and, by World War II, had become a "rallying cry" that "captured the imagination and loyalty of most American Jews" (Diner 2003: 88). When Israel was founded in 1948, more than a million American Jews belonged to a Zionist organization.

For centuries, African American revolutionary ideologies flourished in NYC. Throughout the city's history, segregated neighborhoods provided safe spaces for African Americans to exercise their cultural traditions and voice social critiques without being circumscribed by white oppression (Bush 1999). A variety of community-based institutions, such as churches, voluntary organizations, and businesses, allowed for autonomous discourse regarding identity, oppression, and social change. With five African American newspapers, NYC was also the nation's African American publishing center (Scheiner 1965).

As Zionism captured the nationalist imagination of American Jews, African Americans looked to African independence movements and images of Mother Africa (Von Eschen 1997). This connection to Africa, deeply rooted in slave culture, rose to the surface of African American consciousness during the early 1900s and remained prominent for the rest of the century. Highlighting African Americans' noble African roots, Marcus Garvey and his Universal Negro Improvement Association fostered cross-class solidarity through rallies, parades, and opportunities to purchase stock in the Black Star Line, devoted to returning African Americans to Africa. Garvey's efforts pointed African Americans east, toward Africa's independence movements and left an indelible impression on their collective psyches.

During the Harlem Renaissance, an outpouring of art, music, and literature emphasized African Americans' experiences in the United States. Most highlighted African Americans' double consciousness as descendents of forced migrants indelibly stamped with slavery and discrimination in America. Rather than the pervasive popular stereotypes of plantation slaves shucking and jiving, artists and writers highlighted African Americans' emotions, daily life experiences, and struggles against an all-encompassing repressive system. Zora Neale Hurston, Ralph Ellison, Langston Hughes, Claude McKay, and Alain Locke spurned white assumptions for racial consciousness and pride in the face of one of the world's most oppressive racial systems.

Cultural Consciousness to Collective Action

Jews and African Americans used newly developed and long-standing local networks and communal ties to challenge economic marginalization and exploitation. While African Americans consolidated across class lines to target NYC's white power structure, class divisions found Jewish protests targeting powerful figures both within and external to their community.

Most Russian Jewish immigrants worked in German Jewish–run industries, where they faced low wages and poor working conditions. Seeking workplace control and the removal of the task system that increased production without increasing wages, many Russian Jews joined and organized unions in the Jewish-dominated garment industry. Assailing their "slave wages" received as "white slaves," Jews demanded clocks on factory floors, sewing machines, free electricity, and regular pay (Kosak 2000: 112). By 1910, 400,000 of NYC's Jewish men and women (nearly one quarter) belonged to a union and, between 1911 and 1913, participated in 304 strikes (Dubofsky 1968; Kosak 2000; Rischin 1978). Using synagogues as free spaces to address secular concerns, Jews improved their wages and working conditions and enhanced a collective solidarity based on the socialist tradition of challenging unfair social conditions. Simultaneously, Jewish women successfully organized against price gauging in the kosher meat industry while enhancing informal networks to increase participation and share recipes for meatless meals with their neighbors (Ewen 1985; Hyman 1980; Sterba 2003).

Shut out of most unions, African Americans did not sit idly by as the poverty and unemployment of the Depression struck their community the hardest. African Americans drew on their cultures of resistance and traditions of activism to protest the racist system confining them to one of America's worst urban ghettoes. Fired first at the Depression's onset, the African American unemployment rate remained at 60 percent until World War II. Tensions loomed large during the Depression and the war as economic stability eluded African Americans. White institutions held African Americans in financial servitude through control of local businesses and hiring, apartment rentals, and retail establishments. To combat price gouging and discriminatory hiring practices, Harlemites waged a "Don't Buy Where You Can't Work" campaign, successfully boycotting white department stores until they hired African American clerks. In addition to whites' financial control over African Americans, police brutality and surveillance kept African Americans trapped in an urban colonialist outpost. African American frustration erupted during the 1935 and 1943 Harlem riots. These commodity riots, with participation spanning classes, ages, and genders, grew directly out of African American desires for self-rule and anger with white ownership and police discrimination.[11]

World War: Ambivalence, Opposition, and Honorable Service

Jews' experiences during World War I resemble African Americans' experiences during World War II. In both cases, existing racism and developing oppositional cultures and consciousnesses rooted in cultural knowledge of past oppression collided to generate activism and networks of solidarity. Jews and African Americans responded to World Wars I and II, respectively, with both ambivalence and activism. During World War I, Jews initially supported Germany, who they perceived as more lenient than their former Russian oppressors. But with many family and friends still living overseas, and in the war zone, American Jews concerned for their co-religionists' safety founded organizations to send money to them. On the home front, having lost their families' primary breadwinners and with military paychecks often delayed, Jews spent the war years in poverty. For many African Americans, World War II—and American's involvement with the military campaign to free European and Asian peoples from oppression—seemed irrelevant and hypocritical given the resemblance between American racism and Hitler's anti-Semitism. Indeed, some African Americans believed their lives would improve if Germany or Japan won the war. Others supported the Japanese for standing up to Western imperialism. These attitudes reveal the extent to which African Americans experienced alienation from American society and its institutions.[12]

The American military discriminated against Jews during the First World War and African Americans during both wars. In basic training, Jews contended with language differences, a lack of kosher food and rabbis, and open anti-Semitism among officers and fellow soldiers. Even in the trenches, overt anti-Semitism kept Jewish officers to a minimum and covert discrimination resulted in isolation from fellow doughboys. From the battlefronts to the armament industries, white officers ensured African Americans participated in World War II at the lowest and most menial levels. Segregated in hard labor units, most African American soldiers spent the war in traditional servile roles building barracks, hauling wood, and serving as cooks and janitors. Not until late in the war did the War Department activate African Americans for armed duty, but even then, refusing to give bullets to infantrymen until they were on the front lines. At home, the army treated African American citizen soldiers worse than Japanese interns and captured Nazi prisoners of war. During prisoner transports, the army sat African Americans in second-class cars while Nazis rode in first class, as whites.[13]

Jews' and African Americans' networks of activism and support provided them with the cultural tools necessary to, respectively, protest the draft and wage a war against discrimination at home and abroad in a wide-reaching Double V campaign. American Jews opposed the draft because of their experiences with forced conscription in Russia, which tore apart families and destroyed Jewish communities. Community-based draft boards reminded NYC's Jews of the Kehillah, Jewish leaders in the Pale who decided which young men to draft, making them complicit in their community's destruction. Socialist papers, including the *New York Call*, the *Masses*, and the Yiddish *Jewish Daily Forward*, ran editorials opposing the draft while local organizations staged public protests. Nevertheless, young Jewish men joined at similar rates as other immigrant groups, revealing their desires to defend their country and prove their fitness for American citizenship in the face of rising discrimination.

African American frustrations simmered during World War II as whites nationwide subjected them to racial violence, including lynching uniformed servicemen, even as they risked their lives for their country. The Double V campaign targeted racism at home and fascism overseas. Nationally, newspapers, the NAACP, the National Urban League, and everyday citizens demanded an end to segregation in the army and its industries, as well as in housing, employment, education, and public services (Dalfiume 1968; Kersten 2002). Recognizing their potential to expose racism during a war against fascism, the biggest victory came following A. Philip Randolph's threat to march on Washington. In June 1941, President Franklin Roosevelt signed Executive Order 8802 banning racial discrimination in government employment and defense industries. The order mildly improved conditions for war industries employees but not for African American soldiers.[14]

By the end of World War II, NYC's Jewish and African American populations had gone through dramatic ideological shifts. Jews developed ties to America through social institutions, such as banks (to purchase Liberty Bonds) and draft offices, and through political engagement. After serving the country along-side men from dozens of national backgrounds, in all military branches, Jews achieved a small degree of acceptance but continued to face discrimination and anti-Semitism, particularly as the Depression unfolded. African Americans performed gallantly on World War II's battlefields, came face-to-face with Euro-pean fascism while liberating Jews from concentration camps, and triumphed as France paraded them through the streets as heroes (against the army's wishes and fears that it would buoy African Americans' hopes of racial redemption at home). These overseas victories, combined with the Double V campaign, resulted in a newfound determination to uproot the racist political system at home. With both groups registering to vote in record numbers, Jews and African Americans continued to be perceived as racial outsiders but had laid the groundwork for future mobilization.

New York's Racial Outsiders

A variety of experiences and events reveal that, in the early twentieth century and the post–World War II era, Jews and African Americans, respectively, existed as racialized others. Complex processes of racialization attributed particular characteristics to each group, resulting in perceived differences between them and other Americans. Discriminatory images in popular culture reinforced their perceived physical differences and legitimated exclusionary policies and prac-tices. As a system of oppression embedded in social institutions (Bonilla-Silva 1997, 2006; Feagin 2001, 2006), racial identities and meanings structured all aspects of Jews' and African Americans' daily lives. Iris Young (1990) describes five features of oppression—exploitation, marginalization, powerlessness, cultural imperialism (how groups are perceived of and depicted by the domi-nant group), and violence. Jews were consistently subject to four and African Americans, all five.

America's racist social constructions of African Americans ascribed nega-tive behavioral and psychological characteristics to them, thus ensuring white social, political, and economic dominance. Meanings of whiteness developed in opposition to impugned, and then "scientifically" proven, characteristics that attributed laziness, physicality, and mental inferiority to African Americans. As a result, conceptions of whiteness and American citizenship embodying rationality, intelligence, and a strong work ethic depended upon negative conceptions of "Blackness" (Fredrickson 1971; Gould 1996). As whites defined the American identity "as white, a negation of racialized otherness" (Omi & Winant 1994: 66), law, customs, public institutions, and cultural representations reinforced notions of difference, justified oppression from slavery to the present day, and inhibited African Americans' full citizenship. Together, these laws, practices, and ideologies ensured economic domination and oppression while maintaining white privilege.

Like racism, anti-Semitism is deeply rooted in American history, traditions, and ideology (Higham 1969). Jews' economic success belied a strong undercurrent of ideological anti-Semitism that contributed to stereotypes of Jews as greedy and controlling businessmen. Even as they assimilated, Americans always considered Jews dissimilar from Christians. As immigration increased, perceived Jewish differences in dress, manners, and language found real-life examples on the streets of NYC. When a large influx of poor Eastern European Jews arrived, whites rescinded any advances Jews had made in becoming white, resulting in renewed racialization.

Local and national discrimination relegated Jews to a subordinated position in the racial hierarchy and consigned them to social conditions often identified with African Americans. Quotas and statutes limited Jews' access to jobs, universities, hotels, resorts, restaurants, and social and country clubs (Brodkin 1999). Restrictive covenants excluded them from land and property ownership in the same "Sundown Towns" that barred African Americans (Loewen 2006). No other European ethnic group experienced the same type of legal restrictions to their freedoms. In 1913 Georgia, whites lynched Leo Frank, a Jew, after a jury found an African American man inherently more honest than Jews when it came to rape (Dinnerstein 1994). Decades later, during World War II, as reports of Jewish extermination appeared in American papers, anti-Semitism raged at home. Public opinion polls found the majority of Americans maintained highly anti-Semitic views. Most Americans saw Jews as different from themselves, even more so than Irish, Italians, Poles, Spanish, Czechs, Armenians, and American Indians (Bogardus 1968). To avoid discrimination and "pass" as white, many Jews changed their hair color, nose structure, and name (Diner 1998, 2003; Goldstein 2006).

Compounding Jews' complicated relationship with other Americans, prior to World War II, Jews perceived themselves as religiously, culturally, and racially different from whites. Conceiving of themselves as members of the Jewish race, they engaged in cultural practices and ideologies to resist assimilation into the dominant white mainstream. Many Jews considered all non-Jews *goyim*, a group to which they neither desired nor aspired to belong. Even the most acculturated Jews stressed their distinctive values and maintained their insular community by resisting intermarriage.[15]

American conceptions of whiteness did not rest on Jews' identity as it did for African Americans. Jews, though racialized, never faced a systemic ideological backdrop predicating access to rights and resources on not being African American. Jews nevertheless faced considerable hurdles in achieving equal status with other Americans. Their ultimate outcome as whites was not guaranteed. Exploited, marginalized, powerless, and victims of cultural imperialism, Jews' and African Americans' experiences in NYC perpetuated their similar positions on the racial ladder. They existed, and the American people and institutions perceived them, as racialized others, outside the boundaries of full American citizenship and therefore lacking the privileges existing therein. Central to maintaining these racial distinctions and oppression were American public schools.

Education for Racial Subordination

NYC's educational bureaucracy subjected Jewish and African American students to significant inequities. They attended segregated and unequal schools with overcrowded vocational classes, crumbling facilities, discriminatory teachers, double-sessions, and denigrating school cultures. Enforced by administrators and teachers, those phenomena created cultural tensions for Jewish and African American students, even as each group expounded the value of education for their children's future. The schools' white Protestant culture resulted in discrimination against Jewish students and potential teachers. The board classified Jewish children as delinquent, backward, and "unteachable" and placed them in the lowest level classes (Brumberg 1986; Greer 1972; Moore 1981; Tyack 1974). Thirty years later, the board treated African Americans exactly the same way (Taylor 1997). Discrimination pushed Jewish and African American children out of schools, resulting in high drop-out and juvenile delinquency rates within each community (Greer 1972; Tyack 1974; Ravitch 1968; Rogers 1968). Combined, these phenomena reveal NYC's schools' failure to provide Jewish and African American students with education sufficient to allow them to become upwardly mobile citizens.

Jewish Experiences in NYC's Public Schools

Jewish immigrant children faced considerable difficulties in NYC's public schools. Many children could not even enroll. "When the first wave of Eastern European Jews began to arrive in the United States in 1881, a migration of proletarians and peddlers, education was not a channel of social mobility. Most children were at work in factories" (Gorelick 1981: 4). Until 1896, not a single high school existed in Manhattan, nor did elementary schools teach the academic subjects necessary for college admission. Many Jewish parents did their best to enroll their children, often going right from the docks to the schools to register. Unprepared for the waves of immigrant children, and faced with new compulsory education laws, NYC's board often turned immigrant children away (Callcott 1931; Ensign 1921; Palmer 1905).

The rapid influx of immigrants taxed the public schools to their limits (Berrol 1976). In 1914, the children of Southern and Eastern European immigrants represented 75.1 percent of all children in NYC. Of these, at 37 percent of 808,000 (277,000 students), Jews were the largest group and accounted for 46 percent of Manhattan's elementary school students. In the city's most crowded schools in the Lower East Side, Brooklyn, and the Bronx, nearly 150,000 students attended schools on double sessions, an arrangement during which half of the school's students had class in the morning and the other half in the afternoon (Lewisohn 1965). This reduced students' time in school to four hours. In each classroom, 60–100 students sat three to a desk, on benches, and on the floor. Across town, middle-class nonimmigrant schools stood at half capacity. While the normal enrollment age was seven, overcrowded schools deferred enrollment until children were eight or older. Since students could acquire working papers to leave school at age twelve, many immigrant children left school with only three to four years of education and minimal literacy skills.

Once in school, Jewish children were treated by the Board of Education as racial outsiders. Teachers and students ridiculed their cultures and customs. Their thick accents and unfamiliarity with English made sounding "American," and avoiding conflict, difficult. Determined to Americanize children, the schools forbade traditional Jewish customs, such as wearing a head covering, and served unkosher food in newly built cafeterias. Academically, Jewish students' low IQ scores through the 1930s found them disproportionately placed in "retarded" (more than two years behind grade level) classes (Gorelick 1975; Tyack 1974). Dejected, many dropped out. In the first decades of the twentieth century, dropout panics swept through Lower East Side schools with 99 percent Hebrew enrollment (Greer 1972). Only 16 percent of Jewish students entering first grade graduated from high school (Cohen 1970; Van Denburg 1912).

The public schools maintained three different high school programs: manual, commercial, and academic. Manual high schools promoted entry into "trades," preparing most students to assume their parents' positions in low-wage factory jobs. Commercial high schools prepared students for low-level service jobs as secretaries, typists, and clerks. Academic schools provided students with the skills and courses necessary for college entrance. The board primarily assigned Jews to manual and commercial schools. Not until the Depression did they enter academic schools in significant numbers.

Because public schools were not designed to propel students into the professions, first-generation German Jews did not achieve upward mobility through the schools. Germans preferred their children enter firms employing family members rather than attending college. Thus, they became upwardly mobile in much the same way immigrants do today, through familial networks and entrepreneurship. Although middle-class German Jews began entering American colleges in the 1920s (at rates so high that many prestigious colleges and universities instituted quotas), most Russian Jews were still two generations away from campus life. For the poorest segments of the Jewish community, economic survival was their foremost concern. Since many Jewish youth forsook high school to work and contribute to family budgets, they lacked the preparation and finances to attend college. Children and grandchildren of small business owners went to college, not poor immigrants. For Jews, the schools' focus on only basic literacy resulted in academic and economic stagnation. Before and during the Depression, NYC Jews advanced through unions, strikes, and increasing economic opportunity, not the public schools.[16]

City College's role in promoting economic success for poor immigrant Jews is a myth. While often lauded as the singular reason for Jewish success, City College only accepted a few hundred students of all ethnic backgrounds each year. Therefore, the idea that millions of Jews passed through its doors, enough to allow the entire community to become upwardly mobile, is mathematically impossible. The few Jews attending City College in the early 1900s were not poor Eastern European Jews but their native-born German co-religionists. Nearly two decades later, in 1919, when many children who attended Gary Plan schools began to reach college age, the proportion of Jews entering college was growing, but "what is forgotten is that although more and more students were *Jews*, very few Jews were *students*" (Gorelick 1981: 123, emphasis in original). City College graduated twenty-five to fifty students of all backgrounds each year, a drop in the bucket compared to the 2 million Jews living in NYC. As a result, City College played only a small role in promoting upward mobility for Jewish youth during the first three decades of the twentieth century. The 1920s saw larger Eastern European Jewish enrollments, but increased anti-Semitism during the Depression inhibited Jews from using their degrees to dig themselves and their families out of poverty. Economic duress and overt anti-Semitism held Jews on the lower rungs of the economic and occupational ladder until after World War II, when ideologies about race in general, and Jews in particular, shifted such that they could access the most useful government policies promoting mobility (the G.I. Bill for college and the FHA's low-interest loans for purchasing suburban homes). Only then could Jews use their diplomas to become upwardly mobile.

To amend social and economic inequalities resulting from their racial and social status, Jews targeted NYC's public schools to acquire resources granted to other American citizens (Brumberg 1986; Goren 1999; Greer 1972; Howe 1976;

Moore 1981). Jews' collective success in organizing the garment industry in the first two decades of the twentieth century had produced networks of solidarity and community but never significantly improved their economic situation. Using strikes to target the schools at the turn of the century, Jewish parents protested the lack of Jewish teachers, and the many Irish Catholic teachers who perceived Jewish children as criminal and delinquent. They also protested the schools' use of Protestant curriculum and the dismissal of classes on Christian holidays, such as Christmas and Easter, but not on Rosh Hashanah, Yom Kippur, and Passover. However, these protests neither addressed the issue nor convinced the board to provide Jewish children with education sufficient to transcend the debilitating ghetto poverty.

NYC's Jim Crow Schools

African Americans' fight to achieve equal education in NYC began in 1857, a year before the newly established Board of Education assumed control over African Free Schools, with protests against their assignment to segregated schools when they lived in integrated neighborhoods (Johnson 1991). In 1900, Governor Theodore Roosevelt officially outlawed segregated schools with a bill prohibiting "the exclusion of any individual from any public school in the state because of his race or color" (Goldaber 1965: 10). Yet segregation, and inequality, persisted as educational authorities routinely ignored this law. In early twentieth-century NYC, dropout rates among African Americans were *lower* than those of white immigrants (Greenberg 1991), but discrimination kept many from achieving employment sufficient to improve their economic position.

At the onset of the Great Depression more African American children lived in NYC than in any other city in the world—75,000 under the age of fifteen, 40,000 in Manhattan. The illegality of segregated schools notwithstanding, African American children attended poor-quality, "unsanitary, dilapidated," segregated schools "replete with fire hazards" (Goldaber 1965: 11–12). The Mayor's Commission on Conditions in Harlem found overcrowding, insufficient schools, poor teaching, inadequate equipment and curriculum, poverty, and high rates of truancy and delinquency.

As Jewish parents, with their children, moved to the suburbs to access their better public schools during and after World War II, educational segregation increased for African Americans. The board often redrew boundaries to cordon them off from high-quality schools, often only a short walk away from their homes, and ensure racially segregated schools. With only one school built in Harlem since the turn of the century, the board allocated only $400,000 of $121 million for new schools in African American neighborhoods. Even into the 1950s, the government's reinvestment in science and math curriculum after the USSR's successful launch of *Sputnik*, left African American students in poorly funded vocational schools further behind their white peers than ever before.

Mid-century, quality education eluded African American children. As one of the most residentially segregated cities in the Northeast, many of NYC's schools enrolled not a single white student and declined in physical and educational quality with every passing year, much to the dismay of African American residents. The city's segregated schools subjected African American children, whether in Harlem, Brownsville, Bedford-Stuyvesant, or Jamaica, Queens, to inferior and inadequate education. In Harlem, where children could most benefit from preschool training, not a single nursery school existed. Only one high school and one annex of a vocational training school awaited graduates of twenty-two elementary and junior high schools.

In 1954, the Mayor's Committee on Unity issued a report finding that African Americans' schools had not improved since the Depression. In fact, they had gotten worse. For example, at the New York Vocational High School, holes in the roof and walls created pools of stagnant water, rendering classrooms unusable; falling plaster sent students and teachers to the hospital; and students used faulty 1909-edition drill presses and lathes and unsanitary kitchen and health facilities. Led by teachers who believed Harlem's children were "less ambitious than . . . white children," NYC's African American students scored more than two years below grade level in reading and in math and had an average IQ of 83, considered "dull." Parents argued that the schools' refusal to administer tests to students for elite high school admission, sequestering them in vocational schools, discouraged children's ambitions.[17]

Validating local parents' concerns and the mayor's report, Kenneth and Mamie Clark's Northside Center presented *Children Apart*, a meticulous study of Harlem schools, in 1954 during a citywide conference (Clark 1989; Markowitz & Rosner 1999). The findings were dismal. Inexperienced and substitute teachers taught most classes, and not a single white student attended Harlem's sole high school. Harlem schools featured 103 classes for "retarded" children (those more than two years behind grade level), but only 5 for gifted students. Illegally, guidance counselors placed African American children in "retarded" classes based on the entire group's test results. School district gerrymandering and placement of schools at the far edges of segregated neighborhoods, rather than centrally located near their enjoinment, precluded integration of schools in adjacent neighborhoods. After offering key testimony on segregated schools' effect on Southern children during the *Brown* trial, Clark contended that Harlem's segregated schools were no different.[18]

NYC's educational establishment disagreed. When the Supreme Court unanimously declared, "segregated schools are inherently unequal," NYC's school superintendent claimed segregation in Harlem differed from that in the South, in that it was "natural." He claimed, "there are no effects on the children if it is not purposeful." Refusing to acknowledge any problem, the board did nothing to counteract NYC's severe segregation and inequality, instead citing, when pressed, residential segregation, rather than board action, as the root of the problem. Less than one year later, the nonprofit research advocacy group Public Education Association (PEA) published a searing exposé documenting pervasive segregation and severe differences in educational quality between African American and white schools in NYC.[19]

The PEA found most African Americans in not just segregated, but hyper-segregated (95 percent of students of one race), schools of far lower quality than those for white students. Nine junior high schools were over 95 percent minority and forty were more than 95 percent white. Of 127 junior high schools, 16 had a minority population of 85 percent or greater while 52 had a white population of 85 percent or greater. Ten times more white schools than minority schools had faculties with more than 80 percent experienced teachers and small class sizes. Perhaps most devastating, the PEA found that, each year, the Board of Education spent $65.10 on each white child but only $21.10 on each minority child, making the funding differences nearly indistinct from those in the South.

As a result of these funding differences, African Americans' schools were worse than whites' on every measure (Public Education Association 1955). The average ages of elementary and junior high schools in white neighborhoods were thirty-one and fifteen years, while that of African American schools was forty-three and thirty-five, respectively. The board averaged 17.2 and 4.3 years to renovate African Americans' older and more dilapidated elementary and junior high schools but improved whites' in 9.8 and 0.7 years, respectively. Schools with 85 percent or more African American students maintained teacher vacancy rates of 49.5 percent, meaning that substitutes comprised almost half of all teachers in these schools. In white schools, the vacancy rate stood at 29.6 percent. Two-thirds (66.7 percent) of junior high schools with 85 percent or more whites had gifted classes but not a single class existed for gifted children in schools with more than 85 percent African American students. In these schools, African American students encountered only four hours of instruction (rather than the state-mandated six), ineffective teachers longing to be transferred to white schools, and insufficient and age-inappropriate textbooks.[20]

These spending, staffing, and resource-based deficiencies had devastating effects on African American students' academic performance (Clark 1989; Markowitz & Rosner 1999; Public Education Association 1955; Wilson 1971). While white children consistently tested above grade level in reading and math, African Americans not only scored lower but their IQ scores *declined* between the third and sixth grades, resulting in an increasing gap between African Americans' and white scores at each grade level. Poor schooling and high drop-out rates pushed African American youth toward criminal activity, as it had done to Jews nearly fifty years earlier.

The PEA report, combined with Clark's report and the *Brown* decision, fostered sufficient outcry from NYC's African American and educational communities to compel the Board of Education to establish a Commission on Integration. Each subcommission of the Commission on Integration (COI) featured local and national educational experts and African American New Yorkers who took their role in evaluating and recommending improvements seriously. Each report identified numerous structural reasons for educational inequalities and recognized that equalizing resources between African American and white schools was insufficient to correct existing inequalities. All recommended increased spending.[21]

Each subcommission substantiated the PEA report through interviews, visits, and consultations with parents, teachers, and school administrators, and data from the board's Bureau of Reference, Research, and Statistics. For example, the Sub-commission on Physical Plant and Maintenance recommended that the board should completely replace 22 percent and modernize 24 percent of African American schools, while only 1 percent of white schools needed replacement and 12 percent needed updating. Any new schools should be in locations maximizing diversity. They also confirmed a longstanding parental complaint, the proliferation of double-, and even triple-sessions. An overwhelming 361 African American, and only 21 white, classes were on double-sessions. Confirming the high rate of substitutes in African American schools, the Sub-commission on Teachers Assignments and Personnel also found many teachers, unfriendly and resenting their placement in these schools, harmed rather than helped minority children.

Highly critical reports from the Sub-commissions on Zoning, Teachers and Personnel, Guidance, Educational Stimulation and Placement, Physical Plant and Maintenance, Educational Curriculum and Standards, and Community Relations and Information all took seriously the schools' conditions and offered innovative solutions to a wide range of problems. The Sub-commission on Zoning recommended that the board make integration the primary objective in creating residential boundaries for school attendance through a Central Zoning Unit and cultivate community and parental support. The Sub-commission on Teachers and Personnel described numerous solutions to ensure the best teachers' placement and retention in the neediest schools. The Sub-commission on Community Relations recommended that the board first develop a centralized Community Relations Unit to promote positive relations between racial, ethnic, and religious groups, and then find, hire, and train school personal to promote this goal. It also recommended neighborhood and school-community councils to disseminate information to the public and collaborate with parents' organizations.

Curricular differences plagued students in African American schools. The Sub-commission on Guidance, Educational Stimulation and Placement found an "appallingly low" level of African American college candidates. An additional five dollars per pupil per year would significantly improve their guidance programs with more minority guidance personnel, bias-free aptitude tests for third, sixth, eighth, and tenth graders, programs to raise student interest and educational aspirations in low-income schools, and a Demonstration Guidance program. This program would train teachers to seek out high potential students in low-income areas and provide them with resources and counseling to promote college attendance. The Sub-commission on Educational Standards and Curriculum, which included Kenneth Clark, recommended an intensive curriculum to improve minority students' academic performance, the reexamination of students in "retarded" programs, and curriculum standardization across the city. Conspicuously, it did not address discriminatory curriculum.

The board's actions following these reports did not live up to parents' expectations. Having testified at public hearings and followed their progress in the African American press, parents were both well-informed of educational deficiencies (and therefore the board's knowledge of them) and galvanized by the board's reticence to address them. Armed with in-depth knowledge of their children's inadequate schools from both personal experience and interaction with these committees, Harlem mothers embarked on a movement to alter public school conditions that forever changed the face of African American protest in the North and race relations in NYC.

Hoping to encounter a wide-open Golden Door promoting their children's educational advancement in a new city, Jews and African Americans were sorely disappointed with the reception their children received at the hands of both the city and the Board of Education at different points in New York City's history. However, they did not sit back and watch as local schools subjected their children to the worst education that reified the racial order. Protests against resource inequality and recognition of identity through curricular representation reveal each group's determination to alter the state of education in NYC, and their own racial identities, to expand boundaries of citizenship.

2

Resources, Riots, and Race

The Gary Plan and the Harlem 9

As dawn broke on October 17, 1917, thousands of Jewish children and their parents crowded the streets of the Lower East Side, Brownsville, and Flatbush. In Yiddish and English, they chanted and carried signs reading "Down with the Gary System!" They passed women and boys on street corners railing against a plan that condemned half a million Jewish children to crowded and crumbling schools that featured vocational, rather than academic, curriculum. As immigrant children and parents converged in front of schools converted to the Gary Plan, they showered the buildings with stones and bricks. For a week, Jewish children turned their aim on city policemen and school administrators. These headline-grabbing actions testified to Jews' frustration with social and educational discrimination in the only language to which the city would listen. These riots were the culmination of three years of ignored protests by Jewish parents to reverse the infiltration of the Gary Plan into dozens of predominantly Jewish schools around the city. And now, days before an election in which Mayor John Purroy Mitchel, who implemented the Gary Plan, could be voted out of office, the Board of Education was finally paying attention to Jewish protests.

Almost exactly forty years later, on September 19, 1957, hundreds of African American parents descended on City Hall. Organized by the Harlem 9, mothers chanted and carried picket signs urging the city to end segregation, improve inferior schools, and allow their children to attend integrated schools. For five years, these women rallied hundreds of other parents to challenge the board's policy of de facto segregation of African American youth. As they had done to Jews forty years earlier, the board refused to acknowledge African American parents' protests against crowded, crumbling schools with unqualified and racist teachers where children were subject to vocational, rather than academic, curriculum. So the Harlem 9 sued the board for $1 million, filed hundreds of charges against the board in dozens of city, state, and federal civil rights agencies and courts, and boycotted the schools for an entire school year, sending their children to Freedom Schools. In the years after *Brown* and the height of the civil rights movement, these highly public tactics turned the eyes of the nation away from the streets of Birmingham and Selma and toward Harlem.

Though years apart, these protests by Jewish and African American parents utilized similar tactics and narratives resulting in similar movement trajectories and reactions from the Board of Education. By the end of each protest, the school system had retrenched racialized identities for each group through unequal resource allocation.

The Gary Plan

Developed by Gary, Indiana's Superintendent of Schools, William Wirt, the Gary Plan was loosely modeled on John Dewey's progressive beliefs that classrooms should educate children for life. In Gary, Wirt's plan was guided by the necessity of Americanizing the 63.4 percent of the children in the schools with immigrant parents. The plan was designed to shape children's behavior and produce what later critics called "loyal citizens and docile workers" (Cohen & Mohl 1979: 86). In immigrant-dominated Gary schools, children were stripped of their languages and cultures and subjected to industrial and manual training classes that deemphasized academic subjects such as math, history, science, and geography. Girls learned cooking, sewing, and bookkeeping while boys learned metal work, cabinetry, woodworking, painting, printing, shoemaking, and plumbing. The schools intended these programs to prepare immigrant children for work in factories rather than upward mobility.[1]

Mitchel hired Wirt to introduce the plan into NYC's schools, which were rapidly filling with immigrant children. Rather than building new schools, the Gary Plan would save the city money by utilizing all rooms in existing schools by rotating children through classrooms, auditoriums, playgrounds, and gymnasiums. Changing classrooms became routine as specialized teachers instructed children in one subject and then sent them on their way.

The initial impetus for the Gary Plan in NYC came before Mitchel was elected mayor but at his behest as a member of the Board of Estimate, which controlled the funds for the Board of Education. Attuned to the progressive initiatives occurring throughout the country, and concerned with the increasing cost of educating a continuously expanding immigrant population, Mitchel directed the board's Committee on School Inquiry to hire Harvard professor Paul H. Hanus to study the schools and recommend changes. The report recommended increasing economic efficiency by altering the curriculum and structure of the schools. With his knowledge of the schools, Mitchel ran for mayor, won, and used the report's suggestions to install the Gary Plan in NYC's public schools.[2]

Mitchel met William Wirt at a conference during the Hanus investigation in October of 1912. Two wealthy German Jews supported the plan. Abraham Flexner, of the Public Education Association (PEA) and the Rockefeller-financed General Education Board, openly campaigned for the program. Ira S. Wile, a wealthy Board of Education member, initiated a study of vocational needs in the public schools with Alice Barrows, Wirt's secretary and PEA member. In March, a number of PEA, Board of Education, and city officials traveled to Gary, Indiana, to observe the schools. By June, the city had hired William Wirt as consultant. Mitchel doubled his $6,000 salary in Gary and paid him $10,000, the same as NYC School Superintendent William Maxwell's full-time salary. School alterations quickly followed.

During the summer of 1914, Wirt converted two schools, P.S. 45 in the Bronx and P.S. 89 in Brooklyn, to the Gary Plan for the upcoming school year. Both schools were located in heavily Jewish neighborhoods. Without waiting for reports of academic improvement, Mitchel quickly expanded the program. In December 1914, Mitchel asked Wirt for conversion plans to install the Gary Plan in all eleven Bronx elementary schools and every overcrowded elementary school the following school year. Immigrant neighborhoods with high Jewish enrollments contained the majority of overcrowded schools.[3]

The board told parents that the Gary Plan and vocational education was best for their children. Now its full-time promoter and publicist, Barrows launched a full-blown media campaign for the Gary Plan. She convinced progressive journals, such as *Survey*, the *New Republic*, the *Masses*, and the *Liberator*, to publish positive editorials of the educational and economic benefits of the plan for immigrant children and enlisted muckraking journalist Rheta Childe Dorr of the *New York Mail* to publish a regular column. Barrows also directed the creation and publicity of movies, newspapers, pamphlets, magazines, posters, and leaflets distributed and published in English, Yiddish, German, and Italian. Barrows's salary was drawn from a $10,000 per year donation to William Wirt from U.S. Steel to promote the plan, an industry connection upon which activists would later capitalize (Cohen & Mohl 1979).

The local media set the discursive agenda about the Gary Plan by telling readers what to think about it while simultaneously ignoring protest. Some newspapers reported positively about the Gary Plan, others remained silent. The widely read *New York Sun*, *New York Times*, and *Brooklyn Daily Eagle* ignored protests against the Gary Plan until nearly two years into its installation. Parents were left to determine on their own, with little public information from the media, whether the plan benefited students. Rather than promoting activism, the media silenced potential activists with the appearance that, not only was the plan working, but that little protest existed around it. In doing so, newspapers encouraged acquiescence to the status quo by isolating potential activists unaware of existing protest.[4]

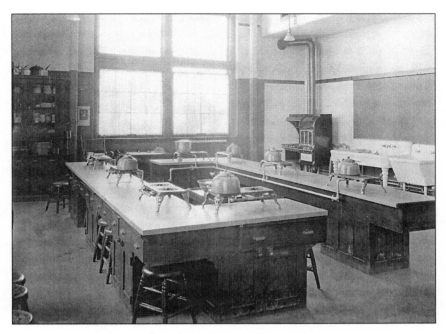

FIGURE 1 Cooking room, P.S. 45 (Bronx).
Courtesy NYC Municipal Archives

FIGURE 2 Pottery shop, P.S. 45 (Bronx).
Courtesy NYC Municipal Archives

But Jewish parents were neither fooled nor convinced. They recognized the Gary Plan for what it was, an economy scheme that turned their children into "cogs" through assimilatory and vocational curriculum that hindered academic success. Historically, schools tracked minority and immigrant children into vocational classes that replicated their place on the lowest rungs of the social and economic ladder. The Gary Plan did exactly this, just as large numbers of Jews had begun to gain entrance into local and national colleges. In addition to vocational education, "the monitor system" compensated for the lack of teachers by placing older students in supervisory positions over younger ones in study halls, assemblies, and lunch periods. This inadequate supervision of younger children also decreased older students' classroom time. As the plan progressed, the board added military training and lengthened the school day, hindering students from working, going to Hebrew schools, and participating in sports and clubs. The days became longer and more tedious—just like in the factories. Jews realized that alone, each one of these programs limited their children's academic potential. Together, the Gary Plan arose as the largest roadblock to Jewish educational mobility since leaving the Pale.[5]

To take on the Gary Plan and the exhaustive resources of the Board of Education, Wirt, Barrows, and the mayor, Jewish parents formed the Federation of Parents Association, the Mothers' Council of the Public Schools of the City of New York, and citywide branches of Mothers' Anti-Gary Leagues. For Jewish members of the Long Island Council of Women's Clubs (which represented 12,000 members in seventy-eight clubs), the School Welfare Association, and the East Side Neighborhoods Association (ESNA), opposing the Gary Plan became their leading cause. Together, these organizations represented a citywide multiethnic backbone of activism to diffuse grievances and tactical innovations throughout the city, with Jews at its helm.[6]

Religion in the Public Schools?

Jewish protest began almost immediately after the Gary Plan was first introduced into P.S. 89 in Flatbush, Brooklyn, and P.S. 45 in the Bronx, their neighborhood schools. Although angered by the vocational aspect of the plan, parents first targeted the most direct affront to their children's status as equals in the public schools, the inclusion of religion. The board's description of this component was vague. At first, it appeared schools would label children with tags stating their religion, let them out early on Wednesdays, and deliver them to their respective minister, priest, or rabbi. Other reports stated that children would receive religious training in the public schools. This secrecy would characterize all Gary programs. The board never stated the content of the curriculum but, given the Protestant norms of the schools, Jews sensed their children might face proselyetization and be forced to learn the New Testament. Regardless of course content, Jews most feared differentiation based on religion.[7]

Jewish parents, fresh from the pogroms of Eastern Europe, worried their children would face violence in their new homeland. They were right—fights between boys of different religious backgrounds broke out in Gary schools shortly after religion was introduced. Jewish community leaders, Leon Malkiel, of the Socialist Party of New York, and Samuel Cahan, of District 2's local School Board, used local meetings to protest sanctioned religion in the public schools. Others brought their complaints to former board member, labor leader, and fellow Jew, Joseph Barondess. His letters to the mayor on behalf of Jewish parents reveal their deep fears of discrimination against their children and cautioned the mayor not to attribute their reactions to "over-sensitivity." He explained that religion in the public schools "would deprive them of the right to practice their religion in the manner they deem proper, a right for which they had struggled for nearly two thousand years." That Jews connected the Gary Plan to their long history of oppression reveals the severity with which they viewed this new curriculum.[8]

Arguing that religion in the public schools was diametrically opposed to America's educational ideals, rabbis and Jewish community leaders protested from their synagogue pulpits, at PA meetings, and in the Jewish press. At P.S. 45, Rabbi Alexander Lyons (of the Eighth Avenue Temple) condemned the plan for "strengthening denominationalism and denominational divisions, which are contributory to a prejudice and unfraternity with which we are already excessively burdened and cursed." Rabbi Rudolph Grossman (of Temple Rodeph Shalom) argued, "to recognize religious differences in the Public School, is in my judgment, to endanger that sacred principle of the total separation of Church and State, upon whose maintenance our American liberty primarily depends." Rabbis Nathan Krass and Joseph Silverman and Henry Neuman, president of the Brooklyn Society for Ethical Culture, also opposed the religious features of the Gary Plan.[9]

Established Jewish organizations also condemned the Gary Plan. The largest of these was the Kehillah, an umbrella organization of NYC's Jewish organizations. The Kehillah opposed the Gary Plan because "public education must be non-sectarian and non-religious" and the extended school day inhibited Jewish parents from sending their children to Hebrew School later in the afternoon. During these prewar years, Jews faced a number of problems—poverty, overcrowded neighborhoods, unemployment, and anti-Semitism. That they spent so much time and effort on the Gary Plan reveals the severity with which Jews viewed this educational program. However, only the religious feature attracted the attention of Jewish community's elites, including Joseph Barondess and Jewish Board members Ira S. Wile and Isadore Montefiore Levy.[10]

Realizing their potential role in quelling concerns in simmering Jewish neighborhoods, these prominent Jewish figures caught school administrators' attention. The school superintendent, assistant superintendents, the school board president, and William Wirt himself attended debates and conferences held by Jewish leaders. Wirt eventually met with religious leaders to ensure them that religion was not essential to the plan and hinted at its impending removal. But reports of religious education appeared for the duration of the Gary Plan.[11]

Reactions to Jews "Jim Crowed" in NYC Schools

As African Americans would forty years later, Jews found themselves relegated to inferior and overcrowded schools with the installation of the Gary Plan. After the religious issue was "settled," Jewish members and leaders of community organizations and Parents Associations (PAs) denounced the plan as a scheme to save the city money without improving their children's education by building more schools and hiring better teachers. Held almost nightly across the city, in synagogues, schools, or civic halls, PA meetings usually attracted between 500 and 700, but sometimes as many as 1,200, parents. These gatherings usually began at 8 P.M. and ended after midnight. Attending a four-hour-long meeting after working twelve or more hours in backbreaking and eye-straining sweat-shops reveal the sacrifices parents made to ensure their children received the best education possible. Each meeting usually featured a well-known principal, local board member, rabbi, or labor leader to oppose the plan while one of Wirt's associates often attended to challenge parents' arguments. The meetings closed with resolutions against the GP, demands for more and better schools and meetings with the board, and calls for sustained mobilization. For example, an ESNA meeting on November 11, 1916, generated resolutions complaining about religion, overcrowding, the longer school day, and teachers' inability to develop close relationships with students because students changed classes so often. They appealed to the Board of Education "not to introduce the said Gary Plan either into the school system of the City of New York, or more particularly, into the schools of the east side." Another meeting, held by the Hebrew Educational Society, closed with resolutions against the plan and a commitment to organize protests throughout the city.[12]

Civic organizations featuring the strong Jewish leadership of Gregory Weinstein, Max Wolff, Louis H. Pink, and Harry Robitzek also opposed the plan. Activists mobilized based on their perception that, as property owners and taxpayers, they maintained a right to oppose the board's spending logic. The Flatbush Taxpayers Association, the Taxpayers Association of Vanderveer Park, and the Cypress Hills Taxpayers' Association, all in Brooklyn, opposed the Gary Plan's "theory, practice, expense, and operation." The Bronx Chamber of Commerce scored the plan and sought a state investigation into the poor quality of the schools and the high cost of the GP. The Brooklyn Civic Club repeatedly demanded more and better schools. The Long Island Council of Women opposed the city's expenditure of $5 million without revealing how school children would benefit.[13]

Jewish educators criticized the Gary Plan in local newspapers and public meetings for its exorbitant cost and failure to improve children's educational opportunities. Speaking from their own experience and research, Jewish principals brought important insight to parents' meetings. Leon Goldrich, principal of P.S. 62 (Lower East Side) traversed the boroughs to argue against Gary proponents Howard W. Nudd, Alice Ritter, and Rheta Childe Dorr at dozens of schools and parent, neighborhood, and civic organization meetings. Repeatedly, he denounced the Gary Plan as "the Devil's own hand cut loose" and published a series of articles in the *Globe* attacking the plan's academic deficiencies. Principals Simon Hirdansky (P.S. 4, Bronx), Herman S. Platt (P.S. 46), and Gabriel Mason (P.S. 37, Bronx) used local schools and their own synagogues as pulpits to alert parents and rail against the plan. At a P.S. 46 PA meeting, Platt "cautioned the parents to look out for the insidious plan of simply doubling classes and calling it the Gary plan." A few weeks later, at P.S. 163, he "protested vehemently" that the GP was "forced upon the people before the schools are properly equipped for it, and that confusion and failure are the result, with very natural and proper rebellion on the part of pupils and parents." In a report to the Board of Education, Jewish principals scored the plan on the basis of its cost, the lack of academic work, increased administrative work for teachers, the lack of children's supervision and resulting safety concerns, large class sizes, and idle time students encountered during "auditorium periods."[14]

For over a year, these organizations met throughout the city but were uncoordinated in their efforts to oppose the Gary Plan. Realizing the difficulty in achieving their goals without establishing networks between parents' organizations, the Federation of Parents' Associations (FPA) began coordinating PAs in the fall of 1915. New PAs held frequent and widely attended meetings and debates at Public Schools 10, 46, 62, 20, 39, 89, 93, 109, 184, and 171 in densely populated Jewish neighborhoods in Manhattan, Brooklyn, and the Bronx. For example, P.S. 46's (Washington Heights) PA held weekly meetings and attracted between eight and nine hundred parents to oppose the Gary Plan as "an economy proposal rather than as a means of affording the children richer educational opportunities." P.S. 10's PA, one of the city's largest and predominantly Jewish, passed resolutions relating to both the cost of the plan and its "very grave danger to this community as a whole" because of the religious feature. A flier advertising a PA meeting at P.S. 62, a predominantly Jewish school on the Lower East Side, encouraged parents' participation by reminding them, "The school belongs to the parents; the parents should have something to say about the conduct of the school."[15]

In January 1916, the Board of Education released a report finding students attending Gary Plan schools performed worse than those in "non-Garyized schools" (Buckingham 1916). Days later, Mitchel, despite knowing the plan diminished educational achievement, announced its installation in twelve more Bronx schools. Infuriated, mothers redoubled their efforts to remove the plan. They wondered how the plan could continue to spread when it disadvantaged children. And they demanded to know how the board could approve luxury items like swimming pools in some public schools while Jewish children attended old, overcrowded schools lacking modern improvements.[16]

Ready for action, PA representatives from across NYC met at the home of Mrs. Meyer Frankel, president of the School Welfare Association, to voice their concern. That afternoon, they discussed overcrowding, long hours, frequent changing of classes, neglect of academic work, the monitor system, the play period required regardless of weather, and religious instruction. Immediately after the meeting, they joined the Mothers' Anti-Gary League of Flatbush in canvassing the neighborhood for signatures on a petition demanding an end to a plan that negatively affected their children. In two days, they collected 419 signatures on a petition they submitted at the Board's January 13 meeting. League members argued they could have gotten more signatures if they were not trying to submit the petition in time for the meeting. Petition signers gathered at P.S. 89 the next day to voice their concerns about the plan with the school's unsympathetic Principal Alice Ritter. Ritter's only response was that the plan was working in her school and she saw no reason to change it.[17]

In April 1916, a contingent of fifty-eight Jewish, mostly immigrant, organizations met at P.S. 62 on the Lower East Side. These Jewish lodges, congregations, and *Landsmanshaftn*, deeply rooted in Old World traditions and "the building blocks of the Jewish community," represented a "crucial reservoir of mass support" for communal undertakings. Opposing the plan because of its cost and detrimental effect on their children's educational welfare, they "protest[ed] against any further extension of the Gary system of public school organization until such time as the said plan, which is now only in its experimental stage in a few schools, has given sufficient evidence of its value and efficiency to warrant its further extension and adoption." The membership of these organizations significantly aided future protest as existing networks of activism embraced non-English-speaking Jewish parents.[18]

After this meeting, Yiddish language use within the Jewish community became a powerful determinant of protest. Both pro- and anti-Gary activists distributed fliers in Yiddish. Meetings were advertised by pamphlets printed in Yiddish. At meetings, Jewish parents found Yiddish posters condemning the plan tacked to auditorium walls. During meetings, parents listened intently to speeches in Yiddish sprinkled with broken English. Newspaper reports of meetings often noted that parents brought their children along to translate for them.[19]

Countering Jewish Protest

For all their efforts, the board paid little attention to these activists. They denied meetings or sent associate and assistant superintendents, rather than board leaders, with little power to enact changes. In March 1916, after engaging in a four-month study of the schools, the Council of Mothers Clubs officially sought a public hearing with the Board of Education. Organizations represented by the FPA joined the call. The board denied their request and instead requested, and received, more funds to expand the Gary Plan into new schools. Board President William G. Willcox then rebuked mothers for seeking a meeting, "assured" them "that he would consider it further," and stated that the religious feature was no longer included in the Gary "experiment." But the Gary Plan had long since become more than an experiment; it was a full-blown restructuring of the public schools in America's biggest city with potentially national ramifications for urban education policy. Willcox later agreed to meet with representatives of the Council of Mothers Clubs of NYC to discuss a public hearing on March 27. This meeting never happened. The board refused even a meeting to discuss meeting with activists.[20]

To counter growing protest, Barrows created the Gary School League with 100 other upper-class women to disseminate pro–Gary Plan propaganda. In addition to attending parents' forums to discuss the plan, Barrows created a school for speakers to learn pro-Gary speeches in different languages (Cohen & Mohl 1979). Never actually listening to parents' concerns, Barrows assumed that she and other reformers knew best. She sent street corner speakers to immigrant neighborhoods and editorials targeting city mothers to the *Harlem Home News*, the *Bronx Home News*, and the *Brooklyn Home News*. These efforts did not sway Jewish mothers' opinions of the plan.[21]

Fed up with parents' letters and demands, the board responded to the FPA, the Council of Mothers' Clubs, the Parents' Federation of the 18th District, PAs from different schools, representatives of organized labor, and local school boards with a single letter denying all requests. These groups were "astounded." This was "the first time in the history of the Board of Education that a request from any considerable number of parents for an opportunity to be heard upon an important question before the board has been denied."[22]

The board finally announced a hearing for Friday, April 7. But it would only last one hour. To keep turnout low, the board did not print a public announcement in city papers, as was normal procedure. Board President Willcox, who "found no evidence of any widespread desire for public hearing in regard to the extension of the Gary plan," notified the FPA of the meeting by mail. The FPA forwarded the letter to the *Globe*'s education editor, Tristam Walker Metcalfe, a longtime Gary Plan opponent, who used his position to broadcast the meeting widely.[23]

Mothers traveled from around the city to condemn the board for experimenting with and exploiting their children rather than educating them. ESNA, the FPA, Mothers' Anti-Gary Leagues, and PAs of dozens of schools attended, as did representatives of local labor and school boards. Not a single parent supported the plan. Instead, they emotionally argued against the Gary Plan's further installation in their children's schools. One mother complained in broken English, "They are our children that you are experimenting with and now it is proposed to exploit them." Another reminded the board that "official report after official report" had condemned the plan. But the board didn't care. Four days later, it announced that twelve local schools would be closed and replaced with Gary schools.[24]

Digging in Their Heels

Jewish protest did not abate. Increased repression resulted in increased resistance. For the next year Jewish parents continued to organize against the plan. Parents flooded the mayor's office, newspapers, and the Board of Education with letters and petitions. They cited the need for more schools, academic instruction, and mothers' input into their children's education. They complained about the poor conditions in their children's schools, the monitor system, and the lengthened school day. Calling attention to the "injustice" done to "hundreds of thousands" of citizens, George Friefeld of Brooklyn asked the mayor, at the end of a lengthy letter detailing problems and shortcomings in schools in his neighborhood, whether "you would send your little boy or your tender little daughter to such a school? If you were poor and helpless your boy or girl would be compelled to go."[25]

America's entry into World War I brought protests by Jewish children, their parents, and community leaders to end the newly established mandatory military training in Gary schools. Students at Eastern District High School, where many of the boys were Jewish, organized the Anti-Military Training League. A letter to the *Brooklyn Daily Eagle* from Jewish father Henry Saum argued that militarism was a barrier to "democracy, progress, and civilization." Two months later, Rabbi Stephen S. Wise of the Free Synagogue spoke at Carnegie Hall against this end.[26]

Letters also complained of Jewish children in Gary schools forced to sing Christian songs and hymns and unable to attend Hebrew schools due to extended school hours. Although the board had publicly declared an end to the religious feature, letters to the mayor and Barondess suggested otherwise. Milton Diamond, principal of the Flatbush Hebrew School, writing to Barondess, noted "the practice of compelling children of our faith to join in the rehearsal of religious songs and hymns has been renewed." Other schools refused applications of Jewish students, such as Elias Stern of Boys' High, to attend morning classes so they could enroll in afternoon Hebrew School classes.[27]

Neither the mayor nor the board responded to parents' letters or petitions. Instead, they denied receiving them. But these documents, found in the archives, filed away by their secretaries, scared the mayor and board representatives. Internal memos communicated fear and apprehension of potential violence by angry parents.[28]

The board's fears were quickly realized. In April 1917, the board announced it would transfer children attending P.S. 31, an uncrowded school near their homes, to P.S. 126, a Gary school over thirteen blocks away. "Unalterably opposed" parents did "not want their children considered as so many sacks of meal to be packed into" this Gary school. A new tactic arose—the boycott. On May 1, 1917, more than 600 students boycotted P.S. 126. A week later, the board served mothers, determined to "fight to the end," with truant notices to appear in Domestic Relations Court. Although the board transferred their children anyway, these mothers became local celebrities in the Gary fight and continued their efforts by speaking at PSBL meetings and holding mass meetings.[29]

Galvanized by the boycott's attention to the plan, parents renewed their weekly protest meetings. A widely attended meeting at the Bronx Borough Hall condemned the lack of academic training in Gary schools. A week later the Bronx Chamber of Commerce requested a state investigation of these schools. The Brooklyn Civic Club devoted an evening to discussing how money used to convert schools to the Gary Plan left nothing for building new schools or properly outfitting existing ones. For a year, the board ignored these protests, believing that Jews did not understand the positive reasons for the plan. They also recognized Jews' powerlessness to affect change. This became particularly apparent when Jews attempted to halt the spread of the Gary Plan at its root, the Board of Estimate, which distributed money to convert schools.[30]

In June 1917, PAs attended a Board of Estimate meeting to confront the exorbitant cost to taxpayers to convert schools to the GP. Prior to the meeting, P.S. 27's (Bronx) PA delivered a petition to the mayor opposing the "Garyizing" of the school. At the meeting, Gregory Weinstein, president of the Flatbush Taxpayers Association, assailed the Gary Plan, "almost universally opposed by the parents," yet still "forced upon the schools." Their pleas fell on deaf ears. The board voted 10 to 6 to expand the Gary Plan to 51 additional schools for $1.5 million.[31]

"Parents Rising Against Gary Plan"

To unite "all Parents' Associations, mothers' clubs, and civic organizations interested in public education in a city-wide campaign to improve conditions in public schools," Mayer Goldman organized the Parents' School Betterment League (PSBL).[32] At its first meeting, John D. Rosenbrock "emphasized the necessity of doing things aside from holding protest meetings. He urged parents to appear in large delegations before the Boards of Education and Estimate to voice their protests." When they did so and still received no response, parents deployed new tactics to attract board attention.[33]

During the summer of 1917, PAs citywide met daily to generate oppositional tactics. In Harlem, Brooklyn, Bronx, Queens, and Midtown Manhattan, parents hoped to gain the board's attention through widely disseminated opposition. By mid-July, over 200 immigrant parents, fluent in Yiddish, traversed the city, speaking out against the Gary Plan on street corners and PA meetings and handing out fliers in Yiddish and English to reach a wide segment of Jewish immigrants. Wealthier Jewish PA members donated money and cars to pay speakers to offset the costs of missing work and bring them to meetings. To sustain momentum and maintain networks of activism and information, FNA members attended PA meetings and held biweekly meetings.[34]

Rather than small meetings with individual PAs, activists utilized community-based organizational spaces to expand attendance. Inviting educational authorities to the meetings, they became debates where Jews articulated their opposition to the plan before bureaucratic insiders. Parents used reports of educational failure in Gary schools as ammunition to demand a return to academic programs. One of the biggest debates was held in the working-class Jewish neighborhood of Brownsville, in the Civic Forum of P.S. 84, on March 26. The debate featured proponents Howard Nudd and Alice Ritter on one side and, on the other, Principal William E. Grady and Tristam Walker Metcalfe. With architects of the plan in attendance, mothers shouted down proponent's justifications that vocational education was better for their children. A tide had turned.[35]

Surveying this new activism, the mayor's representatives found "the bulk of the Jewish population of Greater New York," particularly in the Bronx, Brownsville, and the Lower East Side, adamantly opposed to the system, but believed this was because they did not understand it.[36] But NYC's Jews understood completely. They recognized the similarities between their contemporary treatment in America and Russia, where they were first welcomed but then subject to laws intended to destroy their cultures and communities. They also understood that their children were being trained to take their places in the city's factories.

Appearing to spite Jewish parents for their increasingly public tactics, the board instituted Friday night (the beginning of the Jewish Sabbath) sessions for evening high schools. Jewish parents were incensed. A letter to the mayor warned, "For the love of Mike get the Board of Education to revoke their recent order regarding Friday night session of the evening high schools—on the East Side. The people around here are sore as blazes. They will not permit their children to attend on Friday night and feel that it is not fair for them to lose the credit which other pupils who are not religious will enjoy." The mayor continued to deny any anti-Jewish intentions by stating as late as the end of October 1917 that "the Gary System . . . in this City has no religious features whatever."[37]

Voting Out the Gary Plan

Completely ignored by the Board of Education, Jews realized that if they wanted to end the GP, they had to end Mitchel's mayoral term during the 1917 election. Making their intentions clear, Henry Klein announced that the FNA would interview all mayoral candidates about their position on the Gary Plan. P.S. 93's PA formed a new organization, "For Our Children's Sake." They urged parents to vote against Mitchel and "the men who would force this system upon us, whether or not the parents want it." Principals encouraged children to bring the message home to their fathers and brothers (since women had not yet gained the franchise), "anyone who had a vote," to remove Mitchel from office.[38]

Recognizing the political danger of parents' activities, the Mayor's Office distributed pamphlets with blatant mistruths about the Gary Plan and its opposition. One pamphlet claimed, "No parents' organization in any school which has been reorganized on the Gary Plan has gone on record against it." In fact, dozens of schools had done just this and sent the mayor their resolutions, petitions, and letters plainly stating their opposition. Three years of citywide meetings confirmed parents' mobilized and vocal opposition. Given the over-whelming, and public, activism of the previous two years, that anyone believed no PA opposed the plan seems an absurd and intentional effect to completely ignore thousands of parents' years-long mobilization.[39]

But parents' protest was working. Every candidate saturated the media with speeches and statements regarding their position on the plan. The Gary Plan had become the single most important issue of the election.

Morris Hillquit, a Jewish Socialist candidate, argued that the Gary Plan was a capitalist scheme to keep tax money from the masses. Keenly aware of the role the schools played, through vocational and industrial curriculum, in churning out factory workers for the capitalist industries, Hillquit highlighted links between the Board of Education and the Rockefeller Corporation and U.S. Steel. He told his audiences that capitalist organizations supported vocational training to produce an endless supply of young workers. Rather than simply rejecting the GP, Hillquit developed an ambitious school-based program to amend class-based disadvantages. The program included the immediate construction of schools, class size reduction, more teachers, more teacher control over school gover-nance, free medical care, dental care, clothing, and food, free evening schools and public lectures, and the abolition of military training. To promote these ideas, Hillquit created the Non-Partisan Committee of 1,000 for the Children of New York City and Their Schools.[40]

Tammany-backed Judge John F. Hylan spoke at dozens of parents' meetings, particularly those attended by Jewish parents. He argued that the plan decreased the cost of education without improving children's education. Like Hillquit, Hylan highlighted connections between the board and Rockefeller interests and U.S. Steel. Opposing the plan, he promised, if elected, to listen to parents and remove the GP from every school. When Hylan could not attend meetings, he composed letters stating his views, to be read there.[41]

"Down with the Gary System"

For two years, school administrators refused to meet with students about the GP. On October 11, 1917, amid swirling strike rumors, Board President Willcox, Superintendent Maxwell, and other school officials met with students from Wadleigh, Commerce, and DeWitt Clinton High Schools. With Jewish Aldermanic Chairman Harry Robitzek, the students submitted a petition opposing both the Gary Plan, especially the lengthened school day, and a school strike. Willcox directed the students to the Committee on High Schools. Robitzek argued that they had spoken with this committee two days earlier and, brushing them aside, recommended they meet with Willcox and Maxwell. The students committed to opposing a strike, but the board would not shorten the school day. Their unwillingness to take Jewish parents, students, and politicians seriously would have disastrous effects for both the city and the mayor.[42]

On October 17, 1917, student strikes exploded across the city. For the next week and a half, thousands of students boycotted classes and, with their parents, flooded the streets of Harlem, the Lower East Side, Brownsville, Flatbush, and Washington Heights. On street corners across the city, mothers, students, and other activists in broken English and Yiddish attacked the plan. From sidewalks, students vandalized dozens of schools while children on rooftops showered school administrators and policemen with rocks and bricks.[43]

Mothers and students began their strikes in Harlem, Yorkville, and Washington Heights in front of Public Schools 37, 72, 109, and 171. Young women preaching on soapboxes drew such large crowds that streets had to be closed and police brought in to disperse the assemblies. Police arrested Jewish parents who refused to leave the scene. Principal Myron J. Wilson invited parents to P.S. 171 to organize. After a brief introduction, Jewish mothers and fathers rushed the stage, condemning in Yiddish the vocational aspects of the plan. Across the city at P.S. 72, Mrs. Rubinowitz argued for academic courses. "If I wanted the child to be a dancer," she told the Board, "I would send her to a dancing school." Instead, the law compelled parents to send their children to school while ignoring their wishes. During the meeting, 300 boys showered P.S. 54 with stones, breaking the school's windows. High school boys on street corners urged parents and children to stay out of the schools until the board met their demands.[44]

This dramatic new form of protest spread rapidly from the margins and diffused across the city. To the shock and dismay of school officials and conservative newspapers, the strikes continued for days. On the morning of October 18, protest spread to the Bronx, where between four and five thousand children, accompanied by their mothers, marched in front of P.S. 50 and 54 shouting "Down with the Gary System!" and "We won't go back until Gary gets out!" Three hundred boys marched to P.S. 6 to gather more troops. When police shooed them away, they marched to P.S. 44 and accosted police with sticks and stones. In Brooklyn, students shattered P.S. 20's windows. Police chased students away, often into shops and basements. The next day, a Jewish father complained that police scared his striking daughter by chasing her into a basement, but defended the strikes since the board "won't hear us any other way."[45]

The third day of school strikes required extra police details. Toting anti-Gary placards, hundreds of children and their mothers rallied outside of Public Schools 42, 55, 53 in the Bronx and 50, 109, 125, 165, and 175 in Brownsville and East New York, Brooklyn. Children broke 100 panes of glass at P.S. 50, where, a few months earlier, Jewish women had sobbed and protested the military draft. At P.S. 165, police officers suffered cuts and internal injuries from stones and bricks thrown from nearby buildings. As children poured out of schools to join the marchers, parents watched proudly as their children refused education in "factories" while street orators took positions on soapboxes, encouraging students and parents to "stand fast against the Gary system."[46]

On October 21, a meeting of nearly 700 parents and children at P.S. 147 (Brooklyn) descended into shouting as board members refused to even discuss parents' concerns. During board member Oswald Schlockow's speech, a woman yelled from the back of the room, "We came here to hear something about the Gary Plan. . . . If you won't tell these parents what they want to know, I will and I will tell them about it in Yiddish, a language they all understand."[47]

The next day, October 22, students from six high schools (Boys High, Eastern District, Bushwick, DeWitt Clinton, Commerce, and Wadleigh) met with the Board of Education to deliver a petition protesting lengthened school hours. Speaking for the group, Anna Lederer explained that this feature resulted in discriminatory hiring practices (seeking students from non-Gary schools which ended at 1 P.M., store windows read: "Stuyvesant boys apply only"), a lack of extra-curricular activities, school crowding, and less study time. The board suggested students present their case to the "proper official channels," but did not specify who this was. The students were confused, thinking that the Board of Education *was* the proper official channel. City officials noted students' eloquent and refined arguments and fluency in English despite their heavy Yiddish accents but, like John Whalen, Chairmen of the Committee on High Schools with whom that had previously met, refused any changes. Distraught by the board's reaction, nearly 10,000 students from DeWitt Clinton, Wadleigh, and Commerce conducted mass meetings and voted to strike.[48]

Elsewhere in the city, more than 10,000 children struck in Brownsville, Brooklyn, and the Lower East Side. Students and their mothers paraded up and down the streets and in front of Public Schools 84, 167, 174 and 175 (Brownsville) and 25, 63, 79 and 91 (Manhattan) carrying banners reading "Down with the Gary System" and "Down with Mitchel." On the Lower East Side, children supplemented their parades and pickets with showers of stones that smashed school windows. Student strikes in the Bronx subsided as attendance reached 80 percent, but 300 mothers gathered in front of P.S. 42 to denounce the Gary Plan. To complement students' protests, the FNA announced a series of protest meetings for the following week. The board countered these meetings by holding their own meetings at the same times.[49]

A week after protests broke out, attendance officers began rounding up children and brought them directly to Division Superintendent and the schools' informal "trial judge," Charles Gartland, who saw 600 students the first day. Soon, the board reconsidered and sent children to appear before Children's Court justices. Of seven boys brought in on October 20, five were Jewish and ranged from eight to thirteen years old. In Brooklyn, when five Jewish boys between the ages of twelve and fourteen were arrested, their friends followed them to the station. Many children answered affirmatively when asked if their fathers were members of the Socialist party. George Bergen, president of the Junior Ideal Socialist Club, claimed responsibility for "engineering the movement." Bergen repeated this claim to Justice Robert F. Wilkin at the Children's Court while identifying six Jewish boys and two Jewish girls as his co-organizers. These youth faced serious repercussions. Principals expelled striking high-schoolers and either suspended or put younger children on probation.[50]

The city remained in turmoil as the fast pace of mobilization continued. Between the end of the strikes and the election, parents' groups met to protest the plan and generate votes against Mitchel to abolish the GP. Unable to vote but wanting to influence the election, high school students opened Gary Plan debates to the public. On October 26, 1917, a Bronx County Grand Jury released a report finding that the Gary Plan had failed to alleviate school congestion. Recognizing that Mitchel would probably not be elected for another term, the board voted to wait until after the election to meet. No longer could the board argue that the plan had widespread support from parents or that the plan was working. Occurring only weeks, and then days, before the 1917 mayoral election, these protests had a mobilizing effect on Jewish electoral politics. Students and mothers, though unable to vote in the upcoming city elections, played a key role in ultimately deciding NYC's next mayor. Mitchel's death knell had sounded.[51]

On November 6, 1917, Mitchel was voted out of office by a two-to-one margin. Hylan carried the vote with 297,282 votes to Mitchel's 149,307. Hylan's opponents contended that Jews blindly supported him because of his connections with Tammany Hall or coaching by Socialists. This was untrue.[52]

The president of the Board of Education met with members of the Junior Anti-Gary League of the Bronx, who clearly articulated their logic for protesting: The Gary Plan interfered with their ability to hold jobs and participate in extracurricular activities and clubs. Teachers rallied around the students, telling reporters, "These boys read the newspapers intelligently and know what is going on in the world. If you could have talked to as many of them as I you would know they mean business. This city will see something unique in the history of education this week if the boys feel that what they want is denied them. Many boys have told me they had to leave school because of the longer day."[53] Jewish protests did not arise from Socialist or Tammany agitation. Their protests predated the election and Tammany's involvement by years. Jews' demands reflected a keen understanding of both the situation in the schools and their place in a deeply structured racial and religious hierarchy.

As mayor, Hylan immediately conferred with the board to remove the Gary Plan, fire Wirt as educational consultant, and build new schools to end double-sessions in overcrowded schools. But a month into his term, he was frustrated by the Board of Estimate, which claimed it could not remove the GP *and* build new schools. It wanted to "proceed cautiously in abolishing" the plan. To save money, the board slightly modified Gary schools through conversion to the Ettinger Plan. Under this "new" plan, elementary students received academic training, but vocational curriculum persisted in the upper grades. Jews had protested this plan on the same grounds as the GP years earlier; it grouped children based on class into rich and poor schools.[54] Their schools remained inferior training grounds for the factories, not the colleges.

The Harlem 9

Unequal Schools Found in Harlem

In 1954 and 1955, immediately before and after the Supreme Court decided *Brown*, two organizations released reports detailing exhaustive problems in NYC's schools. They both found that NYC's African American students faced the same inequalities as children in the South. Kenneth and Mamie Clark's organization, the Northside Center, released *Children Apart* in 1954. Presented at a citywide conference, the report documented inexperienced teachers, district gerrymandering to promote segregation, overcrowded classes, dilapidated schools, and 103 classes for "retarded" children to which African American children were assigned, illegally, based on the entire group's test scores (rather than the individuals), but not a single gifted class (Markowitz & Rosner 1996). The Public Education Association's (PEA) 1954 report complemented *Children Apart* by condemning the board for promoting segregation and inequality and exposing severe differences in educational quality between NYC's African American and white schools. The PEA found most of NYC's schools hyper-segregated, containing more than 95 percent of students of one race. Segregation resulted in dramatic spending differences, with the board spending $65.10 on each white child but only $21.10 on each minority child. As a result of spending, staffing, and resource-based deficiencies, students in segregated African American schools tested nearly two years below their grade level at all ages, with the gap increasing as children aged.[55]

The research and findings of these reports notwithstanding, in May 1954, immediately after the Supreme Court's *Brown* decision, School Superintendent William Jansen declared segregation in Harlem different from that in the South, since it was "natural." He claimed, "there are no [negative] effects on the children if it is not purposeful." Disbelieving a problem even existed, much less that the board was responsible, the educational establishment made no efforts to counteract the severe segregation and inequality in NYC schools.[56]

FIGURE 3 Crumbling interior, JHS 88 (Harlem), 1961.
Courtesy NYC Municipal Archives

Challenging Northern Jim Crow

These reports legitimized what Harlem parents had long known—that their children attended hyper-segregated, overcrowded, physically dangerous schools with teachers who considered the students heathens. In most cases, these were the same large and crumbling schools that Mitchel had converted to the Gary Plan when Jews attended them forty years earlier. Harlem's parents, like Jewish ones decades earlier, realized that if their children had any hope of quality education, they would have to fight for it.

Nine Harlem mothers, Mae Mallory, Lulu Robinson, Shirley Rector, Bernice Skipwith, Mrs. Donald Ware, Mrs. Isaac Prioleau, Mrs. Livingston Bryant, Viola Waddy, and Gloria Carter, along with newly minted attorney, Paul B. Zuber, organized the Parents' Committee for Better Education (PCBE) in June 1956. Their children attended Public Schools 10, 133, and 197, and were assigned to segregated Junior High Schools (JHS) 120, 136, and 139 in the fall. These schools' racial composition, 99 percent "Negro," warranted a "most difficult" classification from the Board's Bureau of Education and Vocational Guidance. Within a year, Harlem's newspapers dubbed these women "the Harlem 9." This title explicitly connected these mothers' struggles for improved schools in the North to Southern desegregation battles, particularly in Little Rock, Arkansas, where

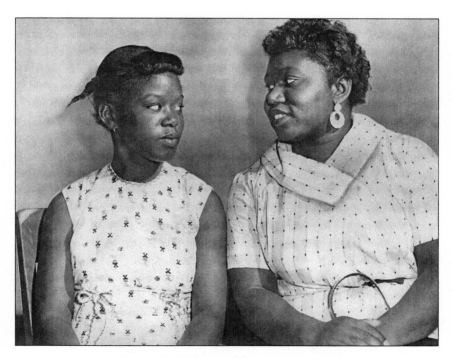

FIGURE 4 Mae Mallory and her daughter, Patricia.
Robert Walker/The New York Times/Redux

students, known as the Little Rock 9, desegregated Central High. Richard Parrish, the president of the Negro Teachers Association, and the NAACP's Ella Baker worked closely with these parents to improve educational quality through both integration and improved resources, better teachers, facilities, and curriculum in their neighborhood's schools.[57]

Leading the Harlem 9 and PCBE was Mae Mallory, an outspoken single mother with two children and former president of P.S. 10's PTA. Mallory lived in the same working-class housing project, the Lincoln Houses, at 2110 Madison Avenue, as other PCBE members. Mallory's children, Keefer and Patricia, attended school with the children of Phyllis Simmons, Ethel Ray, Mr. and Mrs. Stanley Skipwith, Carrie Haynes, Ruby Sims, Mrs. Donald Ware, Mrs. Isaac Prioleau, and Louise Baxter. Other members of the Harlem 9 lived close by—Viola and Elijah Waddy lived two blocks south at 1980 Park Avenue, and Shirley Rector lived two blocks east at 217 Park Avenue. Meetings were often held at the housing project's community center or next door at the Salvation Army Community Center.[58]

Searching for Solutions

Zuber declared the beginning of the Harlem 9's campaign in a letter to Mayor Robert F. Wagner. Referencing the recent PEA report, he charged the board with knowing about and sanctioning inequality, segregation, and its negative effects on minority children. Anticipating the board's argument that residential segregation, not the board, caused educational inequality, Zuber wrote, "This is the same excuse that will be used ten years from now." Zuber demanded that before the 1956–57 school year began, the board improve academic achievement, hire more experienced and licensed teachers (particularly for reading), build new schools in areas promoting integration, keep schools in overcrowded neighborhoods open, transfer African American students to underused schools in white neighborhoods, and allow for community control through parent representation in all school districts. Zuber closed the letter by admonishing, "neither you nor the other elected individuals have kept good faith with the thousands of voters in Harlem, Bedford-Stuyvesant, Lower Bronx, and South Jamaica who helped put you into office. We intend to present this fact to every Negro and Puerto Rican parent who has a child attending an 'all colored' elementary or junior high school in the City of New York and give them something to consider seriously for future elections." And for the next five years, this group would repeat these demands before every city and educational authority they encountered.[59]

To amend these inequalities, Zuber and the PCBE scoured the city to meet with anyone with the power to improve the schools. For months, they attempted to meet with the president of the Board of Education, Charles Silver, and Frank Horne, the executive director of the Mayor's Intergroup Commission, and for months these men rebuffed them. Finally, in November, Silver granted the

PCBE a meeting. There, parents requested integration and local school improvements. Silver promised to look into the problems. Zuber and the parents had "waited patiently for the city administration to correct the unequal conditions that exist in the school system." Receiving only verbal commitments, parents appealed to "a higher authority, namely the State Legislature," to investigate NYC's public schools for their "definite denial of the constitutional rights" of African American children. Their complaints fell on deaf ears.[60]

A unique opportunity arose for the Harlem 9 in January 1957. On the heels of *Brown* and the PEA report, the Board of Education created a Commission on Integration, perhaps believing that problems in NYC schools were minimal, easily addressed, or both. To gather data for the reports, each sub-commission held public hearings where parents and city residents could testify. The Harlem 9 and dozens of other African American parents turned out in full force at the Sub-commission hearings on Zoning and Teacher Assessment and Personnel.

Deftly and emotionally, parents articulated the need for more schools, better teachers, better curriculum, smaller classes, and zoning policy changes so their children could attend high quality schools in white neighborhoods. Mae Mallory, Gloria Carter, Richard Parrish, Paul Zuber, and Leolive Tucker denounced conditions in Harlem schools. Carter argued the irony of their children being bussed within the border of Harlem from one overcrowded school to another, both of which were on double-sessions, while the board refused to bus them to less crowded white schools. "We are fed up," declared Carter. "We are taxpayers and don't think we should be subject to these conditions." In a poignant moment, a JHS 136 PTA member revealed, "we are the parents of children in 136 and are products of the Harlem school system and we don't want to see our children continue in those schools."[61]

Mae Mallory recounted a recent incident in her neighborhood—a truck killed a small child playing with classmates in the street because the school lacked a playground. The principal told Mallory that P.S. 10, which she compared to the segregated school she attended in Macon, Georgia, was just as good as any other school in the community. Given the conditions in surrounding schools, Mallory viewed this statement as "comparing one crumb with another. . . . We do not want to be another crumb. We want to be compared with the whole loaf, the schools that [the mayor's] children go to." She then reminded the audience that a few years earlier Harlem was "saturated" with policemen to stem rising crime rates. "Whether the policemen wanted to come or not, they had to come." Mallory demanded to know, "why can't competent teachers be sent to combat ignorance?" The crowd cheered as Mallory took her seat. The parents' damaging testimony resulted in the sub-commissions' reports recommending exhaustive changes to zoning procedures and teacher selection. The board, however, refused to implement a single one.[62]

The mothers, having attended these and other segregated schools and participated in the public hearings, fully grasped both the extent of the problems (and therefore the board's knowledge of them) and the board's reticence to address them. Armed with in-depth knowledge of the public schools' problems, galvanized Harlem mothers embarked on a movement to alter public school conditions that ultimately led to the globally known Ocean Hill–Brownsville strikes and forever changed the face of African American protest in the North and race relations in NYC. The board's willful ignorance of a known problem, later termed "benign neglect," and paternalistic arguments that inferior, vocational education in segregated schools benefited African American children, only reinforced parents' oppositional consciousness and conviction in their righteousness.

The Harlem 9 Confront the Mayor

African American parents experienced the same cold shoulder from city and board representatives as had Jews earlier in the century. As the Harlem 9's activism became increasingly visible and widespread, it became more difficult for them to meet with the mayor. Wagner, like board members forty years earlier when confronted with Jewish anger, reacted by ignoring letters and petitions, canceling appearances with parents, and sending subordinates.

The mayor's actions only further incensed African Americans, increasing their resistance and diversifying their movement tactics to force educational authorities to deal with them. They flooded City Hall and his Gracie Mansion home with telegrams demanding he listen to their concerns. After miles of telegraph tape, the mayor finally agreed to meet with parents on July 11, 1957. But parents were unsure he would show. They sent dozens of telegraphs urging him to keep his promise. One wrote, "we will consider it a catastrophe if you are not present tomorrow." Another wrote, "I fervently ask urge [sic] you to keep your promise to Parents in Action Against Educational Discrimination and be present at the forthcoming conference." Others noted the meeting's date and time.[63]

To prepare for the meeting, the PAAED convened parents at the Mid-Harlem Community Parrish. First, they rallied parents to attend and generate ideas for the July 11 meeting. Parents contributed questions for the mayor regarding teacher assignment, curriculum and education standards, guidance procedures, and the schools' physical conditions.[64]

At three in the afternoon on July 11, fifty-four parents, Baker, Zuber, Parrish, and Rev. Milton Galamison (also the Brooklyn NAACP's president), crowded into the mayor's chambers at City Hall. Together, they represented 16,000 parents, 32 PTAs, the Manhattan, Brooklyn, Jamaica, and the Bronx NAACP branches, the 369th Veteran's Association, the Negro Teachers Association, and the PCBE. Inside City Hall, the parents "unhesitatingly . . . charged the city fathers stood by and permitted the Board of Education to give their children 'substandard educations.'" Phyllis Simmons, president of JHS 139's PTA, opened the meeting by telling the mayor, "We as parents have waited long enough for the Board of Education to do something about this deplorable situation. We have reached a point where we cannot and will not wait any longer." One after another, these mothers tearfully revealed their frustrations. "We have had so many problems and so little performance. . . . How long are we expected to sit back patiently and sacrifice the future of our children? Our children are zoned in, they haven't a chance unless you, Mr. Mayor, do something immediately."[65]

Baker explained that they approached the mayor because he sat "in the seat which governs the action of all city agencies and it is within your power to question the negligence and indifference shown to a group of citizens of this city by Dr. William Jansen and the Board of Education." Another parent, describing Jansen's indifference to their plight, was interrupted by Wagner, who declared that, "Dr. Jansen runs the Board of Education; I do not." Parents quickly rose to ask, "'Who appoints Dr. Jansen as superintendent of schools?' The mayor answered as quickly. 'The Office of the Mayor.' On the heels of his answer, another parent asked, 'And who puts the mayor in office, your honor?' Answering the question herself, the lady added, 'We voters do, don't we?'"

Silenced for the moment, the mayor listened as parents reeled off demands for the 1957–58 school year. They wanted "better curricula, the end of flexible curricula which varies from school to school in New York City, more qualified and capable teachers, every effort put forth to bring children up to their maximum potentialities and proper and adequate guidance personnel." Parents testified to their children's overrepresentation in vocational classes and to hate groups in Queens attempting to keep African American children out of white schools. They also wanted the board to draw up plans for integration. The meeting closed with Wagner promising to look into the allegations as "quickly as possible," speak with Jansen, and schedule another meeting with a smaller group. The parents noticed that he did not promise to actually do anything about the poor conditions in their schools.

Parents in Action

Sensing the long struggle ahead, in the summer of 1957 African American parents renamed the PCBE to Parents in Action Against Educational Discrimination (PAAED). This evoked perpetual mobilization, agency, and results-oriented efforts to enact change more than their earlier name connoting passive commitment. Ella Baker, on leave from the NAACP to focus exclusively on NYC issues, took up the Harlem 9's cause. Her letter to the mayor notified him of PAAED's launch of a citywide mass action drive for improved education. The *New York Times* estimated PAAED membership at 500. The *Amsterdam News* claimed thousands.[66]

The evening after the Wagner meeting, the PAAED met at the Mid-Harlem Community Parrish to inform local parents of their progress. The mayor's lack of interest in their children's education angered these parents, who recognized change was unlikely without sustained pressure on the board. That night they began planning for a demonstration at City Hall and a boycott in September to target both the mayor and the board.[67]

Like the irate Jewish mothers protesting the Gary Plan, the Harlem 9 met throughout the summer to sustain momentum. Fliers let parents know, "we are now off to a good start on our plans for the summer and fall; but real success depends on you." Just days after the meeting with Wagner, the PAAED began using a longstanding Harlem tradition, street corner meetings, to ensure maximum participation. Throughout Harlem new, angry, red and yellow fliers encouraged new parents to join in the fight for Jansen's resignation because of his many failures. He had failed African American children of NYC by failing to provide experienced teachers, change zoning policies to promote integration, build new schools to end double sessions, provide guidance programs or act on the integration commission reports. The fliers screamed to parents, "Jansen must go!!!" "He should be retired now!!!"[68]

In addition to street corner meetings, the PAAED took cues from the Southern civil rights movement to sustain "direct mass action" by distributing petitions, writing complaints to the Board of Education, and organizing and advertising the September demonstration. A local radio station, WLIB, broadcast recordings of the meetings for those unable to attend. By mid-July, almost every flier advertised that attendees would be "very, very comfortable" in the air-conditioned Mid-Harlem Community Parrish. In the long heat of Harlem summers, this was an important incentive.[69]

The summer ended but protest did not. The PAAED encouraged parents to "come and get in the act" by notifying organizers of additional locations for potential meetings. The fliers listed phone numbers for every borough but Staten Island. On the night of August 21, the PAAED held seven meetings at seven different locations. As the rally drew near, fliers reminded parents of the mass rally at City Hall. They urged parents to "Tell the Mayor!" that Harlem children deserved an equal share of experienced teachers, no part-time sessions, smaller classes, standard curriculum, more remedial teachers (to repair the damage already done) and integration now." Ultimately, the PAAED wanted to "Retire Jansen now!" and "Bring in a Superintendent of Schools who believes in equality."[70]

The Harlem 9 was not surprised when the 1957 school year began without any of the board's promised changes. In a direct rebuff to parents' demands for more experienced teachers, the board announced it would place 1,150 inexperienced teachers in Harlem schools.[71]

Under blue skies, hundreds of parents descended on City Hall on Thursday, September 19, 1957, to protest their children's unequal and inferior education. They carried picket signs and chanted slogans demanding the end of segregation in Harlem's schools. Inside, Baker reiterated demands made during the July meeting—immediate desegregation through rezoning and intradistrict transfers, more experienced and remedial teachers, an end to double sessions, higher quality curriculum, and more schools.[72]

The parents had gotten the mayor's attention. He agreed to meet with them and the board on Monday, September 30, at the board headquarters in Brooklyn. Baker also requested that the city's powerful educational commanders, Board President Charles Silver, Superintendent Jansen, and Commission on Integration Sub-committee chairmen, be invited. But Wagner's attendance was crucial. Parents recognized the mayor's power over members of the board and, in turn, their own power as voters in the upcoming election. Again fearing that the mayor would not show, parents telegraphed the mayor at his home and office to remind him of the meeting and encourage his attendance.[73]

For three hours, fifteen parents, accompanied by City Councilman Earl Brown, met with the mayor, Jansen, Silver, and other board members. The parents had new, more radical demands. They wanted the board to fire Jansen and replace him with a superintendent who would proactively support equal schools for African American children. They also requested regular meetings with board members to hold them accountable—if they had to report on their progress, there had to *be* progress. At the meeting's end, Ella Baker, standing in the doorframe of the mayor's chambers, turned to remind him of the upcoming election and the parents' voter registration drive to elect the candidate most concerned with their children's education.

Tactical Pokes to Compel Board Action

Parents' early protest against inferior conditions in the schools usually occurred through board-created channels. The board's indifference to parents' protests soon found them bypassing routine decision-makers to force reaction to their demands outside the established arenas of educational power (Ellingson 1995). Parents' highly public tactics adopted the government's language to champion their constitutional rights in the courts and election booths (McAdam 1983).

Seeing the possibility of *Brown* applied to NYC schools, the Harlem 9 forced a trial. Requesting transfers to white schools under permissive zoning statues, Mallory and Robinson argued that if white children could be bused *away* from predominantly African American schools at the city's expense, their children should be allowed to walk to higher quality predominantly white schools near their homes. Principals, district superintendents, and Jansen denied their requests. Mallory and Robinson then brought suit against the schools in State

Supreme Court on behalf of all other "similarly situated" parents. This was not just an attempt to enroll two children in high-quality schools. This was a test case to set precedents and change school policy to ensure that no African American child would suffer de facto segregation.[74]

During the trial, Zuber alleged ninety-six separate charges of neglect. Entering into evidence the PEA and COI reports of inherent differences in educational quality and intentional segregation, he argued that the unconstitutionality of the board's policy assigning African American children to inferior schools would result in "irreparable damage" to the children's "intellectual, rational and psychological development." But Justice Samuel Gold was unconvinced that African American youth experienced inferior education or segregated schools. The ruling shocked parents given the mountain of evidence to the contrary.[75]

As 1958 dawned, the Harlem 9 used increasingly public tactics to compel the board to take them seriously. In February, they visited their children's schools to report on their condition. In addition to being 100 percent "Negro," JHS 136 and 139 lacked hot lunches, sufficient cafeteria space, and exams for academic high schools. The schools were "not fit" for their children. Returning from their investigation, parents considered filing charges in federal court against the Board of Education and the City of New York. Instead, they spread fifty complaints over every agency with power over the schools—the Board of Education, ten federal and state courts, and forty city- and state-based civil rights agencies. Notifying the board, parents delivered eleven demands related to three key issues: improved education through better teachers, curriculum, and integration; parental control of the schools; and textbooks that included Black history and culture. Receiving verbal commitment for only one, gifted classes, parents dismissed the offer. Instead, they filed seventy-two charges with the state attorney general requesting the Board of Education revisit its neighborhood school policy to allow their children to attend schools outside their district.[76]

Boycott! The First of Many

On May 16, 1958, in honor of the fourth anniversary of the *Brown* decision, the Harlem 9 organized a school boycott, calling it "School Integration Day." The protest called attention to "inferior educational standards in Harlem schools," the board's "intentional segregated school policy," inexperienced teachers, and ineffective curriculum. Parents, recognizing that their children had "been shunted into vocational and trade schools for the past 20 years," would no longer accept these assignments. To encourage other parents to join them, PAAED members stood outside schools publicizing their protest. Nearly two-thirds of students at P.S. 133 and 197 boycotted. But the board remained unmoved. Recognizing the collective strength of their community, the Harlem 9 announced boycotts for June and September, hoping that repeated strikes would force the board to address their demands.[77]

In an even more public tactic, the Harlem 9 sued the City of New York for $1 million for failing to provide African American children with adequate education. Filed by Zuber on behalf of Viola Waddy, Mae Mallory, Bertha Ware, and Dorothy Braun, this action drew full and front-page coverage from the *Age* and *Amsterdam News*. Even the *New York Times*, which rarely covered the Harlem 9's efforts, reported on the lawsuit.[78]

New York City's Brown *Decision*

Appropriating the board's threats to charge them with violating the Compulsory Education Law, parents boycotted the schools for nearly two school years and at one point even halted their Freedom Schools (a legal alternative to public education) to force the board's hand. Rather than allowing the board to co-opt their tactics, the Harlem 9 co-opted the board's tactics. When the board threatened legal action, the parents took them up on their offer. After the September 1958 boycott, the board charged the Harlem 9 with violating the law. They appeared before the same Children's Court in which, forty years earlier, boycotting Jewish mothers found themselves. There, they faced Justices Justine Wise Polier and Nathaniel Kaplan.[79]

Polier, a well-known child and labor advocate, was the youngest municipal judge in the country and one of only a few women holding this position. Writing of her early years as a judge, Polier reflected, "I saw the vast chasms between our rhetoric of freedom, equality and charity, and what we were doing to, or not doing for, poor people, especially children" (Diner 2003: 77). Hearing the case of Mr. and Mrs. Stanley Skipwith, parents of Charlene, and Shirley Rector, mother of Carla, Polier's lifelong consideration of class- and race-based discrimination resulted in a stunning ideological victory for the Harlem 9. Polier later wrote that of all the cases she heard in her long career at the Children's Court, two stuck out most in her mind; this was one of them (Polier 1989).[80]

In court, parents testified about the poor education their children received in Harlem and Bronx schools. Corroborating their testimony, Arnold Nussbaum, principal of JHS 136, revealed that most teachers lacked licenses, and that, compared to every other school in this city, his had more substitute teachers and ranked in the lowest tenth. Most eighth-grade students tested at least two years behind students in predominantly white schools in reading and math. Undeterred by factual evidence, Dr. R. Wayne Wrightstone, the board's director of the Bureau of Education, offered arguments rooted in scientific racism. He claimed that children in Harlem's schools were behind their white peers because of "biological factors in the post-natal period." Kenneth Clark gave some of the most damaging testimony. He argued that students in Harlem were behind grade-level because they attended inferior segregated schools with "low caliber teachers, watered-down curriculum" and, taking on Wrightstone directly, the board's institutional prejudice regarding African Americans' ability to learn.[81]

Though hearing nearly identical testimony, the two judges issued opposite rulings. On December 3, 1958, Kaplan ruled against seven sets of parents and threatened to take away their children if they did not returned to school in twenty-five days. A week and a half later, on December 15, Polier ruled in Skip-with and Rector's favor. She upheld their "constitutionally guaranteed right" to withhold their children from Harlem's "discriminatorily inferior education," rooted in the board's policies of racial segregation and neglect. Hearing the decision, the Harlem 9 gratefully telegraphed Polier while African Americans across NYC celebrated the decision as if *Brown* had been handed down in Harlem. The same week, the court transferred Kaplan's case to Phillip Thurston after newspapers revealed Kaplan's earlier role as Board of Education secretary, a clear conflict of interest.[82]

It looked as if the tide was turning in the parents' favor. Within days, more than two hundred mothers wrote to the Board of Education requesting trans-fers for their children. Even before the verdict was announced, Carrie Haynes declared the era of segregated and inferior schools over; now, the board must face the inevitable responsibility of changing inferior standards. But the board remained firm. First, they rejected all transfer requests. Then, they made a deci-sion that brought national attention.[83]

Rather than shifting toward equality by addressing unequal segregated education documented by the PEA and COI and reaffirmed by Polier's decision, the board immediately announced it would appeal Polier's ruling. The lone African American board member, Rev. Dr. Gardner Taylor, protested vehemently. He telegraphed the mayor, "community resentment to Board of Education decision to appeal Polier ruling in school case becoming a tidal wave. Serious and far reaching consequences for all Americans are involved." Calling the situation an "educational Scottsboro," Taylor told the *Age*, "I never thought I'd see the day when the NAACP which symbolizes the struggle of the Negro's rights everywhere would have to divert money from its fight in the South to New York City."[84]

Taylor was not the only one upset by the board's decision. Local and national civil rights organizations' attention turned to NYC. Sympathetic support and financial aid poured in. The Empire State Baptist Convention (representing 340 churches and 250,000 congregants), the National NAACP, Harlem Representa-tive Adam Clayton Powell Jr., and Manhattan Borough President Hulan Jack went on record against the appeal. Thurgood Marshall, disgusted that the Southern fight for equality should be suspended to confront Northern racism, offered Zuber aid in arguing the appeal. The *Age* publicized a citywide fundraising drive to support the parents' future court dates. Parents, supported by the African

American community, planned a march on City Hall and an eighty-five-school boycott for February 20.[85]

Heightened national publicity raised the specter of NYC becoming a test case for Northern school desegregation. To resolve the dispute and staunch national attention, in February 1959, Zuber and the new school superintendent, John J. Theobald, issued a joint statement at a press conference. The superintendent would assign the Harlem 9's children to new schools. The board committed to more experienced teachers, guidance counselors, reading, math, science, and language specialists, more accurate tests to judge students' abilities, gifted classes, more remedial classes to get African American children up to speed, and community workers to increase parents' participation in school programs in five schools in Harlem (JHS 120, 136, 139, 171) and Queens (JHS 142). The board also committed to "constantly modify and improve these programs in light of experience and to extend them to other schools throughout the city." Parents called off the boycott.[86]

On the surface, the board capitulated to growing African American outrage and regular media coverage. But in reality, the board remained committed to segregated schools. Parents continued to petition the board for transfers to white schools in Riverdale (Bronx) and Inwood (Manhattan), and the board continued to reject them.[87]

Out of the Public Schools, Into the Freedom Schools

The Harlem 9 brought national attention to Harlem once and, receiving none of the promises issued in the Zuber-Theobald compromise, they planned to do it again. They proposed boycotting the entire 1959–60 school year. Initially, the NAACP supported the parents and allowed them to use their Manhattan Branch office for planning. In a dramatic turn, a month later, the NAACP revoked their support. NAACP leaders demanded parents postpone the boycott, critiqued them for their radical efforts, and blamed their children's poor academic performance (which was never stated) on their own militancy. The NAACP preferred a "wait and see" approach and a "thorough study" of the board's proposals.[88]

Two hundred and fifty mothers voted to proceed with the strike. The board had recently released new proposals to improve the schools that, mothers noted, were nearly identical to those of the Zuber-Theobald compromise. One mother stated, "This just isn't enough. Take a look at these proposals and compare them to the proposals of last February. They're the same thing. The Board of Education never implemented the proposals they promised." Aware of the board's empty promises, these mothers were ready to fight. And so were hundreds of others. The *Age* editorialized, "If something isn't done quickly to alleviate the inadequate physical and educational standards of the Harlem schools, next year, it's going to be the 'Harlem 1,000.'"[89]

In September of 1959, the Harlem 9 and another 250 mothers attempted to enroll their children in Riverdale's JHS 141. When turned away, parents boycotted. On the first day of the strike, over 250 students from JHS 136 and 139 boycotted. The second day, parents sought a meeting with the school board demanding better teachers, not substitutes or recent graduates, the same curriculum found in white schools, and permissive zoning for all junior high school students to avoid segregated schools. The board refused to negotiate.[90]

Long-term planning placed boycotting children in Freedom Schools. Local college students and teachers, Paul Zuber, and his wife, held classes in local churches. Students took classes in English, math, social studies, science, music, Spanish, French, local and world events, and African American history. Parents paid for textbooks and supplies so, unlike in the public schools, children could take books home to complete their assignments.[91]

The boycott lasted through the 1959–60 school year. In December 1959, four months into the boycott, parents remained committed. "We will never send our children to 136 and 139," a mother told a reporter. Shocked at parents' persistence, the board resorted to harassment. The Harlem 9 received harassing phone calls at 5 A.M. Others were charged with welfare fraud dating back ten years. The Fire Department raided Zuber's Freedom School at the Abyssinian Baptist Church and, charging that the doors opened in the wrong direction, closed the school. Mothers remained vigilant, fearing that returning their children to school would result in reprisals. They continued their boycott demanding immediate integration, more experienced teachers, higher educational standards, and community control with parents appointed to local school boards and a committee of African American leaders to design improvements in Harlem schools. Parents also refused to comply with Thurston's order to return their children to school or lose custody.[92]

During the boycott, New York State Supreme Court Justice Henry Clay Greenberg required the board and Superintendent Theobald to show justifiable cause why it refused the children admission to JHS 141 and 52. Neither the board nor Theobald complied. Nor would Theobald transfer the Harlem 9's children to JHS 141. Instead, he agreed to transfer 450 other students to an all-white Yorkville school. For three days, white parents on the Upper East Side reacted with the same vitriol as had white parents in Little Rock. The *Amsterdam News* praised Theobald and admiringly noted the photographs of African American and white children playing and studying together. But for the majority of African American students there was no victory. The schools remained segregated and the Harlem 9's children remained on strike while the board claimed victory in the battle over the schools. Though these strikes, like those of the Jews, disrupted the city's social order and briefly created crisis situations, the board used its power to neutralize protests.[93]

The Board's "Solution"

In January 1960, Thurston reversed his decision and, rather than removing striking children from their parents' custody, ordered the Board of Education to accept their children in new schools within twenty-one days. The next month, the board announced the transfer of 1,450 African American and Puerto Rican children from their overcrowded schools to Harlem's newly renovated P.S. 100. Concerned that this was a logistic rather than a qualitative shift, since teachers often refused assignments in Harlem (or were sent there as punishment from white schools), parents demanded to meet with the principal. He assured them that the school would receive experienced teachers from other schools, had the area's largest library, and would not be on double sessions. While the Harlem 9's children eventually attended integrated schools, either public ones to which the board assigned them or private ones, the overall quality of education in Harlem had worsened, exacerbated by white flight.[94]

Prior to the 1960–61 school year, the board announced a new program, Open Enrollment. This, theoretically, offered children entering the seventh grade in overcrowded schools the opportunity to transfer to predominantly white schools with vacant seats. The *Amsterdam News* published a letter from Theobald and a list of schools to and from which African American children could transfer, but not terms of acceptance for transfers. African American parents were responsible for transportation. This was notable since the board bussed white students away from African American schools. The first year, the board told parents that 3,500 of the approximately 600,000 African American and Puerto Rican children could transfer, but only accepted 105. By 1962, 5,000 students had transferred to schools outside of their neighborhoods. But many were white students using the Open Enrollment program as a cover to flee African American schools and enroll in segregated all-white schools. This left at least half a million African American children in crumbling, inferior, underfunded, and still-segregated schools. The board's rhetoric of neighborhood schools maintained segregation and relegated another generation of African American children to repeat the cycle of their parents.[95]

Harlem's African American children, whose parents remained concentrated in low-skill jobs earning half the income of whites, desperately needed higher quality schools. But they remained segregated. Many junior high schools in Manhattan, Brooklyn, Queens, and the Bronx were 75 to 98 percent African American while others were between 90 and 95 percent white. Between 1959 and 1963, segregation doubled and conditions in segregated schools deteriorated. A state-funded report cautioned that if the board continued to ignore the problem, segregation would double every five years leading to increased African American drop-out rates. The board could have used its power to halt this

FIGURE 5   Assembly at All-African American JHS 139 (Harlem), 1961.
Courtesy NYC Municipal Archives

alarming trend by changing feeder patterns, redistricting schools, constructing comprehensive high schools outside of ghetto areas, increasing teacher training, and creating educational complexes with both elementary and middle schools. Instead it did nothing.[96]

Parallel Protests

Together, these protests reveal the similar ways in which two different marginalized groups challenged institutional inequalities in the public schools to deliver resources to their children. Transgressive contentious politics targeting the government by newly self-identified political actors employed innovative collective action tactics to promote equality in the schools and enhance democratic education. Jews' and African Americans' protests were structured by reactive sequences, what Mahoney (2000) describes as "chains of temporally ordered and causally connected events" (509). But at each turn of each protest, the Board of Education's reactive sequence of countertactics minimized and neutralized Jews' and African Americans' efforts to rearticulate existing structures of inequality and stabilized the existing racial order. Therefore, these cases reveal the similar ways in which state institutions reaffirmed and ascribed racial identities by silencing resistance and reconstructing policies to enhance racial differences.[97]

Similar environmental and cognitive mechanisms provoked Jewish and African American protest. Large-scale Jewish and African American immigration to NYC from the Russian Pale and the South, respectively, lead to large populations of immigrants with high expectations for their children's educational opportunities. These expectations foundered when parents and children faced the realities of an overcrowded school system that treated its Jewish and African American students as second-class citizens. External events in conjunction with cognitive recognition of impending and existing inequalities in the schools resulted in the educational system's loss of legitimacy in Jewish and African American parents' eyes. This knowledge, combined with large populations of similarly situated citizens living in close quarters, resulted in important mobilization opportunities.[98]

Accurately perceiving threats to their livelihoods in America and opportunities to promote change, these subordinated racial groups capitalized on political opportunities as they set out to increase educational democracy for their children. The Gary Plan, a suddenly imposed grievance, threatened Jewish upward mobility but revealed the board's openness to changes to the public schools' structure and curriculum. For the Harlem 9, the *Brown* ruling, the board's willingness to establish the Commission on Integration, consistent reports of educational inequality by legitimate authorities, such as the Commission on Integration and Justice Polier, and the concurrent civil rights movement, all suggested existing opportunities to influence the schools to promote educational equality for their children. They were wrong.

From Many Organizations, One Cause: Neighborhood and Parents' Organizations Appear

Crowded into poor, ethnic neighborhoods, Jewish and African American activists living in the same buildings nurtured a sense of community rooted in similar economic circumstances and ideologies about education. They formed a tight-knit mesh of community-based relationships and networks of activism to share resources during mobilization. In these social and political "free spaces," Jews and African Americans nurtured and maintained oppositional cultures of solidarity rooted in working-class communities. These world outlooks emphasized communal strength and resistance to the dominant culture's oppression through overt and covert protest.[99]

Jewish and African American parents relied on existing and newly created parent, religious, and neighborhood organizations and networks to challenge the school system. These mobilizing structures, by brokering connections between existing formal and informal networks, organizations, and individuals expanded protest potential. As vehicles of protest, these organizations provided activists with the resources, manpower, networks, and "informal connective structures" necessary to deploy oppositional consciousness and tactics challenging educational inequalities.[100]

Mothers' nontangible resources, such as time, social networks, and sheer rage at the system, were central in protest organization and activity. At the center of their families' lives, poverty-stricken but conscientious Jewish and African American mothers passed down stories of oppression and survival. To improve their children's education in America, mothers interwove existing narratives of their resilient ancestors with culturally-rooted tactics to challenge state-sanctioned inequality. African Americans added an additional strand to this narrative, knowledge of generations of neglect by the Board of Education. Parents passed these stories on to their children and empowered them to organize both separately and alongside of their parents to improve their educational futures.[101]

Ignoring Indignation

The Board of Education did not believe that Jews' and African Americans' demands were legitimate problems worthy of attention. During the Gary Plan, the board was incredulous that Jewish parents, whose children previously lacked seats due to overcrowded schools, had legitimate complaints. They therefore dismissed their efforts as misdirected and uninformed. The board engaged in logistical gymnastics to first deny that inequality existed for African American youth and then blame others when reports, which they quietly dismissed, found the opposite. It affirmed *Brown*, but did not believe it applied to Northern schools. Its Central Zoning Unit created school zones maximizing, rather than eliminating, segregated schools and then blamed segregated schools on housing "preferences." When the board conceded existing problems, it refused any proactive measures.

Secret plans and incrementalism in adding new programs to the schools characterized the board's opposition to parents' activism. Without consulting parents, or any public announcements, the board lengthened the school day and institutionalized mandatory military training and changing of classes in Gary schools. This reactive policy making was a direct effort to staunch protest and retrench inequalities. African American's experiences with the board highlighted their complete lack of legitimacy as citizens in the board's eyes. The board locked their children in the worst and oldest schools in the city and denied parents any influence over their educational destinies. Although institutional tactics in silencing activists' protest differed (Paul, Mahler & Schwartz 1997), the results were the same—continued educational inequality for Jewish and African American children and continued protest from each community.

Movement Trajectories: Mobilization, Media, Breakpoints, and Emotions

Jewish and African American activists generated similar repertoires of contention, tactical actions, to challenge the Board of Education to promote educational equality. But local PA meetings, and meetings with board representatives and the mayor, quickly became routine and ineffective. Lacking contention and elements of surprise, these events barely generated a response from the board or mayor. On the losing end of the educational battle more than two years into their respective protests, Jews and African Americans reorganized to develop and deploy new tactics. Innovative forms of contention developed from improvisation and interaction with different audiences and activists.

Certification, validation of activists' grievances by external authorities, provided additional ammunition for activists to sustain mobilization (McAdam, Tarrow & Tilly 2001). Reports of the Gary Plan's failure to improve students' educational outcomes and Polier's ruling that the board subjected African American children to segregated and inferior schools highlighted the board's central role in sustaining unequal education for Jewish and African American children. These findings legitimized existing cognitive mechanisms, generating protest events to galvanize activists and sustain mobilization in the face of continued board repression.

Both groups used the summers prior to the 1917 and 1957 school years to generate citywide support through regular open-air public meetings. Cumulative rejections became transformative events that loomed large in activists' collective consciousness. Frequent meetings heightened interactions among parents to increase the flow of information across the city. New tactics reflected activists' recognition of the board and mayor's circumventive decision-making that completely excluded their sentiments. The next protests promised to be larger, more organized, and, more importantly, draw intense media scrutiny.

As activists geared up to bring new forms of protest to the city's streets, community-based newspapers sustained activism. The sole newspaper opposing the GP, the *New York Daily Globe*, contained a daily School Page edited by Tristam Walker Metcalfe, an outspoken critic of the plan. Both African American newspapers, the *New York Age* and *New York Amsterdam News,* supported the parents. These papers printed regular reports of dissent and contributed significantly to mobilization, particularly the frequency and intensity of protest. Printing information regarding problems in the schools, notifying parents of upcoming protest opportunities, and then reporting on protest events sustained momentum and activists' sense of accomplishment. Parents frequently turned to these newspapers to publicize events, generate movement participation, and investigate the schools. Circulating movement ideas, these newspapers offered "communities in print," publishing letters to the editor and editorials, and opened a new front, the public forum, of social protest.[102]

Parents' protest event sequences, coupled with the board's rejections, transected with outside trajectories—the upcoming mayoral election and the board's decision to appeal Polier's ruling—to produce what Mahoney (2000) and Abbott (2001) call "breakpoints" or "turning point" events, citywide protests. The city and board knew in advance of activists' plans. But they were caught off guard at the extent and duration of each groups' protest strikes. Unprepared for activists' convictions in their cause, and the national attention it would bring, the board maintained their policies of unequal schools, refusing to budge even an inch.

During these citywide, media-generating, and highly visible events, activists converted cultural traditions and tactics into political tools to gain political power. Boycotts and mass protests, which were high in ritual solidarity, became dominant tactics in each case to force a breakdown in public order, forcing the board to deal with activists outside of their traditional channels of authority. Activists consolidated centuries of social protest, including recent efforts to unionize the trade industry, protest America's involvement in World War I, seek women's suffrage, and desegregate public schools and other accommodations, to challenge unequal schools in NYC.[103]

Throughout these protests, emotions compelled action forward. Alienation from the board and the educational establishment, shock about repeated rejection (even as reports, Sub-commission investigations, and court rulings validated their concerns), and moral outrage at the inherently unequal schools to which the board subjected their children all acted as crucial ingredients for the protestors. Reports of schools training Jewish children for factories, and of horrific educational deficiencies in Harlem, resulted in moral shocks that generated initial movement participation. As protests progressed, activists channeled their shock and shame at being subjected to inferior education into protest-generating anger. Angry outbursts in front of educational authorities and the mayor reveal Jews' and African Americans' recognition of these powerful figures' perceptions of their place in the racial hierarchy and parents' complete rejection of this positioning. This anger, many social movements scholars argue, is essential to mobilization and persistent engagement. Articulated on neighborhood street corners and in written and verbal denunciations of educational inequality, anger fueled parents' unwillingness to acquiesce to the status quo and dig in their heels and challenge it. The emotional tone of protest signaled a heightened sense of structural dislocation, contributed to their sense of injustice, and amplified the intensity and duration of the school strikes and boycotts. These intensified emotions generated citywide boycotts and riots unlike anything the city had seen since the Catholic school riots of the 1800s.[104]

Highly visible disruptive confrontations, which rapidly diffused across the city, put pressure on the board and the city to negotiate outside their established arenas of power. As innovative repertoires of contention, these strikes and boycotts were not precise scripts of action but altered depending on which activists and targets attended, where it was located, and reactions from authorities (Sewell 1996; Tarrow 1998). Communitywide protest was a significant tactical escalation and resulted from activists' recognition that their routinized tactics had become ineffective. These strikes created a crisis situation for the board and the city, necessitating action to either allow educational and extra-educational structures to shift to promote equality or retrench existing inequalities. Both educational and citywide institutions (the police, the courts, and the media), acted in concert to retrench existing social structures, generate new policies, and maintain educational inequality.

Absorption and Diffusion: Entrenched Educational Inequalities

Jews and African Americans waged years-long campaigns against the public schools, even, in the case of the Gary Plan, voting the architect out of office. But this mobilization could not open the Golden Door of equal education for their children. Jewish and African American agency encountered powerful racist structures imposed, and countertactics deployed, by the Board of Education and the City of New York that, in concert, maintained the racial order. New names for old inequality contained contention and retrenched educational repression. By acquiescing to minor demands that did little to change Jews' and African Americans' educational realities, the city and Board of Education achieved symbolic victories over both the parents and debates over unequal education.[105]

Their sizable populations notwithstanding, both groups achieved only incremental and symbolic "lowest common denominator" (Tarrow 1998: 163) changes that imposed and satisfied external critics. The Board of Education remanded Jewish and African American children to inferior schools and made every effort to ensure that, as racialized groups, they exercised no control over their children's schools. These cases reveal the difficulty in enacting change in large bureaucratic educational institutions and the limited extent to which these organizations are amenable to change when sought by social outsiders. The board's policies actively ensured that Jewish and African American success and progress would be impeded for at least one more generation as they took their place on the lowest rungs of the racial ladder, while white and nonimmigrant youth maintained a sense of racial superiority and privilege.

3

Resource Equalization and Citizenship Rights

> For over 80% of U.S. history, its laws declared most of the world's population to be ineligible for full American citizenship solely because of their race, original nationality or gender. For at least two-thirds of American history, the majority of the domestic adult population was also ineligible for full citizenship for the same reasons.
>
> —Rogers M. Smith, "Beyond Tocquevilles, Myrdal, and Hartz: The Multiple Traditions in America," 1993

America's public schools have consistently embraced some students while marginalizing immigrant and minority children as racial others. Vocational classes, discriminatory teachers, and poor resources relegated minority children, who were consequentially unable to compete for college acceptance and white-collar professions, to second-class citizenship. NYC's Board of Education relegated Jews and African Americans to the worst schools, with the meagerest resources, and the most discriminatory teachers and curriculum. Jewish children experienced an intensifying decline of resources in the schools, which replicated their position on the lower rungs of the economic ladder, coupled with citizenship training to strip them of their culture. Schools subjected African American children to systematic educational disenfranchisement. Denied quality education, the state limited these groups' equal participation in the American democracy. Rather than allowing for upward mobility and equal citizenship, schools institutionalized power relations, resource inequalities, class differences, and racial identities, all of which were inextricably interconnected. In doing so, the schools reinforced the whiteness of citizenship by excluding racialized Jews and African Americans, inhibiting them from social, political, and economic success.[1]

Neither Jews, as recent immigrants, nor African Americans, as members of a historically oppressed group, were considered members of the larger American political community during these eras. Yet both groups sought membership in this community through the expansion of educational rights and resources.

Arguing on behalf of their children, activists used inclusive language that spoke to the general idea that *all children*, including their own, should be treated equally through a politics of semblance. However, particular histories of oppression necessitated a politics of difference to realize fully social justice and equality. Group narratives articulated during each protest reveal how Jews and African Americans conceived of their own identities.[2]

Schools for Citizenship

Both Jews and African Americans believed in the schools' potential for accessing citizenship rights. When considering rights as resources, attempts to acquire them amounts to efforts to realign social relationships to include Jewish and African Americans within the folds of citizenship. Parents hoped the schools would fulfill their duty as "citadels for good citizenship" and a "bulwark of democracy, the fashioner and the inspirer of civic and national unity." In a legal brief, Paul Zuber summed up Jewish and African American parents' attitudes toward education:

> Today, education is perhaps the most important function of state and local governments. Compulsory school attendance laws and the great expenditures for education both demonstrate our recognition of the importance of education to our democratic society. It is required in the performance of our most basic public responsibilities. . . . It is the very foundation of good citizenship. Today it is the principal instrument in awakening the child to cultural values, in preparing him for later professional training, and in helping him to adjust normally to his environment. In these days, it is doubtful that any child may reasonably be expected to succeed in life if he is denied the opportunity of an education. Such an opportunity, where the state has undertaken to provide it, is a right which must be made available to all on equal terms.

Weaving ideas of democracy, equal opportunity, and citizenship together, the Harlem 9 and Jewish activists articulated clear understandings of the centrality of a quality education to success in America and, as citizens, their entitlement to this resource. Parents hoped to overcome structural barriers to educational success and thus realize social equality.[3]

Participatory Citizenship: Taxpayer Entitlement and Power

Using a universalist discourse appealing for equal, rather than special, treatment, Jews and African Americans expressed their beliefs that, as citizens of

America who paid taxes (which paid the mayor's and Board of Education's salaries), owned property, and voted, the Board of Education and the City of New York were accountable to them and their children. This mobilizing frame is consistent with broad civil rights rhetoric used by a wide variety of marginalized groups throughout American history. Activists questioned the establishment's morality and legitimacy through frequent and public complaints that politicized the education of marginalized and oppressed groups.[4]

As members of taxpayer and civic organizations, Jewish and African American activists challenged the American dilemma of racially based exclusion and second-class citizenship status for nonwhites. Aiming to remove second-class citizenship markers, Jews and African Americans participated in a variety of civic virtues, such as voting, paying taxes, and active membership in neighborhood organizations. Though activists perceived themselves as full citizens, the state clearly did not. If it did, activists would not need constantly to remind it. However, race limited and constrained groups' access to citizenship rights such that universalist rhetoric rooted in the American creed did not translate into educational access.[5]

As taxpayers, voters, property owners, and civically virtuous members of the community, Jews and African Americans seeking equal educational resources for their children targeted not only the board, but also the entire white power structure. Issuing nearly identical narratives, Jews and African Americans demanded "to be considered citizens and taxpayers of New York City." They believed that, "as citizens of New York . . . merely striving to obtain the very best school system possible," they were entitled to a say in how the city spent their money. Jews frequently demanded the board's justification for millions of dollars spent to alter existing schools in nonimmigrant neighborhoods when their schools were either overcrowded or nonexistent. African Americans asked for the same thing, demanding equalization of funding between schools in white neighborhoods and their own.[6]

Voluntary organizations, often referred to as "schools for citizenship," featured prominently in these efforts. Unable to own property in their former countries, Jews took great pains to purchase homes in America. They believed this accomplishment signified both the nation's freedom and their status as full members of the community, invested in its well-being. As new homeowners, Jews organized property-owner and taxpayer associations to formalize their status as participatory citizens. As leaders and members of those organizations, Jews demanded that the city's administrative powers respond to their demands.

Many Jews also belonged to local neighborhood and citywide parents' organizations reflecting their commitment to their local and metropolitan communities. These organizational affiliations allowed them to unite with parents of different ethnic backgrounds to engage in participatory democracy to control their children's education. Jews, with other groups, and as "citizens of New York, [were] merely striving to obtain the very best school system possible—rather than to tolerate an inadequate system."[7]

Like Jews, African Americans asserted their citizenship through forceful narratives referencing their status as taxpayers and voters. This was imperative, since the Civil Rights Act of 1964 had yet to institutionalize these equalities. African American activists linked their demands for citizenship rights with larger civil rights struggles through a universalistic discourse embedded in contemporary political realities that highlighted the need for quality education for future economic success. Repeatedly, in both public and private, the Harlem 9 declared and enacted their citizenship for the public's witness.

At public hearings, African Americans demanded the same high-quality schools as whites. Parents wanted to be "considered citizens and taxpayers of New York City, and in dealing with these problems the Board of Education must look at it that way. If they do, they will realize that all we want is the same things that every other child within the City of New York gets." Robert Parrish, president of the Negro Teachers Association, delivered an impassioned plea at a COI hearing that the board fulfill its duty and uphold their rights:

> Now more than ever before must the classroom be the citadel of good citizenship and teacher and supervisor alike furnish the acid test of good faith. . . . Not only school administrations, parents, students but citizens of every color the country over have their eyes and ears fixed upon our deliberations here today. We have no doubt that if you persist in obeying the spirit of the Supreme Court decision of May 17, 1954, that the great people of New York City who now are so correctly and magnanimously opening their hearts to the freedom-loving refugees from Communism will support you in according our own citizens their constitutional rights.

This democratic rhetoric tied African Americans' demands to the struggle against global communism during an era of heightened alarm and HUAC hearings.[8]

Parents delivered the same claims to the mayor. Addressing him in a 1956 letter, parents argued that local schools perpetuated African Americans' second-class citizenship status and denied their children "constitutional rights." The PCBE told Wagner, "the residents of Harlem must pay taxes and they are entitled to their share of equality in the benefits that accrue from the disbursement of funds. . . . We feel it is unjust for the major portion of the tax dollar to be used to pay experienced teachers high salaries and then refuse to come to our community to teach our children." The Harlem 9 was no less adamant when speaking to Mayor Wagner personally. In his chambers, they told him, "We are taxpayers. We do not think that we should have to supplement the teaching of subject matter at home, or with tutors. We do not think we should have to send our children to private schools. We do not think that the whims of a teacher regarding where he or she want to teach are more important that the needs of our children. We are fed up with sending our children to inferior schools and we urge you to correct these injustices." Throughout these educational skirmishes, African Americans had been denied their rights as citizens and city residents. At the beginning of their citywide boycott, activists notified the mayor that "there will be no compromise this year—we're going to hold out for our rights." Repeating this claim five months into a year-long boycott, the Harlem 9 told him they would "not let up in the fight for first class citizenship in every area of American life."[9]

Unable to vote or hold politicians accountable until moving to NYC, both groups exercised the vote, a tool of citizenship to which they had never before had access, in their protests. Interestingly, Jewish mothers featured prominently in efforts to remove the Gary Plan and the pre-election riots even though suffrage had not yet brought women into the voting fold. It is significant that, when Jews voted in large numbers for the first time in American history, it was to acquire resources for their children. Similarly, as the Harlem 9's protests commenced in 1956, national practices consistently denied the franchise to African Americans. As migrants from the South, many in the Harlem 9 had never been able to exercise this right.

Throughout their protests, Jewish and African American activists leveraged their power as voters to impress upon the mayor their dissatisfaction with the schools. This was logical given that the mayor appointed board members, and, in the case of the Gary Plan, was its primary advocate. Over forty years apart, Jewish and African American activists repeatedly delivered nearly identical letters, telegrams, and petitions to Mayors Mitchel and Wagner, implicitly and explicitly referencing their power as voters and challenging the government to deliver quality education to their children. Demanding meetings and concessions, these documents reminded the mayor of his accountability to them and their power to remove him from office.[10]

When their demands went unmet, Jews and African Americans enacted "get out the vote" campaigns. For months prior to the 1917 mayoral election, Jewish activists urged parents to support a non-Gary candidate at the polls. Their tactics worked and they voted Mitchel out of office. The Harlem 9 waged a political war on the mayor. A letter to the mayor notified him of their effort:

> It appears to us that these individuals to whom you have delegated authority are proceeding in a manner contrary to the program and policy you promised all voters regardless of race, color or creed. We feel that it is incumbent upon us to bring these facts to the attention of the voters of the community. We shall also present to the

residents of our community the record, and what is more important, the action that has been taken on the mandate from the voters when they were elected to their respective offices to protect their interests. . . . Neither you nor the other elected officials have kept good faith with the thousands of voters in Harlem, Bedford-Stuyvesant, Lower Bronx, and South Jamaica who helped to put you into office. We intend to present this fact to every Negro and Puerto Rican parent who has a child attending an "all colored" elementary or junior high school in the city of New York and thereby give them something to consider seriously for future elections.

Contesting school conditions, parents engaged in a verbal tug-of-war with Mayor Wagner, arguing that they put him into office and they could take him out. Parents understood the power structure in NYC and, in demanding it be accountable to them as voters, though holding no institutional power, they articulated perceptions of themselves, through the ballot, as holding power equal to that of other citizens, regardless of skin color.[11]

Repeated claims for citizenship, though they convinced neither city nor educational officials of these citizens' equal belonging and entitlement to benefits, had a deep impact on activists' psyches. Claiming and enacting citizenship, Jews' and African Americans' collective citizenship-based identities coalesced during these movements such that even if the state did not believe they were citizens, they did.

Multicultural Participation in the American Dream

The American creed posits that every citizen should have an equal opportunity to life, liberty, and the pursuit of happiness—"the American Dream." None of these was possible for Jewish and African American children without the same education as whites. Jewish and African American parents and community leaders appealed to powerful state and educational representatives to redefine citizenship so that it lived up to its own democratic principles and no longer precluded their children from accessing particular resources.

Academic attention to multiculturalist rhetoric, referencing the extension of citizenship and political rights to oppressed groups, is relatively new.[12] However, throughout American history disadvantaged groups have consistently sought to participate in the larger American political community without dissociating themselves from their cultural community of origin. Jews' and African Americans' demands for control over their children's education through sanctioned participation in the democratic decision-making process acknowledged cultural and identity-related differences alongside membership in the larger national community. Though the national rhetoric emphasized

Americanization, assimilation, and integration, parents believed that only if the schools recognized group differences could their children participate as equal citizens in a multiracial America. Had this occurred, the board and the city would have expanded the definition of who was American and removed negative connotations of difference associated with each identity. Rigid racial structures, however, impeded this rearticulation.

The City's Children

Seeking full rights granted to citizens, Jews and African Americans connected the narratives of their community's children with that of children throughout the city. Demanding high-quality education for all children, Jewish parents spoke of a universal child, represented by the diversity of backgrounds in NYC's schools. A Jewish mother asserted, "This plan may work very well in the small factory town where it originated. But in New York City, where classes are large, and the children in the classes come from such widely different homes, will it work well? I, for one, think not." In a series of anti-Gary articles published in the widely read *New York Daily Globe*, Jewish principal Leon Goldrich repeatedly referred to all children living in NYC, not just Jewish ones, as "our children."[13]

In predominantly Jewish neighborhoods, activist groups with Jewish officers and large Jewish memberships sought change using universalist frames and a politics of semblance. With parents citywide, Jews demanded that the board do what was best for NYC's children rather than institute an "economic scheme" that undercut their education through policies privileging the bottom line. The Parents' School Betterment League (PSBL), featuring strong Jewish leaders and membership, united "all parents' associations, mothers' clubs and civic organizations interested in public education in a city-wide campaign, to improve conditions in the public schools."[14]

The Harlem 9 explicitly and repeatedly sought to improve educational conditions for the entire community, not just their own children. Speaking for every child in segregated schools, Mallory and Robinson's petitions sought quality education for all "others similarly situated."[15] This case was not just about two children. Lawsuits filed against the Board of Education and City of New York, mass meetings on the streets of Harlem, and protest rallies on the steps of City Hall all drew on African Americans' historical efforts to improve their children's education.

Support from the Empire State Baptist Convention and the national NAACP following the board's decision to appeal the Polier ruling galvanized a vast segment of the local and national African American community. This directly linked the Harlem 9 to the national civil rights movement, "unit[ing] the community as never before." Rev. George Lawrence, chairman of the Special Harlem School Crisis Committee for the Baptists, stated that his organization felt "this is a very serious matter affecting all Negroes."[16]

The Harlem 9 took advantage of the publicity generated from these cases to enact participatory ideologies and mobilize protest relationships within and outside of the African American community. African Americans and Puerto Ricans across boroughs acted together to "obtain better educational facilities for the children in our community through the united organization and unified train of thought of the parents and residents of the community." Organizing a school strike beginning in September 1959, parents declared, "if they don't give us what we want immediately, with no 'ifs, ands or buts,' we'll keep on striking. We're united this year." Together, they threatened the board with publicity-generating mass action, declaring, "until schools in Harlem are brought up to the level where they can be called schools, we're going to strike."[17]

American Race Relations

Addressing contemporary American race relations and global conflict (World War I and the rise of independent African nations), activists highlighted the necessity of every child's ability to participate in building the nation's position in an expanding global economy. This universalist frame was particularly salient given contemporary politics during each case. Appealing to the democratic sentiment of leaders, and indirectly denying their own perceived ties to communist and socialist organizations, Jews and African Americans, like other disenfranchised groups, used a democratic frame featuring a politics of semblance to mobilize for social change.

REMOVING RELIGIOUS DISTINCTIONS. Jewish activists sought to eradicate religious distinctions and training in the public schools, as these tended to encourage differentiation, discrimination, and decrease their children's access to citizenship-based resources both in school and in the future. Religion may have been uncontroversial in Gary, Indiana, where most students were Christian, but in NYC this possibility provoked outrage among Jews less than a decade removed from anti-Semitic pogroms. Rabbi Rudolph Grossman articulated fears of many parents, asking, "especially ought we Jews as a minority, be very chary in accepting a scheme that might be utilized for the purpose of proselytism and that might tend to foster racial antipathies and religious prejudices?"[18] In opposing publicly enacted religion, Jews challenged the schools to view all children as similar and a part of the larger NYC and American community.

Jews believed combining religion with the public schools was diametrically opposed to America's principles of religious freedom, and they marshaled the First Amendment to contest the Gary Plan. Calling the plan "undemocratic" and "un-American," Grossman argued that the religious feature of the Gary Plan was "subversive of the fundamental principle of American liberty . . . mere recognition by the public school of religion and religious differences at once introduces the baneful spirit of sectarianism and weakens, if it does not nullify, the great and mighty principle that is basic to our American life and happiness—the complete separation of Church and State." He believed that the public school system was the "one institution that more than any other, is the expression and the molder and inspirer of the true American spirit, the spirit that knows no distinction between race and creed, between Jew and Gentile, that knows only Americans and aims to fashion only Americans."[19]

In a united statement, a coalition of Jewish religious organizations "adopted a resolution against the religious feature of the Gary Plan as not in accord with the American cardinal principle of complete separation of secular education and religion." Instead, they believed it would "prove detrimental to the interests and welfare of the children and future citizens of the state." Significantly, the goal of all of these organizations was to perpetuate Jewish culture, albeit in private and community domains.[20]

Perhaps more important than violating a constitutional principle, Jews saw in the Gary Plan "a grave danger to this community as a whole and to the children in particular, because firstly, if adopted as originally intended, the children now in attendance in schools, necessarily will be made conscious of differences between themselves in religious opinions and beliefs." This "creed conscious-ness" could "open the flood gate to a tide of bitterness and hatred." Invoking Jews' history of oppression, Rabbi Alexander Lyons declared, "denomination-alism and denominational divisions . . . are contributory to a prejudice and unfraternity with which we are already excessively burdened and cursed."[21]

Jewish rabbis believed that, rather than create a community among children of "rich and poor, Jew and Gentile, believer and unbeliever," religious training would "divide our children into groups according to their religious affiliations." Ira S. Wile, a prominent German Jewish member of the Board of Education, argued that the Gary Plan "dragged religion into the schools, creating barriers and denominational differences between children, between children and their teachers, and between homes." Rather than obliterating prejudice, the schools would become cauldrons of hate where children would see differences where before they had not. These effects would be most disastrous for Jewish children who "would be made miserable, [and] become the butt and target of [their] fellow beings." Indeed, interracial fights had already broken out in schoolyards citywide.[22]

PREPARING FOR AN INTERRACIAL FUTURE. Historically, equal distribution of resources and equitable educational opportunities have been central foci for African Americans attempting to remove the "badge of slavery" that shackled them to second-class citizenship. African Americans perceived education as key to making it to the "promised land" of equal interracial citizenship and away from the economically depressed and segregated industries in which many found themselves. Central to this possibility was the immediate potential for schools to promote positive race relations. In public, in the courts, and in the presence of the board, activists' demands featured a universal appeal that firmly located African Americans within NYC's citizenry. This civic nationalist frame (Gerstle 2001) highlighted the importance of unfettered access to social institutions without racial distinctions.

Contemporary racial discourse centered on integration during the Harlem 9's activism. Many believed that educational integration would promote multiracial institutions, necessitating interracial communication skills. Therefore, integrated schools would also benefit whites. Zuber pointed out, "the ability to live with and tolerate other races, religions and creeds is as integral a part of an education as reading, writing and arithmetic. . . . The necessity of social communication and understanding is equally important to the white student, it is essential for this education to start at the earliest possible age before the attitudes, concepts and biases become hardened into the child's personality. . . . Segregation of children in schools no matter what the cause does irreparable damage to the emotional, intellectual and psychological development of not only the Negro child but the white child also."[23]

Aware of the changing racial realities in America, African American parents accurately assessed whites' discomfort while interacting across racial lines in social and professional settings. Parents argued that educational integration would strengthen the entire American polity. Hopeful for an integrated future, parents believed that when children got along, so too would parents, although it may take a generation or two. But more importantly, they believed that if the schools treated their children equal to white students, as adults they would have the tools to be, and status of, true American citizens.[24]

Jewish and African American parents believed their children belonged equally to a citywide community and hoped for an interracial future, for the day when every American would see themselves and their children as full members of the American public. As each group articulated these hopes and dreams, their actions (voting, paying taxes, and owning homes) backed up their beliefs that they really were American citizens. Engaging in these actions alongside their racial peers heightened group solidarity and revealed a Du Boisian double consciousness featuring a Jewish or African American identity in conjunction with a viscerally felt American identity.

Plural Visions of Democratic Education: Culturally Influenced Resource Demands

Educational resource inequality, due to perceived racial differences, significantly affected Jews' and African Americans' status as citizens, replicated the racial hierarchy, and fostered white parents' and students' privilege. To amend these conditions, activists drew on histories of oppression and group cultures to assert their rights as American citizens. Narratives linked their historic inability to receive schooling with current economic conditions.

Using a politics of difference, each groups' narratives referenced their particular histories of discrimination to seek policies to remunerate past inequalities. A Jewish father at a parents' meeting argued in Yiddish, "we come from Russia. To us education is a holy thing. Its means so much for my girls and boys. . . . You tell me to join the 'parents' association and it could do nothing. . . . We have only our vote left." During board-sponsored COI hearings, African Americans linked their historical experiences with Jim Crow education in the South and in NYC with their children's contemporary educational lives. Parents referenced group culture, desires for citizenship, and their own civic virtues in opposing the poor quality schools their children had been subject to and disadvantaged by for generations.[25]

Each group publicly exposed and contested explicit discrimination from a school board that subjected their children to unequal and inferior education. Jews opposed the Gary Plan as a cost-cutting scheme designed to cram more immigrant children into already overcrowded schools rather than build more. During protests, Jews urged the board to reallocate funds to build non-Gary schools to alleviate double sessions. Jews considered the board's persistent denial of new schools, explicit discrimination. Alderman Alexander S. Drescher of Brownsville, a poor and working-class Jewish neighborhood, argued that the board neglected Jews by failing to construct new schools there, where all students were on double sessions. He accused the board of "discriminat[ing] against a district whose growth is conceded by all and where school conditions are in a very bad state." In editorials, the mayor's chambers, letters to the editor, and at local meetings, African Americans decried the discrimination to which NYC's schools subjected their children. In January 1959, the Harlem 9 and Zuber called for the complete reconstruction of the Board of Education and removal of Superintendent Theobald, arguing that they ignored discrimination against their children and, in doing so, violated the U.S. Constitution.[26]

Vocational Curriculum: Education for Second-Class Citizenship

The proliferation of vocational classes in their children's schools outraged Jews and African Americans. They fully recognized the necessity of academic training for white-collar and professional jobs promoting social and economic mobility and up the racial and economic hierarchy. Parents also understood that this form of hidden curriculum replicated the unequal division of labor, social relations, and racial inequality by denying their children opportunities to share in the American Dream and compete for coveted jobs. Protesting vocational education, parents frequently referred to the communitywide long-term consequences if their children continued to receive a "segregated and inferior" education. These historically and culturally specific statements relating to Jews' and African

Americans' economic conditions stemmed from Jews' segregation in garment sweatshops and African Americans' roles as domestics and menial laborers. Neither group wanted the schools to reproduce the social order. Instead, they demanded that schools enable their children to overcome it.

Jewish parents did not want their children in the Gary Plan's "educational factories," designed to "train the working class, or, as we have all along declared, to make efficient cogs for [the] industrial machine." Schools devoting time to sewing infuriated Jews, the vast majority of whom worked in sweatshops and in their homes as pieceworkers to fuel the garment industry. Instead, Jewish parents demanded academic curriculum to facilitate qualification for City College. A Jewish mother summed up the attitude against the Gary Plan at a PA meeting at P.S. 171 in the predominantly Jewish Washington Heights section of Manhattan, in broken English and Yiddish: "We want our kinder to learn mit der book, der paper, und der pensil und not mit der sewing und der shop!" At P.S. 126 in Greenpoint Brooklyn, boys who had no interest in the plumbing profession took plumbing lessons but received no training in spelling, composition, or penmanship. When asked about this coursework by a reporter,

FIGURE 6 Machine shop room, P.S. 45 (Bronx).
Courtesy NYC Municipal Archives

Leo Voilenick complained, "We don't want to saw on metal for 100 minutes a day," with his classmates nodding in agreement. Five hundred mothers boycotting this school declared, "We don't want our children raised as automatons but as free and independent citizens." Forty years later, African Americans faced the same treatment.[27]

Vocational/industrial curriculum was a particular thorn in side of African Americans, who knew that whites had subjected them to this curriculum from kindergarten through college since the days of Booker T. Washington. Vocational education had, for generations, condemned African Americans to the lower classes, both nationwide and in NYC. Many Harlem 9 members had firsthand knowledge of this curriculum since they had attended the same schools as their children with curriculum preparing them for lives as domestics, janitors, porters, bellmen, and other menial laborers. At graduation, vocational school students received a High School Certificate. Colleges, which required a High School Diploma, considered the Certificate nothing more than an attendance certificate. African American parents, aware of these realities, struggled to replace vocational classes with academic ones and enroll their children in academic high schools.[28]

Parents recognized that segregated vocational schools "crippled the minds" of African American students. As the "most effective form of exclusion from higher education or specialized training," segregated schools lacking science and engineering curriculum "doomed" African Americans "to an inferior standard of living" through "an inferior competitive position." In America's increasingly technological society that necessitated scientific knowledge, vocational curriculum literally left African Americans in the dust of the last century.[29]

The Harlem 9 deployed a multifaceted challenge to vocational education's every component. First, parents protested against the curriculum itself. Joining the Harlem 9 at City Hall, Phyllis Simmons of the JHS 139 PTA told the mayor, "We realize that we must have plumbers, carpenters and waiters, but we resent limiting these trades to any particular race of people just because they happen to have less money in the bank or because they are forced to live in less favorable sections of the city."[30] Parents then challenged the system's mechanisms.

Guidance counselors often placed African American students in vocational junior and senior high schools and vocational classes in academic schools regardless of their academic track record. Furious, parents took their complaints about "guidance counselors [who] deliberately turn Negro students away from academic courses and place them in vocational schools" to the mayor. He did nothing and this persistent "shunting" of African American children to vocational and trade schools provoked the Harlem 9's September 1958 boycott.[31]

Substandard elementary education inhibited access to elite high schools and college attendance. Entering the fourth month of a school boycott in December 1959, parents charged "the educational standards are so low in those schools that our children can't get into decent high schools." Professional accounts legitimized parents' complaints. Studies consistently found that children graduating from segregated schools rarely attended NYC's elite high schools (Hunter High School, Bronx High School of Science, Brooklyn Technical High School, and Boys' Stuyvesant High School) offering students the best opportunities to enter college. These schools required an entrance exam, which educators refused to most African American students. The *Amsterdam News* charged the Bronx High School of Science with maintaining a quota system to keep out African American children. In the school's twenty-year history, it had admitted 8,000 students; only 90 had been African American. The previous year, the city's elite high schools accepted only three African American students; Bronx Science accepted none. Arnold Nussbaum, principal of JHS 136, admitted that very few students had ever moved from JHS 136 to elite high schools. Notably, it was principals' responsibility to recommend students for the exams and Nussbaum only recommended two of JHS 136's twenty-three National Honor Society members.[32]

Challenging African American students' dramatic underrepresentation at elite high schools, Shirley Rector demanded the schools offer her daughter, Carla, an honor student, and all of her classmates, admission exams. Rector charged school administrators with keeping parents "in the dark" about these tests and their importance for admission to elite high schools. She advised "all Negro parents" that they "insist that their children take these exams." In addition, she demanded that schools provide their children with the academic material necessary to score high enough to gain entrance to elite schools. However, Truda Weil, district superintendent of schools, claimed that unqualified students who took the exams would be "traumatized" and she was "proud" of the curriculum offered at Carla's school (JHS 136). Completely ignoring African American students' potential and instead justifying the watered-down curriculum parents had been fighting for decades, Weil's statement captures the longstanding belief in African American intellectual inferiority. Like adherents to "culture of poverty" arguments, her assumption of African American children's failure blames low educational attainment on the children, rather than the schools.[33]

Finally, parents insisted that the board reevaluate their decisions regarding reclassification of local schools from academic to vocational when the racial composition shifted from white to African American, which also decreased financial resources. At COI hearings, the Harlem 9 testified that every high school in their neighborhoods was vocational. This sentenced African American children to inferior curriculum and reduced funding that reproduced the racial hierarchy through a separate and unequal educational system.[34]

Exacerbating Poverty in the Schools: Jews' Economic Conditions

Jewish poverty fueled critiques of Gary innovations, such as the changing of classes, recess, and increased enrollment that directly and indirectly strained household budgets. Parents complained of lost and stolen clothes and school materials due to shared lockers, frequent clothing replacement when items were lost or dirtied during mandatory recess and gym, and doctor expenses for written excuses from these classes.[35]

More problematic than clothing and doctor visit expenses was the choice the Gary Plan forced many teens to make: complete high school or drop out to work. The lengthened school day compelled Jewish students to quit jobs that vitally contributed to household finances and paid for their future college education. Businesses discriminated by hiring only students from non-Gary schools, mostly non-Jews, since they arrived at work later than students attending non-Gary schools. Students condemned this aspect of the plan for imperiling their and their family's contemporary economic survival and the impact on their future if forced to choose between school and work. In a letter to the *Globe*, Abraham Kahn, a High School of Commerce student, implored the Board of Education to

> think what it means to the thousands of unlucky boys who must hurry as fast [as] they can after school in order to arrive at their places of employment on time, in order to earn an extra few dollars per week, so as to not only help support their families, especially these days, but also make it possible by their earnings to stay in school. At least a large majority of the employers do not want school boys after 3 or 3:30 P.M., the latest, especially in the newspaper business, in which many boys are engaged. . . . I am still willing to continue the struggle. But with the Gary Plan in effect I would have to leave school. Don't forget there are hundreds of similar cases.

Kahn closed by imploring the *Globe* to print the letter to "help the 'anti-Gary Plan campaign'" and improve their educational and economic opportunities. Anna Lederer, a Wadleigh High student, told President Willcox, "the lengthened day had barred pupils from employment after hours and hundreds of boys and girls were being forced out of school as a result." Hoping to move off the lower rungs of NYC's racial hierarchy, Jews young and old struggled against these discriminatory policies.[36]

Flashbacks to the Pale: Mandatory Military Training

Jews viewed mandatory military training in American schools as discriminatory and exploitative based on previous experiences with mandatory enlistment in Russia. Teenage boys at Eastern District High School called on their families' histories as they joined their parents in protest. Well aware of the importance of education, parents nevertheless withdrew their children from school rather than permit them to participate in a program reminiscent of culturally destructive practices that tore their families asunder in the old country. This was an astounding move for parents who came to America for their free public schools.[37]

Though potentially un-American and unpatriotic, Jews perceived their actions as the opposite. Henry Saum, a Jewish father, argued, "unthinking militarism and subservience is a detriment to the democracy in which they seek to live." He and others sought to uphold what they found great about the nation; their children's freedom to choose whether to volunteer for military action, an option not available to them in Russia. In demanding the freedom to choose to serve their country, they also preserved the nation's democratic principles.[38]

Juvenile Delinquency

Juvenile delinquency featured high on the list of social problems within NYC's Jewish and African American communities during the Gary Plan and Harlem 9 protests. During these eras, alienation from school due to racist school cultures and discriminatory teachers, combined with a lack of supervision from parents working multiple jobs, resulted in high dropout rates within each community. While many dropouts joined the workforce to contribute to household economies, others became criminals. Although local politicians often referred to African American children as delinquents, African American parents never uttered this word, perhaps critical of the city's portrayal of members of their community as overrepresented among NYC's criminal element. However, Jewish concerns regarding delinquency reveal the connections between educational disenfranchisement and social disenfranchisement. Parents knew if their children became criminals, as many Jewish youth did, they would lose access to citizenship rights for which they had worked so hard.[39]

Upper-class Jews used the Gary Plan debate to advocate for programs that would ultimately contest demeaning and anti-Semitic images. An editorial in the American Hebrew directed to women argued for religion in the public schools, noting that the idea that, "every child should receive religious instruction is stoutly maintained not only by the clergy, but by all social workers who come in contact with the delinquent. It is found, by actual investigation, that the majority of children brought into the juvenile courts have received little or no religious instruction. One of the first steps toward the reformation of the delinquent is provision for instruction in the religion of his parents."[40]

Though many did not want religion in the public schools, Jews nevertheless believed the time had come to address delinquency within their community. Rabbi Rudolph Grossman wrote in the American Hebrew, "It is high time that our Jewish community awaken to the seriousness of the present chaotic condition. It is in this lack of religious training of our youth that there lies the chief causes of gangsterism and crime. It threatens the future of our faith and brings upon us humiliation and shame. . . . If the present agitation regarding the Gary

System will help to arouse our people to a better realization of the urgent need for the religious education of our own children, it will, to that extent at least, have served a valuable purpose." Agreeing with Grossman, Dr. Samson Benderly (director of the Bureau of Jewish Education), argued that the Jewish community, and not public schools, should invest in religious and recreational centers for their children.[41]

William Wirt, the Gary Plan's architect, played on Jewish fears of criminality and negative stereotypes to convince Jewish leaders of its value. In a letter to Joseph Barondess, a Jewish member of the Board of Education, he argued that extended school hours would replace the "wasted street life of the child." Writing to Benderly, Wirt highlighted the "reduction of 'alley' time" as a key benefit of the Gary Plan so "children would not be exposed as much as they are now to the dangers of the street." Benderly disagreed with Wirt's logic, arguing that the Gary Plan was "drifting toward paternalism." Speaking for the community, he stated, "we Jews feel that, while we want to reduce the influence of the street on the children, this should be done by providing more adequate facilities for Jewish religious instruction, so that the time left to the children, after their public school studies, shall not be used up by them exclusively for recreation, which is, of course, necessary, but also for ethical and religious training, without which their education is incomplete."[42]

Linking the Gary Plan to "factory methods in the schools," Rabbi Joseph Silverman chastised the board for using scare tactics with parents concerned about delinquency. From his pulpit, Silverman declared, "They say it is better the child were in school than on the streets; that the streets are dangerous. If the streets are dangerous, impure, and immoral, then let the city purify our streets." Other parents argued that the Gary Plan would exacerbate, rather than attenuate, delinquency within the community by releasing low-income students to the streets during and after school hours. Since most parents worked, this increased children's opportunities for "truancy and immorality."[43]

Qualified, Compassionate, Capable Teachers

African Americans have consistently sought experienced and culturally sensitive teachers to provide their children with safe spaces in which to gain the knowledge necessary to compete on equal footing with nonimmigrant white students. NYC employed a higher proportion of African American teachers than many other Northern cities but did so disproportionately to that of the African American student population. The board hired most African American teachers as temporary substitutes. In 1949, African Americans made up only 2.5 percent of all teachers in NYC. By 1955, the board reduced that number to 1.08 percent (544 of approximately 50,000 teachers in the system). Of these, 232 held regular appointments and 312 were substitutes.[44]

Therefore, most African American students encountered white teachers who fostered a denigrating school culture and treated them as second-class citizens unentitled to a quality education. Most white teachers had no knowledge of African American culture or the public school's role in perpetuating inequality. As students encountered teachers lacking cultural sensitivity, experience, or knowledge, cultural mismatches facilitated low expectations, low grades, and high dropout rates. While Jews issued few teacher-related grievances, African American parents often complained about their children's inexperienced and insensitive white teachers.

In NYC, white teachers dehumanized and physically disciplined African American children. Monthly photographs in the *Age* and *Amsterdam News* featured African American children beaten and bruised at the hands of their teachers. Parents, lacking political and economic resources, had little recourse. Principals often defended teachers' actions, saying, "Well, if you don't like the way we do things here you can take your children elsewhere."[45]

Compounding the problem of racist teachers, many white teachers assigned to African American schools represented NYC's least qualified, experienced, and effective members of the corps. The PEA, the board, a Mayor's Report on the Schools, the Junior High School Principals Association, and educational experts testified to the lack of qualified and experienced teachers in African American schools. Indeed, half of the teachers at JHS 120, 136, and 139 were substitutes while the board assigned teachers licensed in specific subjects to classes in other areas. White teachers often refused assignments in African American schools or immediately requested transfers to white schools after completing their five-year probation period. The Teachers Union discouraged the board from firing teachers and as a punishment placed poor-performing teachers in schools labeled "difficult" (the Board of Education's designation for predominantly African American). The board also required teachers with the lowest scores on the citywide teacher exam to teach in "difficult" schools. In other words, students who needed the most qualified, experienced, and culturally sensitive teachers often found themselves in classrooms with the worst ones available, or none at all.[46]

The board sanctioned and encouraged these teacher-related problems. Ruling in the Harlem 9's favor, Justice Polier wrote, "the Board of Education is entirely responsible for the existing discrimination in teacher assignments, there is, in my opinion, not the slightest doubt. What the board did was to let the teachers themselves establish the discriminatory pattern. . . . The Board of Education of the City of New York can no more disclaim responsibility for what has occurred in this matter than the State of South Carolina could avoid responsibility for a 'Jim Crow' State Democratic Party which the State did everything possible to render 'private' in character and operation." Assigning blame to the school system for not supplying African American children with a high-quality education, Polier challenged the Board of Education to fulfill its mission regardless, or in spite, of efforts to withhold these benefits.[47]

Parents recognized the dearth of experienced and qualified teachers in their children's schools. At the public hearings of the Commission on Integration Sub-committee on Teachers and Personnel, parents decried discrimination by teachers who did not want to teach in their neighborhoods. Another complained that these teachers assigned homework without any educational value rather than intellectually engaging activities. Throughout their protests, the Harlem 9 affirmed their children's need for more teachers, more aides, and more clerical staff in the schools so teachers could develop innovative classroom activities to engage and instruct their children.[48]

A Racial Census

The board did not keep statistics in the 1940s and 1950s regarding the racial backgrounds of its students. This was likely an intentional effort by the board to remain ignorant of explicit racial differences in quality of education and segregation in the schools. At least that is what African American parents believed. In a board-sponsored hearing, they called for a racial census to generate data to receive state aid for improving schools in their neighborhoods, since the board had recently done this to account for non-English-speaking Puerto Rican students. Seeking "a more democratic education for all children," this demand is a perfect example of African American parents using a politics of difference to seek equal treatment in NYC's schools.[49]

Parents' Committees: Reconciling Cultural Needs with Citizenship Rights

To democratize education, Jewish and African American parents' organizations (such as the PSBL and the PCBE) challenged the hierarchical decision-making structure by seeking direct control over their children's education. Rather than allowing the board to mold their children into the lower and working classes, as members of self-governing parents' groups, Jews and African Americans would promote group representation and equality in a new democratic system of education.[50]

Jewish parents drew a clear boundary between themselves and the powerful white establishment running the schools. They recognized that the board cared little for their desires and saw through the rhetoric of economy used to install a plan that, against their wishes, effectively created two separate and unequal school systems. At a public hearing attended by President Willcox, one mother stated, "They are our children that you are experimenting with and it is not proper to exploit them," while another issued a "vehement denunciation of what 'they are doing mit unserer kinder. Dey are unserer kinder, not theirs.'"[51]

Believing "the time is now ripe for the parents of school children, the true 'guardians' of their interests, to assert themselves in matters of public educa-tion," Jewish parents protested "against the fads and fancies, which under the guise of economy and against the option of educational experts, are being forced into our school system at the insistence of a small group who represent nobody but themselves." After the board refused to meet with them, questioning whether their concerns were sufficiently serious, a Jewish mother retorted: "Well, if you have 500 parents coming to school on that account it might be considered a serious question." In a similar effort, African Americans mobilized parents across the city to produce widely attended demonstrations at City Hall and the board. On the heels of the May 16 school boycott honoring the *Brown* decision, 100 parents met at the Salvation Army Community Center. Their unof-ficial slogan, "Our children will have gray hair if we wait for the board and the city to improve Harlem schools" reflected their frustration with the board and determination to take matters into their own hands.[52]

Struggling for power in an educationally exclusive city, Jewish and African American activists believed the Board of Education should institutionalize parental control through consultation with parental representatives from each community prior to implementing any educational changes. Embedded in their own communities, parents hoped to engage in collective decision-making regarding their children's education. These autonomous decision-making bodies would democratize education by bringing different, and previously marginalized and excluded, voices into the room to compel changes in the public schools to promote upward mobility.

Adamant that educational decisions not be enacted without their input, Jewish and African American parents demanded that the board and the mayor address their concerns. Describing her frustration in a letter to the editor of the *New York Daily Globe*, a Jewish mother in Flatbush wrote, "In reading to-night about the protest the principals and teachers are making against introducing the Gary plan into more schools, it occurred to me that the parents of the children might well be considered. What right has any man or board of men to so revolutionize the school life of the child without consulting the parents? Such a radical change should not be made without giving the parents, mothers particularly, a vote in the matter."[53] Mothers, who had not yet won the right to vote, strongly believed in their entitlement to consideration and response in the education domain.

Jewish parents and community leaders flocked to organizations such as the Mothers' Anti-Gary League and PSBL. Arguing "the time is now ripe for the parents of school children, the true 'guardians' of their interests, to assert themselves in matters of public education," President Goldman explained the

PSBL's mission as "a non-partisan organization which seeks to unite all parents' associations, mothers' clubs, and civic organizations interested in public education in a citywide campaign to improve conditions in the public schools. One of its activities will be a vigorous and organized fight against the extension of the Gary plan. Its board of directors [will present] a united opposition to the school policies of the present administration." Designed for longevity, the PSBL continued "as a permanent organizations of parents to fight year after year for better schools for their children." The Kehillah, an umbrella organization of Jewish organizations, went further. They demanded that the board "establish an advisory committee of Jews . . . to cooperate with it."[54]

Forty years later, a coalition of African American parents expressed the same sentiment as Jews regarding the need to act as a united community to exert control over the public schools. On behalf of the PCBE, Zuber stated, "We believe that we can only obtain better educational facilities for the children in our community through the united organization and unified train of thought of the parents and residents of the community. We realize that if we wish to accomplish certain things we must work to get them ourselves. . . . We intend to apply pressure and continue applying it until our goal is reached. . . . From now on we shall demand action and remain positive in those demands." To institute this practice formally, members of the PAAED sought "a parent committee set up in each school district with authority to visit and inspect every school in the district periodically and file a report of their findings with the Board of Education. And once unfavorable conditions are found the Board will correct it, immediately."[55]

Jewish and African American parents believed that community control of education would subvert the "schooling" their children received at the hands of the dominant group.[56] These innovative demands reveal Jews' and African Americans' perceptions of the schools' symbolic (and, in many ways, actual) meanings in America. Either they could be hegemonic establishments subjecting their children to education for inequality or they could be collaborative institutions promoting democratic education. As part of *their* communities, Jewish and African American parents wanted oversight and ownership over their children's education and everyday life. These proposed parents' auxiliaries represented true equality of citizenship by promoting democratic, rather than hierarchical, decision-making and social justice in the form of high-quality schools attentive to group differences.

Plural Citizenship Visions

Jews' and African Americans' racial status, rooted in cultural differences, existing ideologies, and social practices limited their citizenship in a nation with a long history of preserving boundaries through official and de facto enforcement. Citizenship is not just a legal status. It is, as Evelyn Nakano Glenn explains, "a matter of belonging, including recognition by other members of the community" (2002: 52). Exclusion from one of the key elements of social citizenship, high-quality public education, based on perceived racial differences profoundly effected each group's social, political, and economic participation, their equality, and thus their success in America. The board's decision-making along racial lines reproduced stratified systems of power, state-based benefits, and patterns of resource distribution. Jews and African Americans strongly resisted this selective denial of rights and resources.[57]

During these eras, each group operated as racial outsiders within a civic and racial nationalist state founded on racial principles embedded in racist cultures. Customs, practices, and laws constantly reminded members of each group of their liminal citizenship status. The state, through racist immigration legislature in 1924, excluded Jews from national boundaries of citizenship. Although legally white, customs, practices, and daily discrimination belied this reality for America's Jews. Whites had treated African Americans as "second-class citizens" since slavery's end. Since the state does not voluntarily grant power and privileges to racial outsiders, Jews and African Americans made claims to seize them.[58]

Shut out of jobs, neighborhoods, restaurants, hotels, and many colleges, Jews and African Americans attempted to democratize education and promote social justice by redistributing educational resources, changing the structure of education within NYC to increase inclusivity, challenge cultural stereotypes, and alter the system of hierarchical decision making.[59] Each group's efforts at educationally based racial contestation attempted to alter the structures and change the boundaries of citizenship and racial ideologies so that racial difference did not preclude membership within the folds of the American community.

However, available repertoires of discourse, structured by the racial hierarchy in place during each era, constrained mobilizing frames. These historical junctures, featuring a liminal citizenship status and deeply rooted and daily experienced cultural identities, necessitated activists' use of universalist and particular narratives referencing both cultural and American aspects of activists' identities. This resulted in the simultaneous use of a politics of difference and semblance to generate ideas about rights and entitlement using mobilizing frames of participatory citizenship and multicultural access to the American Dream. To reach multiple groups, each frame aligned closely with contemporary rhetoric of Americanization, inclusion, and integration while drawing on group cultures and histories. Drawing upon collective experiences, Jewish and African American parents developed a changing rhetoric that combined the dominant social narratives of the time with concrete desires to challenge the school systems.[60]

Although unable to generate structural changes within the educational bureaucracy, Jewish and African American involvement transformed each community from scattered to unified networks of activism. Composing constituencies, Jews and African Americans created and disseminated informative tactics among diverse individuals within each group. Examining frames deployed and narratives used in both public and private reveals the deeply held, yet perpetually shifting, multifaceted identities that transformed during each movement. By the end of each movement, each groups' collective identities coalesced into hybrid identities featuring a Du Boisian double consciousness reflecting both American and particular group cultural identities (Hobson 1999; Du Bois 1995 [1903], Weiner & Richards 2008).[61]

Jews and African Americans not only desired to be, but *perceived themselves as*, full American citizens entitled to the privileges existing therein. Enacting citizenship in strikingly similar manners, Jews and African Americans demanded similar rights by seizing on education to create "political opportunities through discursive resources and patterns of mobilization" (Hobson 1999: 153). In public, Jews and African Americans used a politics of semblance to highlight their similarities to other Americans and mobilize widespread support. Narratives linked demands for educational resources and opportunities with future group outcomes and possibilities to participate in America's social, political, and economic spheres. They hoped this would be sufficient to expand boundaries of citizenship to include them, as active participants of the local society rather than disenfranchised subjects of a race-based *herrenvolk* democracy.[62]

Through increased utilization of local, state, and federal institutions available only to citizens, Jews and African Americans asserted their belonging to the national community. Marching together in the streets, formulating letters and petitions to the mayors and the Board of Education, or meeting to discuss the next tactic or just vent about local educational problems, became consciousness-raising experiences for Jewish and African American activists. By mobilizing and then enacting an activist identity based on an American identity, Jews and African Americans "delegitimized negative constructions of themselves" as noncitizens (Hobson 1999: 149). Universalist claims and politics of semblance conveyed their willingness to subvert cultural differences, at least in public, to uphold America's democratic ideologies and values. In doing so, they took on not only NYC's Board of Education but also a system of racial subordination that relied on schools to unequally distribute citizenship rights and resources.

Although activists mobilized and acted as Americans, activists also embedded hidden transcripts and culturally rooted demands in a civil rights master narrative to argue their case in the courts of public opinion and educational and city-based centers of power. In both public and private, activists' politics of difference challenged the Board of Education and the city to commit to principles of social justice, address differences, and promote equality. These hidden transcripts referenced each groups' collective memories of historical oppression, group cultures, nationalist sentiments, and status in NYC to acquire educational resources to which they believed they were entitled. Neither Jews nor African Americans sought to minimize their group cultures; they sought to maintain group differences and cultures while being perceived as full American citizens.

The intertwining of group cultures and histories of oppression with contemporary conditions and citizenship-based narratives while celebrating and enacting hybrid identities highlights the degree to which both groups conceived of themselves as a unique group with separate and distinct cultures and customs. These narratives reveal Jews' and African Americans' plural and democratic vision of American society and citizenship wherein they could participate equally. Jews and African Americans hoped to expand the definition of citizenship to include members of their own group, thereby changing the very meaning of citizenship in America. They believed an equal educational policy would signal to other Americans their status as full citizens and would no longer enable cultural differences to be grounds for exclusion or discrimination. Jews and African Americans therefore expressed a vision of an equal, yet plural, American cultural life. However, faced with Jewish and African American protests, city schools dug in to enforce exclusionary social citizenship.

Citizenship Denied

The American public considered neither African Americans *nor* Jews white during these movement episodes. Lacking membership to this exclusive category, each group encountered the Board of Education's exclusionary practices, which systematically denied them resources, and maintained racial inequality and white privilege. Therefore, Jewish and African American movements to acquire equal education represent what Young (1990) and Winant (1994) would consider radical efforts to promote social justice through the reallocation of educational resources and opportunities in a reimagined and reconstructed racial democracy while simultaneously rearticulating and maintaining racialized identities.

Consistently and explicitly, the United States has reserved democratic rights for whites. In a country where so many groups have *not* been white at some point in their histories, American movements seeking citizenship-based privileges have attempted to expand rights for and extend citizenship status to members of racialized minority groups. African Americans' consistent disenfranchisement throughout American history, and the second-class citizenship to which whites relegated them, limited their potential and freedom to *be* American. Southern and Eastern European Jewish immigrants found themselves in a similar (though not identical) early-twentieth-century NYC. Expanding boundaries of citizenship would amend negative conceptions of difference and contemporary images of Jews and African American within the national imagination. Each group would then have been free to maintain a double consciousness featuring an American and cultural identity.

In NYC, both dominant racial narratives and the board's actions situated Jews and African Americans, unqualified for full citizenship rights, near the bottom of the racial order. These racial narratives, which "'explained' obvious inequalities between whites and African Americans in different ways" (Pride 2002: 7), were critical to America's racial hegemony. Attempting to repudiate the highly complex structure and meanings attached to American citizenship by disengaging it from meanings of whiteness, Jews and African Americans challenged and addressed the very meanings of and connections between citizenship and whiteness in a country that, though based on these links, often fails to address them. Rather than existing as what Barrett and Roediger (1997) call an "in between" or "not-yet-white" group, both Jews and African Americans sought to reconcile their cultural differences with concepts and constructs of being American while maintaining cultural differences.

Demanding the rights to which they were entitled as citizens, each hoped to uncouple citizenship rights from whiteness. As a structural condition, whiteness confers privilege to members while constraining nonmembers' abilities to achieve upward mobility through denial of rights and resources. Though implicitly linked, claiming whiteness and claiming membership to the American citizenship are not necessarily the same—especially since Jews *did not* claim whiteness while claiming citizenship. Instead, Jews sought to reconcile Jewish and American identities by participating in local and national communities while maintaining group differences and cultures. They believed that cultural and citizenship-based group attributes were thoroughly compatible but that "children should develop their religious consciousness and much is done in this direction to-day at the domestic alter in church and synagogue, in the denominational school, all before or after school hours" but not in NYC's "cosmopolitan and democratic public schools."[63]

But Jews' and African Americans' progressive visions of a racial democracy in the educational arena remained unrealized. The City of New York and the Board of Education withheld privileges of citizenship in order to maintain boundaries of both whiteness and American citizenship. By ensuring only nonimmigrant white children's access to quality education, Jews and African Americans remained racial outsiders, outside the realm of full citizenship.

4

Contesting Curriculum

Hebrew and African American History

In 1946, a seventh grade teacher at P.S. 37 in Queens demanded that her only African American student read "Plantation Memories," advising him that if he used the proper emphasis in his oration, he would "receive a good mark." Mrs. Sasser used the poem, describing slaves as "carefree, light-hearted Negroes of the South," to teach her mostly white students "the truth" about "colored people," believing it to be a "beautiful" depiction, "typical of a group of people," which the class received "very well." Aware of the text's racist underpinnings, William Townsend refused to complete the assignment, and upon learning of the book's use, his mother demanded its removal.[1]

Such was a day in the life of a typical African American student in New York City's public schools in the mid-twentieth century. In addition to inadequate educational resources described in previous chapters, both Jews and African Americans contended with curriculum that, at best, rendered their cultures and histories invisible, and, at worst, held them up for ridicule. To ensure their children's academic success and retain their cultural traditions, both groups, during two separate waves of activism, at two separate moments in history, confronted the schools with different sets of demands to combat these curricular shortcomings. Each wave lasted eighteen years, meaning that a child born at their inception would have little hope of encountering the sought-for curriculum before he or she graduated.[2]

Between the onset of the Depression and the end of World War II, Jews demanded that the schools facilitate the development of a language community through the instruction of Hebrew. The decades after the Gary Plan protests found many Jews staying in school longer due to a paucity of well-paying jobs for those skilled only in vocational trades and to anti-Jewish hiring preferences during the Depression. With the decline of immigration from Southern and

Eastern Europe following restrictive legislation enacted in 1924, Jewish youth began to resemble other European groups; they Americanized, assimilated, and developed increasingly secular outlooks. These efforts to combat assimilation and ensure cultural longevity through Hebrew classes in local public schools were also intended to enhance Jewish students' feelings of inclusion in local schools in order to do better academically and be better Americans. But, unlike African Americans' demands, Hebrew demands appeared independent of resource-based demands. In fact, these efforts to violate the constitutional separation of Church and State through the instruction of a religious language (though not the religion itself), stands in sharp contrast to parents' and rabbis' insistence that the schools not differentiate students based on religion during the Gary Plan protests.

Encountering explicitly racist curriculum in the schools, African Americans, during the immediate post–World War II period through the civil rights era (culminating with the passage of the Civil Rights Act of 1964), demanded a holistic reconfiguration of school texts to remove racist images throughout the curriculum and replace them with books and courses that accurately represented their culture and contributions to American and world history. These protests unfolded alongside generations-old efforts to challenge resource inequality, including the Harlem 9's battles. Activists recognized the centrality of cultural misrepresentation to their oppression and often demanded the teaching of African American history in conjunction with resource reform to facilitate a holistic restructuring of their children's education.

Both Jewish and African American curricular reform efforts involved the grassroots, but attracted these activists at lower rates than did resource-related protests. Jews mobilized elite German Jews with longstanding ties to the Jewish community alongside lower-class first-generation Zionist teenagers from Eastern Europe. These groups competed with teens and adults from similar backgrounds hoping to perpetuate Yiddish as the lingua franca of American Jews. Absent from Hebrew protests, unlike all other protests, were Jewish parents who, during the Gary Plan, had proved their mobilization capacity. African American protests emerged from across the community ranging from popular and radical figures such as Dick Gregory and James Baldwin, to teachers' groups, to neighborhood groups, to more conservative community members sitting on newspaper editorial boards. However, in neither African American case could activists secure consistent support from community elites.

Hebrew Language Curriculum

American public schools have taught foreign language courses, particularly classical languages such as Greek and Latin, for centuries. As new immigrants arrived in America at the turn of the twentieth century, public schools, catering to the industrial classes, replaced or supplemented classical languages with modern Romance languages such as French and Spanish. Ethnic Europeans—Jews, Italians, Poles, and Portuguese—saw in the schools' foreign language program an opportunity to promote cultural retention through language preservation (Zimmerman 2002a).

Jewish organizations' efforts to resurrect Hebrew in local schools, beginning in the late 1920s, served two purposes. It asserted the community's sentiment that Jewish heritage was important enough to build into the public school curriculum, and it represented an attempt by a subset of the Jewish community to determine the appropriate way to be "Jewish." Many German Jewish leaders believed that Hebrew, the holy language of rabbis and the proposed language of a future Jewish state, was central to retaining rapidly Americanizing youth within Judaism's folds (Lieberman n.d.). But considerable debate existed within the Jewish community regarding the appropriate language to preserve in America—Hebrew or Yiddish. Established, middle-class, German Jews embraced Hebrew. They considered it a classical language of equal importance to Latin and Greek, with contemporary relevance as the official tongue of the future Jewish nation in Palestine. German Jews looked with contempt at Yiddish, linguistically similar to German and considered a lower-class language. Parallel institutions reflected this diversity of opinion, with Hebrew taught in reform and conservative organizations with a modern Zionist emphasis, such as yeshivas, Talmud Torot, Hebrew high schools, and Hebrew schools. Yiddish was spoken at day schools organized by Jewish labor groups, such as the Shalom Aleichem Folk Schools, "a network of Yiddish-language schools that emphasized Jewish folk culture instead of religion" (Diner 2003: 57; Shandler 2000). The language debate, reflecting different ideas about the future of the religion, was still unsettled as efforts to include Hebrew in the public schools commenced in 1929.

Whichever ideological bent a community member chose, most Jewish education occurred through private institutions such as Hebrew or Yiddish schools, summer camps, neighborhood groups, and clubs designed to attract Jewish adolescents. Social programs encouraged children to play among themselves and marry within the fold. The extracurricular activities also kept Jewish youth off of the streets and out of reform schools, a deep fear within the Jewish community. The most institutionalized form of Jewish education, Hebrew schools, offered thrice-weekly classes to prepare for bar and bat mitzvah. While many parents sent their children to Hebrew schools, the majority did not. Jewish leaders as well as Zionist youth members of Avukah, Young Judaea, and the American Student Zionist Federation expressed deep concern that, of the 200,000 Jewish children in New York City in 1910, only 42,000 (or 21 percent) received any Jewish instruction (Chipkin 1937; Dushkin 1918; Friedlaender 1961).

NYC's public schools offered Ancient Hebrew between 1909 and 1923 as a trial period following the request of Joseph Barondess, a well-respected Jewish leader and NYC's commissioner of education. The Regents rescinded its approval after restrictive immigration legislation curtailed both Jewish newcomers and course enrollment. This ended Regents exams for college entrance, credits, and scholarships and, in NYC, all Hebrew course offerings. The Jewish community urged the board to reconsider, given the expanding number of Jewish students as existing immigrants married and began Jewish families. The board did not oblige.[3]

Efforts to incorporate Hebrew into the public schools arose sporadically between the end of its official recognition in 1923 and its reinstatement in two NYC high schools in September of 1929. Consistent attention to Hebrew began with a 1928 speech by Samuel M. Blumenfield, president of Avukah, the student branch of the American Zionist Federation. In his public address, Blumenfield advocated the teaching of Hebrew classes in high schools and colleges. This speech mobilized a wide swath of NYC's Jewish community, both professional and voluntary organizations, newer and established organizations, and youth and adult organizations, to promote Hebrew classes. These organizations met a few months later to "take practical steps to make Hebrew a part of the high school and college program." Dr. Samson Benderly, president of the Bureau of Jewish Education (BJE) and, later, head of the Jewish Theological Seminary's Teachers Institute, chaired the conference and became a leading figure in efforts to reinstate Hebrew. After Avukah named Blumenfield chairman, he promptly organized committees to, first, convince NYC's Board of Education and the State Regents to include Hebrew and, second, develop curricular materials.[4]

Community leaders, in their difficult task of convincing educational authorities, formed a committee featuring a dozen prominent German Jews. As time went on, responsibility fell to the community's progressive elite, Benderly, Rabbi Stephen S. Wise, of NYC's progressive Free Synagogue, and Israel Chipkin (educational director of the Jewish Education Association [JEA]), which became known as the Hebrew Committee (HC), and their constituent organizations. Student and Zionist organizations focused on increasing student enrollment and persuading principals of students' desire for Hebrew courses.[5]

The committee quickly approached local educational authorities to promote Hebrew's expansion across the city. These authorities acted just as quickly in rejecting the HC's request. Harold G. Campbell, associate superintendent of schools, stated that Hebrew was a religious rather than a secular language, not widely used for communication, insufficiently related to English, appealed only to a limited number of students, and was inappropriate given the schools' shift toward scientific, rather than humanities, curriculum. Also, they noted, most colleges did not teach Hebrew "on an equal footing" with other languages since students could not declare it a major subject.

The HC met with the Board of Superintendents on March 30 but left the meeting unsure of its outcome. In April, still unsure of whether to grant students taking Hebrew courses credits toward graduation, the board approved the subject as an "experimental" elective in two predominantly Jewish high schools, Thomas Jefferson and Abraham Lincoln, after receiving support from each school's Jewish principal. But only students familiar with the language could enroll. A week later, the board voted on the broader, citywide adoption of Hebrew's status as a foreign language in local schools. Hebrew warranted official recognition with other classical and modern languages and would be accepted in partial fulfillment of graduation requirements. To ensure Hebrew's success, the HC worked throughout the summer to develop curriculum materials and train teachers, which the board left up to the Jewish community. This was not an insignificant task given the financial resources required as the Depression bore down on institutions attempting to aid poverty-stricken Jews. Upon accomplishing these tasks, this "radical change" precipitated by Zionist student organizations appeared it might be successful and complete. But this was far from true. The HC still needed to convince the Board of Regents to certify Hebrew language classes for credit toward a College Entrance Diploma and create a Regents examination that tested students' mastery of the subject, a requirement necessary to graduate from all schools in New York to this day.[6]

Hebrew for College Acceptance Credit

Since students needed to pass a foreign language Regents exam to graduate from high school, those enrolled in courses without one needed additional language coursework. State and city colleges also used the scores to determine scholarships. With increasing school enrollment due to immigration and the Depression (few jobs meant many students staying in school longer), the schools objected to classes like Hebrew, on the grounds that they did not facilitate graduation.

Jews, after receiving approval for Hebrew in two schools, targeted the top of the educational hierarchy, the Regents. The Hebrew Committee believed it imperative that the Regents offer an exam and local colleges accept Hebrew classes for entrance credit to legitimize the coursework and not to disadvantage students enrolled in Hebrew courses. For nearly twenty years, beginning in 1930, in letters, phone calls, and meetings, the HC pleaded with the State Board of Education, the Regents' Board of Examinations, and high-ranking officials, such as George M. Wiley, associate commissioner of education, and Dr. Frank Pierrepont Graves, state commissioner of education, to approve Hebrew for college entrance requirements and develop a Regents exam.

When this failed, activists redirected their efforts to the local level to encourage colleges with close ties to the Jewish community to install and accept Hebrew. But local colleges agreed that a Regents exam must exist for them to accept Hebrew courses for credit toward entrance. Nearly all—Manhattan

College, St. John's, City College, Brooklyn College, and Fordham—resolved to "follow the lead of the Regents." For decades, colleges waited for Regents' approval while high schools waited for colleges' acceptance of Hebrew coursework. The Hebrew Committee saw clearly the task ahead of them. Without a Regents exam, Hebrew's expansion and acceptance would be impossible.[7]

While the state and colleges resisted sanctioning Hebrew for entrance credit, local high schools triumphed. At a conference at the Board of Education with Hebrew teachers and their supervisors, Chipkin found those "who were at first doubtful speak in the highest praise of the results obtained as compared with those in other foreign languages." However, all made clear that without official recognition from the state, enrollment in these classes would, and already had begun to, decline, especially with guidance counselors discouraging students from enrolling. Chipkin argued "unless the three local colleges, especially the one in Brooklyn, agree to recognize Hebrew amongst the electives offered for admission to college, I fear that our efforts to go ahead will prove futile. The teachers seem quite discouraged about this obstacle." Knowing of these problems firsthand, Principal Gabriel Mason suggested skipping the middlemen and going directly to the Board of Regents in Albany. Representing the HC, Samson Benderly left the first meeting with the Regents and President Robinson of City College empty-handed.[8]

Undeterred, Chipkin, Wise and Benderly met with presidents and chairmen of foreign language departments of local colleges. Many believed Hebrew's recognition for credits would be unproblematic and initiated its inclusion in their own college's curriculum. But ultimately, inclusion was contingent on the Regent's official recognition with an exam. In June 1932, the Regents officially approved and adopted Hebrew's second-year and third-year syllabi in 1931 and 1932, respectively. Hebrew courses would count toward the College Entrance Diploma. With this, the HC set out to ensure Hebrew's acceptance by the colleges, increase student enrollment, and expand the course throughout the city. By November 1932, the HC realized the inadequacy of the Regents' recognition without an exam.[9]

By January of 1933, six colleges had added Hebrew as a legitimate precollege subject area: St. John's, Manhattan, Hunter, City, Brooklyn, and New York University. But recognition from the most important college for young Jews, City College, was not forthcoming. In a series of letters to the school's president, Frederick B. Robinson, the HC emphasized other colleges' recognition of the course. Robinson responded that while he supported the curriculum, faculty members of the Committee on Curriculum did not. Robinson could have leveraged his authority as president to support Hebrew, but he did not. Simultaneously, Chipkin pressed this line of reason to convince Columbia and Fordham to recognize Hebrew, to no avail.[10]

As these events unfolded in NYC's schools, Hitler rose to power in Germany and began instituting rules and regulations against German Jews unprecedented in modern history. These events did not go unnoticed by the HC, particularly Stephen Wise. At this point, Wise took a step back so that he could give himself "without reservation to the work for our brother-Jews in Germany." Chipkin penned most of his letters after this point. The HC's failure to capitalize on this opportunity to enhance narrative fidelity by linking the necessity of Hebrew and Zionism with this rising global threat to international Jewry, a dominant discourse within the community, likely hindered communitywide support for the classes.[11]

Again attempting to gain official approval for Hebrew with a Regents exam, the HC wrote to a variety of educational authorities in Albany. They argued that since the Regents did not offer a Hebrew exam, students needed an additional foreign language course to fulfill their requirements. Wondering whether their curriculum needed adjustments to gain approval, Chipkin queried Wiley through an ally, Harold C. Campbell, associate superintendent of schools and Board of Education member. Wiley never responded.[12]

To get answers, and Hebrew approved, the Hebrew Committee decided to travel to Albany to meet with educational authorities in person. Anticipating requests by educational officials and knowing that if Hebrew was included in the public school curriculum, it would be by their doing, Greenberg and his colleagues prepared second, third, and fourth year syllabi comparable to other foreign language syllabi and submitted them to Wiley. They also wrote a Regents exam. All they needed was official approval.[13]

Meeting with State Department of Education representatives in Albany, in January 1933, Chipkin, Wise, and Benderly found them averse to approving Hebrew exams. Avery Skinner, director of the Examinations Division, claimed his department lacked Hebrew examiners and that allowing Hebrew opened a window for other groups to demand language parity. Wiley explained that the exam could not be included since the state liked to encourage continuity in educational subjects and most colleges did not offer Hebrew. Recognizing Wiley's circular logic, Wise argued that without Regents and its Examination Board's recognition of Hebrew the colleges would not accept or teach Hebrew. Chipkin reiterated this sentiment later in the meeting and reminded the board that it had given these exams in the past and could reinstate them. He also noted that colleges and universities nationwide taught Hebrew. Benderly argued that students pursuing Hebrew were penalized, and in a city like New York, with over two million Jews, tremendous potential existed for large enrollments.[14]

At the end of the meeting, Wiley informed the HC that they would have to wait nearly a year for an answer. The State Board of Secondary Education had the final say but was guided by the State Examination Board, which would not meet again until December. Wiley suggested that Chipkin, Wise, Benderly, and Greenberg submit a brief to the Examinations Board. When asked if an HC representative could attend, Wiley vacillated, stating only that it was "possible." Graves later granted Wise an invitation but the meeting was to be held on a Saturday, when these observant Jews would be unable to attend. This was all Graves would do for Hebrew.[15]

To prepare for the meeting, the Hebrew Committee, in November 1933, completed and submitted an official memo to the State Board of Regents Examinations requesting Hebrew be recognized "on a parity with other foreign languages" rather than "treated differently." Days before their scheduled meeting in Albany, Wiley notified the HC that Hebrew's syllabi, which Greenberg had submitted nearly a year earlier, did not contain enough reading and that "more Hebrew history and literature should be included," contradicting the board's earlier warning that the course must be secular. Wiley emphasized that all principals, instructors, and pupils should know of Hebrew's ineligibility for an exam because of this insufficiency. Wiley's Board of Examiners placed the final decision in the hands of Frank Graves, the commissioner of education, who had opposed an exam in the past.[16]

Undeterred, Chipkin wrote to Graves explaining that the state had approved syllabi up to the third year, and that the BJE was developing textbooks for the fourth year. He wrote to request that the College Entrance Diploma Section of the Board's Handbook add Hebrew to the list of foreign languages, including Latin, Greek, French, Spanish, German, and Italian that met the state's three-year foreign-language course requirement. Graves, without directly opposing the HC's efforts, transferred the request back to the Board of Examiners, which only met once a year, to decide Hebrew's fate. By not responding to the HC at this point, or any other point for the next fifteen years, the State Board of Examiners denied Hebrew's official recognition.[17]

Lacking an exam, the Hebrew Committee shifted its target from the state-level educational bureaucracy to local school officials. Chipkin met with principals of local junior and senior high schools to persuade them to teach Hebrew. The first, Dr. Robert B. Brodie, principal of Seward Park High School, located in the Jewish Lower East Side, resisted until directly pressured by Wise. The Jewish district superintendent of the junior high schools, Benjamin Veit, disappointed Chipkin when he asserted, Hebrew "does not belong in the junior high schools and it should be limited to senior high school programs" since English, health education, and "other subjects suitable to pupils at the JHS level" were more appropriate at this age.[18]

Curriculum Creation and Teacher Training

Even without Regents' approval, by 1935, enrollment in Hebrew schools had doubled since 1918, increasing to 35 percent of all Jewish children in NYC. To

provide for students' needs, textbook, syllabi, and teacher training responsibility lay with Jewish organizations. Employing resources from the Hebrew
Committee's organizations, the Jewish Education Association, the Bureau of
Jewish Education, and the Jewish Theological Seminary, Jews created entire
syllabi and textbooks, based largely on those used in Hebrew schools, trained
teachers, and created the highly contested Hebrew Regents exam, when the
board would not. For five years, teachers in NYC schools used mimeographed
copies of Hebrew school texts while the HC paid for their development. The
HC's Syllabus Committee released the first-year 400-page textbook, *Elements
of Hebrew* (costing $1.65), in 1934 after consulting with students, teachers, and
the Bureau of Jewish Education. The JEA, with Simha Rubenstein, a well-known
Hebrew scholar, then developed a textbook for second, third, and fourth year
students.[19]

The Jewish community's pursuit of Hebrew courses on its own, sparing no
expense during a time of economic and, in Europe, social crisis, testifies to their
belief in the importance of this language to perpetuating the religion and its
community. Despite the board's best efforts to deter the HC, their determination to do the work of the board's curriculum department allowed them to both
succeed in their efforts and control the curriculum's content. This autonomy
enabled Jews to promote the Jewish faith by including books and material
resembling local Hebrew school curriculum to reach students not enrolled in
these parallel institutions.

Hebrew teachers had to be licensed by the board to teach in the public
schools. To increase those available, in 1935, the Jewish Theological Seminary
and Yeshivah College introduced a Teachers Institute and a Jewish Teachers
school, respectively. NYC's Board of Education also granted the Jewish Theological Seminary responsibility for developing and grading licensure exams. While
many expressed interest in teaching Hebrew, few qualified. Of 153 who took the
exam in 1935, only 19 passed. Those licensed formed an association, the Jewish
Teachers Association, and stayed in close contact with the JEA for support,
maintenance of licensure, and pedagogical innovations. The board offered a
junior and senior high school teacher exam in 1938 but budget shortfalls, due
to the Depression, prevented it from appointing many who passed. Unlike for
other subjects, the board offered Hebrew licensing exams infrequently, again
delaying the subject's progress.[20]

Hebrew Progress Stalled

For the next five years, the Board of Regents equivocated, stalled, or simply
ignored the Hebrew Committee. Trying another route and hoping for a more
direct response, Mason wrote to Skinner. He noted that discrimination barred
students enrolled in Hebrew from competing for scholarships, a dire need for
poor immigrants during the Depression. Mocking the HC's demands, Skinner

repeated his arguments from the January 1933 meeting. "It will be interesting to note in this connection that there has been, from time to time, requests for examinations in other language fields: Swedish, Polish, and most recently, Esperanto. If Hebrew were granted in New York City, why not Swedish examinations for Jamestown, or Polish examinations for Buffalo?" The committee received a similar response from Lawrence A. Wilkins, director of foreign languages in the city high schools. He "slammed" Hebrew, comparing it to Esperanto and Russian, neither of which NYC schools taught. The HC succeeded in including Hebrew in local high schools without Wilkins's support. But without Skinner's support, a Regent's exam and official recognition were impossible.[21]

Given the Board of Examiner's continued rejection, the HC decided to contact Susan Brandeis, daughter of Supreme Court Justice Louis Brandeis and the sole Jewish member of the Board of Regents. Brandeis advised Wise to secure powerful figures, particularly Campbell, to recommend Hebrew to win over the Regents. As the sole Jewish Regent (and a woman), Susan Brandeis lacked the authority to convince her colleagues to install a Regents exam. So this effort also proved futile. While Campbell supported the HC, Graves did not. Graves's persistent disregard of the HC's concerns resulted in their pursuit of a different strategy.[22]

Unable to successfully convince school officials that Hebrew was a valuable foreign language worthy of the same state standards as French or German, the HC sought extracommunity allies to make its case. HC members Samson Benderly and Ralph Marcus suggested that Wise contact religious scholars to either give their written support of their efforts or pass resolutions "commending the Board of Regents of the State of New York and the Board of Education of the City of New York for introducing Hebrew into the Public High Schools." Wise and Chipkin also pursued well-known educators, including John Dewey, who supported this initiative. Although these progressive educators and Semitic language professors supported the HC's efforts, they failed to directly address the board on their behalf, minimizing the potential positive effect of these allies.[23]

Despite student and teacher enthusiasm for Hebrew, a lack of state support left many confused as to the language's exact status. The Hebrew Committee was especially excited by the curriculum's introduction into Morris High School (Bronx) and Samuel J. Tilden High School (Brooklyn) in the fall of 1935. And many students and student groups believed the exams they took at the end of the year were Regents' exams qualifying them for college credits and scholarships. They were distraught upon learning this was not the case. Information about Hebrew classes appeared in the board's official language circular for junior high school students, but Veit turned down principals interested in introducing courses.[24]

Believing that local colleges' lack of recognition might convince high schools to remove, rather than expand, Hebrew courses, the HC changed its tactics yet again. First, it reorganized to include educational and political establishment insiders. New members included Mark Eisner, of the Board of Higher Education, James Marshall of NYC's Board of Education, and Manhattan Borough President Samuel M. Levy. Then, the HC collaborated with Jewish student organizations, particularly the Hebrew Culture Council and the Jewish Culture Council, in a campaign to arouse Jewish students' interest in the program. Finally, they financed the language's introduction in local colleges. New York University agreed to introduce Hebrew if assured of $6,000 over two years. Hoping that NYU's decision would influence other schools, particularly City College, to include Hebrew, Wise responded that he could find "$5,000 to bring this about." Within two years, NYU began teaching the course.[25]

Grassroots Success and Hebrew's Approval

The HC's elite members increasingly saw their efforts, particularly at the grassroots level, outshone by Zionist student groups' youth-oriented events. Avukah's outreach programs and information campaigns, such as an Annual Hebrew Week, promoted "the importance of Hebrew" in its monthly journal. These publications encouraged students to enroll in the courses where offered. In high schools without Hebrew courses, such as James Monroe (Bronx) with 8,000 Jewish students, they advocated "a movement" to generate the 70 students necessary to introduce subjects and for parents to contact principals to demand the course. The JEA, with the BJE, sponsored programs to "stimulate interest in Hebrew among parents and children in several neighborhoods" and organized Hebrew Culture Clubs in high schools. These clubs introduced students to "the cultural treasures of the Jewish past and present" and attempted to attract sufficient student interest to introduce the courses. Their efforts succeeded. This tactical shift, away from community elites and toward local youth, promoted an "imagined community," based on a Jewish state, privileging Jews' religion and culture, and allowed young Jews a safe space free from discrimination. Grassroots-level interest sustained Hebrew's inclusion and facilitated its spread in schools across NYC. Given the board's indifference to the well-known and respected HC, the movement's failure to capture the attention of Jewish parents (for whom the board cared little) likely only minimally affected Hebrew's trajectory.[26]

By April 1939, twenty-six teachers taught 100 classes in eleven senior day high schools, four evening high schools, and three junior high schools. Across the city, 3,195 students took Hebrew classes. NYC's junior and senior high school manuals all included Hebrew listings and descriptions. New York University and Brooklyn College taught Hebrew, while eight colleges, Brooklyn College, City College, Fordham University, Hunter College, Manhattan College, New York University, Queens College, and St. John's College, granted admission credit. But without a Regents exam, guidance counselors continued to staunch student enrollment.[27]

Even without official approval, student interest in Hebrew grew. The Jewish Youth Council, directed by Judah Lapson, one of Benderly's protégés, sponsored semi-annual awards for "scholarship and leadership in Hebrew classes." In 1942, an audience of 600 watched as Lapson awarded 100 students a gold pin in the shape of an ayin (א), the first letter of the Hebrew alphabet and the word for "Hebrew," Ivrith, and read a letter from Albert Einstein praising Hebrew's inclusion in the public schools. Beginning in 1944, 85 students in junior and senior high schools participated in a citywide Contest in Hebrew Culture and Its Contribution to American Life. Interest swelled as the number of students enrolled increased through World War II. By 1947, twenty-three schools taught Hebrew and between the end of the war and 1948, enrollment had increased 17.5 percent, with over 3,000 high school students enrolled each year.[28]

In 1948, after nearly twenty years of pressure from Jewish groups, the year of Israel's birth, and with NYC containing the largest population of Jews in the world, the Board of Regents approved a Modern Hebrew examination. Finally, students studying Hebrew became "eligible for diplomas and scholarship benefits . . . on the same basis as those for other modern languages." Later that year, three more Brooklyn schools added Hebrew, Cunningham Junior High School, Bensonhurst Junior High School, and Winthrop Junior High School, bringing the total to twenty-six schools teaching Hebrew. State approval, contingent on structural change related to Jews' racial status, legitimized the language and allowed for its expansion.[29]

Although lacking Regents' approval, increased enrollment over twenty years signaled the HC's success in their earliest goal, expanding young Jews' interest in Hebrew to ensure Judaism's longevity. Thousands of Jews and non-Jews developed proficiency in a language previously reserved for the rabbinical elite. Particularly significant in this era of rising global anti-Semitism, was non-Jewish enrollment with the potential to diminish anti-Jewish sentiment through increased knowledge of Jewish cultures and customs. Hebrew courses continue to be taught in NYC's schools, and the Regents still offer an exam in the subject. However, most Jews encounter basic Hebrew not in the public schools but in extrascholastic Hebrew schools, and not as a conversation language to promote Zionism, but only in rudimentary form to complete bar or bat mitzvah.

African American History

Since American public schools' inception, curricular depictions of African Americans belied their true contributions to American history, alternating instead between complete absence and utter misrepresentation (Fitzgerald 1979; Moreau 2003; Zimmerman 2002b). While the nation's legal debate, economic independence from England through cotton production, and the physical erection of many landmarks, including the White House, all relied on African

American labor, textbooks rendered African Americans invisible in discussions of the American populace. When African Americans did appear, textbooks perpetuated myths of white superiority and African American savagery in vivid detail or, alternately, as "voiceless appendages to the main story of whites." Texts depicted slavery as a positive experience for African Americans, who passively accepted their oppression as benevolent slave-owners civilized savage and backward African men and women. In this version of American history, slave rebellions, such as that of Nat Turner, did not arise from desires for freedom or attention to concurrent historical revolutions; Northern whites orchestrated them for political gain. Children learned that, after slavery, ignorant African Americans refused to work and that "patriotic" white organizations, such as the Ku Klux Klan, protected white women from violent African Americans who did not understand freedom. These depictions disseminated stereotypes of African Americans, often referred to as "niggers" and "darkies" in texts, as alternately lazy and ignorant sambos or violent brutes but always dangerous to white society.

Challenging these ideologies and depictions since the 1800s, African Americans campaigned for their removal and replacement with accurate images, culture, and history to promote social and economic equality and group solidarity. African American teachers in Southern segregated schools intro-duced culturally relevant curriculum and, where possible, attempted to remove discriminatory texts from white schools. African Americans published books to combat the fundamentally racist lessons of "stupid, incompetent, and comical" African Americans and whites' moral and intellectual superiority found in the widely used McGuffey Readers and *Little Black Sambo*. These books featured stories and poems with "real pictures of Negro children and Negro leaders" to help African American children "learn about their race" (Moreau 2003: 164; Shujaa 1994: 174). These efforts paved the way for scholars such as W.E.B. Du Bois and Carter Godwin Woodson to create and disseminate accurate representations of their culture, history, and life.

The largest institutional change to African American history came with Carter Godwin Woodson's founding of the Association for the Study of Negro Life and History in 1915, the *Journal of Negro History* in 1917, and Negro History Week in 1926. His *Mis-Education of the Negro* articulated a new pedagogy to counteract traditional public school curriculum reproducing African American subservi-ence and emulation of whites, instead, promoting cultural pride. To disseminate African and African American history widely, particularly in schools, Woodson's campaigns against miseducation demanded schools teach African American history, literature, and art. He encouraged parents to insist schools purchase books, magazines, and pictures of African American history and document their own family histories. As progressive educators championed this cause, white schools in the North incorporated into the curriculum Negro History Week, which soon came under fire from African American educators and laypeople, while parents increased demands for African American history coursework and the removal of discriminatory texts.[30]

Reading, Recognizing, and Reacting to NYC's Racist Texts

Contention over discriminatory texts, though not new, increased significantly in the years following World War II. By 1946, African American soldiers, who had achieved valor in battle, experienced acclaim overseas, and developed a new consciousness precluding subservience to whites, had returned home (Brandt 1993; Kelley 1996; Martin 2005). Yet their children's textbooks depicted African Americans as lazy, ignorant, docile, and childlike, reflecting a Southern nostalgia for slavery that legitimized their oppression, reinforced their status as second-class citizens, and decimated their culture on a daily basis. Virulently resistant to these images and all they represented, African Americans demanded their removal to promote their children's pride in their culture and in its contributions to the world, and to minimize white children's beliefs about African American difference. The board resisted the discriminatory texts' removal through evasion, the same tactic used when Jews requested Hebrew courses twenty years earlier.

The first year of the postwar era, 1946, dawned with an "irate" citizens committee confronting Arthur Klein, the principal of Morris High School in the Bronx. The school required reading of *The Yearling*, "which was peppered throughout with . . . uncomplimentary racial slurs," including "nigger." Klein agreed to remove the book but not reprimand the teacher who failed students refusing to read and report on it. That same week, Benjamin J. Davis Jr., an African American Manhattan City Council member, linked political power and curricular representation in demands for an African American representative on the Board of Education and the removal of every "anti-Negro" textbook from school shelves.[31]

With their children regularly confronting overtly racist curriculum, African Americans reviewed board-sanctioned, and -written, texts and demand the removal of offensive and inaccurate ones. The Teachers Union (TU), with a large African American membership, created yearly lists of discriminatory textbooks and curricular recommendations. In February 1947, the TU critiqued two such books, *Lanterns on the Levee—Recollections of a Planter's Son*, by William Alexander Percy, and *How to Create Cartoons*. The former painted a picture of African Americans as sexually aggressive thieves. The latter, in a lesson designed to "create a comedy situation from the following—a Negro savage and an alarm clock," taught children to draw African Americans with exaggerated lips, rolling eyes, and a slovenly appearance.[32]

Along with the removal of racist depictions of African Americans, activists demanded texts include their contributions to American history. In March

1946, the *Amsterdam News* called for the removal of "anti-Negro textbooks" and the institutionalization of "African American History and Culture among the 'required' courses." The editorial demanded "syllabi of American and World History courses edited to include those pertinent of Negro participation in American growth which have been left out."[33]

Although Carter G. Woodson created Negro History Week to foster a greater understanding and pride within the African American community, local content often contradicted these aims. Infuriated parents chastised school administrators when children at JHS 246 participated in minstrel shows, complete with white children portraying African Americans in blackface in "Old Black Joe & darkies in the cotton fields type of Stephen Foster admiration presentation." Strong emphases on George Washington Carver and Booker T. Washington taught African American children success could, and should, be found only in the traditional plantation economy. Extolling Matthew Henson, who accompanied Robert E. Peary to the North Pole, taught African American youth that fame came from helping whites succeed. A play highlighting African American soldiers' contributions to American war efforts from the Revolution to World War II failed to address their segregation in hard labor units serving whites. A near exclusive focus on spirituals and discussions of "Negro's Contribution in Music to American Culture" taught students that African Americans worked happily to build the nation, but that their primary contribution was musical, not intellectual.[34]

By 1950, demands to end Negro History Week appeared alongside notifications of community-based events challenging dominant ideologies. African American activists and community leaders demanded African American history's inclusion in regular history and social studies courses. They argued that African American history *was* American history. Four years later, in 1954, newscaster and *Amsterdam News* managing editor S. W. Garlington, in his Minority News report on radio station WEVD, "demanded an end to the study of 'Negro' History and the observance of Negro History Week as 'side shows.'" A letter to the editor the same week argued for year-round "Negro History" in all schools and a "campaign to have this disgraceful week wiped off the books." Another reader, noting that African American school superintendents in Georgia mandated this curriculum, advised the same in NYC. Recognizing the unlikelihood of change in the public schools, an *Age* reader proposed a private school with "awakened Afro-Americans" to teach African history.[35]

NYC's public schools did not exist in a bubble. Racially and politically conscious teachers ensured that students learned about and, in some cases actually learned from, contemporary social and political figures overcoming racial barriers. TU-published curriculum, radio programs, and community leaders discussed social conditions in America and Africa. In the late 1940s, students at Harlem's 99 percent African American J.H.S. 120 viewed artifacts from their ancestors' cultures in West Africa, learned about the Soviet Union's treatment of African Americans, and African American participation in labor unions. In other schools, African American teachers taught their students of America's racial origins and their ancestors' role in the Civil War. At P.S. 113 (Harlem), students performed "North Star Shining" with Harriet Tubman's niece as a speaker alongside displays of African art. Pathbreaking African Americans Roy Campanella and Jackie Robinson spoke at New York Vocational High School while students at P.S. 83's (Brooklyn) Negro History Club taught their classmates about Governor William Hastie (of the Virgin Islands), Marion Anderson, and Ralph Bunche. The TU's Harlem Committee and CIO Local 555 sponsored a "Negro History Week Celebration" at Harlem's (soon-to-be-Schomburg) public library for the community to hear Brooklyn politician Ada B. Jackson, historian Herbert Aptheker, and NAACP member and W.E.B. Du Bois's assistant, Hugh H. Smythe, speak.[36]

Interracial Organizations Take Notice

Legitimizing African American complaints, established interracial organizations issued reports documenting racism in NYC's texts and encouraging accurate representation of African Americans in the curriculum. In March 1946, Jews and African Americans collaborated on a radio program, "Schoolbooks as a Source of Intolerance," to expose local residents to problems in their children's texts. African Americans, at a weekly evening lecture series at the Schomburg Library, called for all courses to emphasize African American equality, lessen racial tension, and encourage progressive action. In 1947, the Anti-Defamation League sponsored an in-school viewing of their film, *Our People*, depicting the "contributions to the United States of the different cultural groups that make up its population." In 1949, the Carnegie Endowment for International Peace issued a report finding bias in the majority of American textbooks. History texts, in particular, presented "a very small, almost minute amount of information about Negroes since 1876" while value judgments and offensive generalizations "perpetuate[d] racial antagonisms." Although these groups legitimized African Americans' concerns, they had no direct effect on the curriculum. The nationally recognized Carnegie organization offered no direct commentary to NYC's educational authorities, while the potential effect of the Anti-Defamation League's support was minimal, and may have been negative, given Jews' precarious status as whites during the 1950s.[37]

In 1950, the TU's Harlem Committee prepared and released a twenty-six-page pamphlet, *Bias and Prejudice in Textbooks in Use in the New York City Schools*. The committee found dozens of textbooks, including those written and edited by NYC principals and superintendents, with "racist stereotypes, distortion of historical facts, and bias . . . toward allegedly 'inferior' people." Two examples included:

- [The slave's] life was safe; his master must care for him in sickness and provide for him when he was too old for labor. Most Negroes who grew up as slaves were content with their lot, being well-treated, and having no fear of poverty or old age.
- Most Southern people treated their slaves kindly. It was true that most slaves were happy. They did not want to be free. The people of the North did not understand this.

The board ignored the pamphlet but the community did not. It requested dozens of copies and provoked widespread discussion about African American representation in texts.[38]

The TU also criticized the board for ignoring recent complaints by the NAACP and including in their 1951 *List of Approved Text Books* those containing "nigger, fat African American mammies, darky, heebs, dagos" and "unabashed justification of the Ku Klux Klan." After slavery, according to *My Country* by Mace and Hannig, African Americans "thought that freedom meant no more work. They caused much trouble in the South, for sometime they went about the country in gangs, begging, stealing, threatening people and creating disorder." *Short Stories for English Courses*, by R.M.R. Mickels, contained passages such as, "You know a nigger cannot be as good as a white man"; "Yes, I know all niggahs will steal"; and "A drunken nigger is headed this way." *The King's English*, a play by Herbert Bates, described African Americans as savages.[39]

That year, the TU's list of objectionable quotes was so long, they divided it into sections: Stereotypes, Distortions Regarding Slavery, Distortion of Emancipation and Reconstruction, Improper Presentation of Colonial People, and Objectionable Pictures and Cartoons. An addendum featuring in-depth analysis of the most egregious examples of offensive stereotypes included a humor book that synonymized "Negro" with "chicken-stealer" by cross-referencing the two in the index, and displayed African Americans as lazy, razor-carrying thieves incapable of speaking proper English. Receiving no response from the board, in 1952, the TU included an annual four-page NHW supplement to their weekly *Teacher News*, complete with classroom materials. The TU offered to mail up to fifty copies, free of charge, to anyone. Requests came from cities nationwide, from teachers and community activists, and as far away as Africa (Zitron 1968).[40]

Four years later, in May 1956, another TU study found that, while "the prolonged efforts of parents and teachers have had some effect in removing some of the biased and derogatory material from the list of books issued by the Board of Education . . . there are extremely obnoxious books containing harmful material, which are still being issued to the children. . . . Even when books are removed from the approved list, they continue in actual use in the schools . . . since they are available in the supply closets many teachers use these books when there is no replacement available." Ten years of work had yielded minimal progress.[41]

Local Organizations and Media Mobilize

As the 1950s dawned, activists shifted from working with interracial organizations to autonomous community-based action to critique and create curriculum. Neighborhood and community groups established committees to address local schools' textbooks. The Schools Council of Bedford-Stuyvesant-Williamsburg, headed by mother and civic leader Ada B. Jackson, held a conference on biased textbooks in March 1950 with more than thirty PTA representatives. Afterward, they supplied an itemized list of discriminatory statements in textbooks to Education Commissioner Maximillian Moss, NYC School Superintendent William Jansen, and Mayor O'Dywer.[42]

The contact director of the Harlem YMCA, Fannie P. Byrd, complained to the Board of Education that *Verse of Our Days* failed to capitalize "Negro" and characterized African Americans as maintaining a "happy-go-lucky, trusting, child-like Negro nature, enjoying the sunshine and fearing the shadow." According to Byrd, this passage gave "a distorted concept of the Negro and perpetuates a racial stereotype." The board agreed to remove the book from its approved textbooks list because of its age and the recent requirement that all approved textbooks utilize a capital "N" in its spelling of "Negro," but never fulfilled its promise. A report later that year found racist texts still failing to capitalize "Negro" and "Negroes."[43]

Two years later, the Forest Neighborhood Community Group's Committee on Education organized a subcommittee to create an intercultural education course and then demand the Board of Education install it as a required class to replace the voluntary programs in only a few schools. That same year, meeting at the Harlem YMCA, thirteen parents formed the Committee for the Improvement of Texts to correct information in textbooks and include African American history books in public school libraries. A letter to the *Amsterdam News* from the committee's chairman connected the discriminatory treatment of African Americans in textbooks with larger societal discrimination, particularly by housing corporations refusing to rent to African Americans.[44]

Receiving "a large number of phone calls and letters from parents protesting the way many of their children's textbooks referred to and described Negroes," the *Amsterdam News* completed its own in-depth study of NYC's textbooks. Published in 1957, the report documented dozens of racist texts, even after the American Council on Education and Carnegie Corporation recommended their removal or revision and the local TU, every year, submitted a list of discriminatory books to the board.[45]

The *Amsterdam News* study documented derogatory adjectives ("ignorant," "illiterate," "easily led," foolish," "superstitious," "shiftless," "backward," "evil," and "irresponsible") and historical misrepresentations in widely used textbooks. In these texts, African Americans picked banjoes while slapping their feet, lighted up upon seeing "missus" (their former owner), and spoke incoherently. The books depicted former slave owners sympathetically and the Klan as patriotic in upholding order by brutalizing African Americans, while illiterate and unqualified African Americans held office during Reconstruction. The books depicted Africans even worse. *Distant Lands*, a geography text written by School Superintendent William Jansen with Nellie B. Allen, read: "The native people are backward and of mixed races." Another written by Jansen and Allen asserted: "Because the native people of Africa, most of whom belong to the Negro race, are very backward the greater part of the continent has come under control of European nations since its opening up began." Two weeks later, the Negro Teachers Association and the Education Committee of the New York Branch of the NAACP held a conference, "Educational Standards in Our Schools," at the Harlem YMCA. Hoping to unite parents and teachers to oppose discriminatory texts, the conference focused on two types of books: those containing derogatory treatment of African Americans and their history, and positive ones that did the opposite.[46]

Targeting and Training Teachers

The African American community mobilized significant resources to train white teachers in African American culture and contributions to American history. These represent radical efforts to convert white teachers from oppressive to emancipatory figures. The courses, a "sure method of passing on Negro history lessons to pupils," sought to counter derogatory images of African Americans, which many teachers believed, and promote the use of accurate material. For over a decade, the principal of JHS 139, an all-boys, 99 percent African American school in Central Harlem, required the entire faculty to learn about African American history and culture and to receive private lessons about African American culture and history from Schomburg Library's librarians. Schomburg Library also published an annual list of "Books About Negro Life for Children" for interested students and for teachers to request for their classrooms.[47]

Signaling the continued need to educate teachers about their history and culture, Eleanor Sinnette, chief librarian for Harlem schools, instituted teacher courses in 1963. During the course "The Negro: His Role in the Culture and Life of the United States," kindergarten through high school teachers received assignments and developed lesson plans and research projects for students. Guest speakers included local teachers and prominent African Americans such as John Henrik Clarke, Kenneth Clark, and NAACP Legal Defense Fund attorney Constance Baker Motley. During James Baldwin's highly publicized appearance, he lashed out at the board for "the diabolical, calculated scheme to brainwash the Negro into believing that he is inferior."[48]

African American parents and citizens demanded the board fire teachers and principals using racist texts and curriculum. Judge Hubert T. Delaney's daughter "spearheaded the fight for the inclusion of Negro students in the Guard of Honor" at George Washington High School, where Principal Arthur A. Boylan had forbidden them. Arguing Boylan's incompetence, parents cited his refusal to capitalize "Negro" and his effort to discredit famous African American figures such as Crispus Attucks and Phillis Wheatley. Three years later, parents insisted Superintendent Jansen fire May Quinn, a teacher who told students, "Negroes were happy before they knew about racial discrimination" and, in referring to African American students attempting to integrate colleges, "I would not go where I was not wanted." When Jansen refused to fire Quinn, Brooklyn parents scored his "anti-Negro prejudice" in protecting a teacher who "defended segregation of Negroes," highlighted a passage from his text, "the native people of Africa, most of whom belong to the Negro race, are very backward," and called for his resignation.[49]

African American History to the Fore

By the late 1950s, African Americans citywide insisted schools address their role in American history. A conference of local historians and educators published a manifesto calling for "The Negro History Quinquinnial" to augment the current Negro History Week with "a period of intensive study and teaching of the history of the race." Letters to newspapers in the late 1950s and early 1960s urgently advocated African American history. David Holford, an *Amsterdam News* reader, wrote, "African American history, not to be confused with Negro history," and not school desegregation, "would give character pride and dignity" to young African Americans.[50]

In local classrooms, African American teachers, parents, and community groups ceased asking permission from the board to include African American culture and, like Jews, just did it on their own. Parents and teachers in the Bronx developed a holistic curriculum so "whether pupils at P.S. 63 study history, literature, music, science or art, they will know of the role Negroes have played in these fields." A program celebrating this curriculum included prominent community members, including George S. Schulyer, Chuck Stone, and Anne Arnold Hedgeman. Every speaker advocated African American history and a telegram from Jackie Robinson congratulated the school for introducing the subject. While African Americans celebrated these exhaustive efforts, Principal Joseph Levine never approved the curriculum and only allowed its use during Negro History Week. Parents called this a "farce" which "woke up" others to the schools' curricular shortcomings. Levine then barred the PTA's president, Pearl Matthews, from the building and urged other PTA members to vote her out of office. A month later, Levine fired the three African American teachers "who worked tirelessly" in their efforts to create the curriculum. Parents charged

Levine with "recanting on the part of the school on promises to purchase adequate books for purposes of teaching the course," "threatening each teacher individually for sending out 'unauthorized press releases' and for failure to cooperate with white teachers on the committee to bring in the Negro history course." Parents also condemned Levine for "charging that Negro pupils were 'unteachable,' and would be 'frustrated if taught about their history.'" Over ten thousand ministers attending the Baptist Ministers Conference of Greater New York and Vicinity voted to support parents' efforts and the dismissed teachers, but the damage was done. The curriculum disappeared.[51]

At P.S. 93 (Brooklyn), nine teachers created a *Negro History Guide for Teachers*, distributed by the Interborough Negro History Committee. The guide helped "teachers to convey to elementary school children an understanding of the 'contributions of the Negro and the impact of these contributions upon American culture.'" It featured "Afro-American Contributors to America," lists of reference books for teachers, classroom activities for students in kindergarten through sixth grade (in language arts, social studies, science, art, gym, and music classes), and detailed accounts of African American figures in all areas of history.[52]

NHW in the 1960s opened with John Hope Franklin's critique of American history courses and textbooks that excluded African Americans from every phase of American history. In local schools, spirituals and depictions of Booker T. Washington, Harriet Tubman, and George Washington Carver appeared alongside discussions of Jackie Robinson, Althea Gibson, Marion Anderson, Daniel Hale Williams, James Weldon Johnson, Paul Lawrence Dunbar, Countee Cullen, and Langston Hughes's poetry. While some represented traditional assimilationist ideologies, others, particularly contemporary literary figures, critiqued white oppression.[53]

Efforts to institutionalize African American history intensified in 1961. In March, African American historians and educators called for increased attention to their history during the next five years and appointed local community members, including Leolive Tucker and Carrie Haynes of the Harlem 9, to the helm of the organization's film commission. In June, Hortense James Jones, president of the Frederick Douglas Memorial Park, proposed "Our History" Week featuring Douglass, Richard Allen, Mary McLeod Bethune, Harriet Tubman, Martin Luther King Jr., and Adam Clayton Powell. Later that year, the newly established Harlem Forum Committee developed a book featuring Langston Hughes, historian J. A. Rogers, cartoonist Nel Tapley, Horace Carter, and photos and stories from local community members.[54]

Alongside the emergence of radical figures and holistic efforts to include African American history in the curriculum, activists continued calls to remove stereotypical images and racist teachers. In 1961, African American and Jewish members of the Brooklyn Branch of the Association for the Study of Negro Life and History and the Bowen Park Club of the Emma Lazarus Women's Federation co-sponsored a conference and published their findings of racist depictions in school texts. Inaccurate and incomplete descriptions of African American (as well as Asian American, Jewish American, and Latino) history negatively impacted both African American and white children, they argued. The 300 parents, educators, and civic leaders in attendance learned that 98 percent of publishers deliberately misrepresented African Americans and their role in history. That week, John O. Killens, a prominent African American historian, concluded, "we want this practice stopped immediately. We must pressure the Board of Education into refusing to buy and use books in our schoolrooms which are offensive to Negroes and other minority groups, distress them and are misleading and inaccurate as to their American history."[55]

Targeting teachers and administrators, parents demanded an apology from a teacher who referred to African American women's hair as "a greasy mess" and claimed that Africans were "dirty because their hands and feet are always dirty" after watching a film about Africa. Muriel J. Paul reported the incident to the NAACP, the *Amsterdam News*, and filed a complaint with the Board of Education. She later praised the *Amsterdam News* for alerting the community to the "propaganda being spread, sometimes unwittingly and often times deliberately, in our school system." A letter to the editor complained of texts employing "pickaninny," "darky," and "coon" to describe African Americans and students required to sing and march to "Swanee River" and "Dixie." Another letter demanded a "militant" stance by Dr. Calvin E. Gross, the new superintendent of schools appointed in 1963, and texts with "a balanced picture of the contributions of all persons" featuring "prominent Negro military personnel, legislators, writers, and social scientists" to supply African American children with role models and promote interracial respect.[56]

But discriminatory texts lingered on bookroom shelves. Dissatisfied with these, Harlem schools' chief librarian Eleanor Sinnette, responsible for twenty-four schools with 33,000 pupils, worked diligently to improve the availability and quality of relevant books. Frustration also peaked at the highest levels of the African American community. In March 1964, Adam Clayton Powell Jr., Harlem's representative and chairman of the House Education and Labor Committee, introduced legislation in Congress to ensure that, on both a local and national level, African American contributions to American history were presented accurately. The hearings sparked debate but not change.[57]

Persistent protests goaded educational authorities into action. At a 1959 conference sponsored by Superintendent John J. Theobald, *Amsterdam News* reporters revealed a troubling answer to the question of why textbook publishers printed books defaming a large segment of the population. NYC's children read books printed for Southern students because, as the largest segment of textbook purchasers, publishers accommodated their demands for racist revisionist history and abhorrence of integrated history and pictures. Theobald called on over 100 publishers to "remove anti-Negro remarks and to use Negro pictures in books." The same month, the board requested publishers "take further steps toward introducing representation of non-white individuals in illustrations in textbooks . . . for a factually adequate representation of the realities of social life in America today."[58]

Two years later, Theobald notified publishers that the board would not purchase textbooks "which do not adequately treat the roles of the various minority groups in American culture." This would correct their "largely white, Anglo-Saxon view of our society and history" and ignorance of "the interracial, multireligious character of our population." A new Social Studies Textbook Appraisal Committee would scrutinize books to address five issues prior to purchase—space and treatment of minority groups, pluralistic illustrations, inclusion of recent scholarship, presentation of contemporary struggles, and promotion of pluralism in housing, education, and employment. The next day, the publisher, Macmillan, began reviewing their texts to conform to Theobald's demands. Some principals complied by rooting out discriminatory textbooks and furnishing their libraries with books written by, or accurately about, African Americans. Morris Levine, principal of P.S. 111 (Queens), "stimulate[d] interest among pupils in the vast contributions the Negro has made to American life" by "adding books written by Negroes as well as those written about Negroes to the school library." These represented important changes, but racism and discrimination by omission persisted.[59]

Contemporary Struggles Enter the Classroom

As the civil rights movement and African independence movements dominated headlines, activists brought the movement into local classrooms. Encouraging teachers to introduce African history, the Afro-Arts Cultural Center held a Teacher Course beginning in February 1960 entitled "African and World Affairs." Co-sponsored by the Board of Education, African citizens led fifteen sessions about different nations, beginning with Ghana. Exchange students from Kenya and South African, Ghanian United Nations delegates, singers and drummers, and Nigerian and Liberian dancers spoke with students and began exchange programs. In May 1961, 1,500 school children from three Harlem school districts attended a program featuring African dancers, who described rituals, music, dances, and songs. Supplementing in-school events, extrascholastic institutions instructed African American children and adults of their culture and heritage. For example, the African Theological Center held classes in West African "history, language, arts, and philosophy" for everyone interested. Soon, murals of pre-European African societies appeared alongside prominent African

Americans on the walls of local high schools. These innovations reveal the importance of larger national movements to force administrators to implement curricular changes.[60]

As the civil rights movement progressed, so too did teachers' efforts to involve students in the struggle. In 1962, the TU's *Teacher News* featured an analysis of civil rights activists' recent accomplishments. In June 1963, Class 507 at Harlem's P.S. 135 held a "Freedom Bake" "to raise funds to aid the Southern Christian Leadership Conference voter registration crusade in Alabama." They also wrote to President John F. Kennedy opposing the jailing of student civil rights activists in Birmingham. At a memorial program held at Harlem's P.S. 119 to honor the four girls killed in the Birmingham, Alabama, church bombing, school children sang freedom songs and read Langston Hughes's poetry. At the JHS 139 community center, Lawrence Cumberbatch, a sixteen-year-old African American student from NYC, discussed his participation in sit-ins, the 1963 March on Washington, and his walk with other "freedom fighters" from New York to Washington, D.C.[61]

NHW in 1963 and 1964 represented a confluence of contemporary realities and historical African American struggles for equality. Examining freedom fighters since Emancipation, 1963 editions of *Teacher News* linked contemporary struggles with African Americans' long history of resistance. This challenged textbooks' narratives of African American satisfaction with the racial status quo. Rather than complacent assimilatory figures, students learned about historical and contemporary freedom fighters such as Eleanor Roosevelt, Mary McLeod Bethune, James Weldon Johnson, Assemblywoman Bessie Buchanan, Judge Harold Stevens, Lena Horne, Joe Louis, Jackie Robinson, Representative Adam Clayton Powell Jr., Congressman William Dawson, Ralph Bunche, and Walter White.[62]

Freedom struggles also featured prominently during professional organization meetings. In 1962, the Brooklyn NAACP's annual conference examined "Negro History and the New Birth of Freedom." There, the national president of the Association for the Study of Negro Life and History vehemently denounced the Southern view of African American history dominating textbooks and poisoning the minds of African American and white students. The next year, the organization's symposium focused on African American history as "a basis for the new freedom." Attendees learned of former freedom fighters and highlighted revolutionary quotes: W.E.B. Du Bois, "The problem of the twentieth century is the problem of the color line"; John B. Russworm, "Too long have others spoken for us"; Frederick Douglas, "It is not light that is needed but fire"; Harriet Tubman, "I wouldn't trust Uncle Sam with my people no longer"; and Carter G. Woodson, "To enslave a people, you must first rob them of their history." An essay contest allowed children to choose from radical activists Mary McLeod Bethune, Carter G. Woodson, James Weldon Johnson, Samuel Coleridge Taylor,

Benjamin Banneker, Alexander Dumas, Kwame Nkrumah, Hannibal, Alexander Pushkin, Toussaint L'Ouverture, or Dr. Charles Drew.[63]

Predating the Freedom Schools opened during the southern civil rights movement, African Americans in NYC developed parallel institutions to teach African American children about their culture and history. A mother of ten- and twelve-year-old boys who "thirst for knowledge" wrote to the *Amsterdam News* hoping to find a Saturday or afternoon class in "the history of the African American race." P.S. 133's PTA, led by Ruby Sims, held classes in African American history three times a week in their Harlem homes. Simultaneously, adult classes flourished.[64]

Linking Resources and Representation

Calls for improved textbooks aligned and merged with the civil rights movement as activists linked these demands to equalization of resources, experiences, and opportunities in African American schools. In 1963, a crowd of 300 NAACP, labor union, church, and PTA members demonstrated for increased school integration in Corona–East Elmhurst, Queens, and "for textbooks that specified the contributions to the nation by Negroes." African American parents seeking desegregation turned their backs on Superintendent Calvin E. Gross during a meeting in August 1963 to protest his lack of support and demanded the schools adopt the Jamaica NAACP's fourteen-page guide highlighting "minority group contributions to American life." Picketing for school improvements in Harlem's 11th and 12th districts, the Joint Schools Committee for Academic Excellence sought "meaningful" textbooks, including African American history, and the "removal of all textbooks 'which are derogatory and insulting to minority groups from schools now.'"[65]

A Conference on Integration held at Teachers College, Columbia University on May 1 and 2, 1963, attended by 175 "key community and education leaders," addressed the poor educational quality and curriculum in local schools. A follow-up Work Conference on June 14 at Bank Street College of Education generated the following recommendations: discussion of "racial, religious and ethnic dissimilarities to enrich the curriculum and help the child identify with his own image in a positive way," texts for all grades with accurate depictions of "the historical and contemporary roles in our society of different cultural groups," and increased cultural tours and trips for students.[66]

A subcommittee of the Harlem Neighborhood Association, the Parent's Action Committee for Equality (PACE), sought to improve education within Harlem. With curriculum a key platform, PACE publicly attacked discriminatory and inaccurate schoolbooks. In addition to reviewing school texts, PACE developed a list of books containing "the presence and enriching contributions of minority groups" and distributed it within the community. When the board announced in early 1964 that new books would be included, PACE insisted that they not be placed alongside old ones, but be removed from local schools to ensure that only accurate books remained.[67]

Freedom Schools

As the struggle for improved schools continued, and the board resisted integrating NYC schools, boycotting parents opened Freedom Schools, with African American history featured prominently, for their children. During the Harlem 9's boycott, Paul B. Zuber stated, "The kids in Harlem have never had Negro history in school. This is a perfect time to give them some pride in their heritage." In the early 1960s, multiple groups, including the Harlem Parent's Committee, the Citywide Committee for Integrated Schools, and the Parents' Workshop for Inequality, took cues from the Harlem 9 and established Freedom Schools during citywide boycotts. A researcher found that students attending a Freedom School sponsored by the Harlem Parents Committee in 1963 showed increased pride in their heritage and lacked the inferiority complex with which many of them, particularly the boys, arrived.[68]

During a citywide boycott on February 3, 1964, sponsored by the Citywide Committee for Integrated Schools, seventy-five city churches provided regular subject and African American history classes for students. On February 5, the media descended on a 1,500-student Freedom Class at Brooklyn's Siloam Presbyterian Church as comedian, athlete, and civil rights leader Dick Gregory commanded an hour-long session emphasizing African American independence, power, and respect. The Bronx CORE chapter also organized free Saturday afternoon classes in African American history to supplement a Freedom School held at Bethany Lutheran Church.[69]

One Book

At the end of 1964, the Board of Education finally implemented parents' decades-old requests. The board followed their new guidelines for choosing textbooks with new programs to "emphasize civil rights, civil liberties, civic responsibilities, and pride in ethnic heritage." Even more pathbreaking, and culminating these efforts, the board released the 158-page *The Negro in American History*, written by Irving Cohen and John Hope Franklin, for use in NYC's public schools. They stopped short of mandating the book's use throughout the school system.[70]

The Negro in American History, stating, "the current struggle for civil rights may be seen as consequences of social, economic, and political forces reshaping American life" (166), represented a true departure from most books then available. It accurately depicted slavery's role in America's development, Africa's diverse and advanced cultures prior to the slave trade, and acknowledged African American agency in attributing slave revolts to horrific treatment during slavery. Later editions of the book (1967) close with an appendix suggesting ways to incorporate African American history in social studies, key ideas to teach, and myths to dispel (such as, that African Americans were genetically suited for slavery, slavery was only a Southern problem, African Americans greeted slavery with docility, and that racism no longer existed in America). While African American youth reading the book encountered new and important information about early American and African history, it minimized discrimination, institutional racism, and African American efforts to challenge these inequalities since World War II. Treatment of African Americans in NYC, though stated as the book's focus in its introduction, was similarly limited.

Following the inclusion of *The Negro in American History*, the board expanded the availability of texts published by local and national African American organizations. It adopted and ordered 1,100 copies of the NAACP's forty-four-page illustrated booklet, *Negro Heroes of Emancipation*. The Central Harlem Mothers' Association convinced a number of local principals and teachers to adopt their recently published *Great Negroes—Past and Present*, without any board interference to the contrary. However, this curriculum never reached most white children who encountered racist texts that facilitated conceptions of interracial difference and inequality.[71]

Racist Texts Linger, Protests Persist

While the board published and recommended *The Negro in American History*, and issued new textbook guidelines, racist and exclusionary texts lingered on bookroom shelves, resulting in few concrete changes to the curriculum encountered by NYC's multiracial student population. Still angry with "insulting, insipid, and uninspiring" textbooks that neglected "to present Negroes and Puerto Ricans in a proper light," in December 1964 the Joint Schools Committee for Academic Excellence Now decided to create their own textbook with help from local teachers. The committee's chairman, Janet Karlson, also pointed out three books (*Seven Grandmothers*, *A Guide to African History: A General Survey of the African Past from Earliest Times to the Present*, and *A Glorious Age in Africa: The Story of Three Great African Empires*) accurately representing African Americans absent from the board's approved books list.[72]

To combat these books' persistence, NYC writers, parents, educators, and illustrators founded the Council on Interracial Books for Children (CIBC) in 1965 with the "premise that children's literature and learning materials—consciously or unconsciously—carry hidden value messages which either support the inequities of the status quo or pave the way for a more humanistic society." The organization established its national stature in monitoring texts and aiding educators interested in truthful treatment of African American, Latino, Native American, and Asian American history and culture. To promote local involvement, particularly among parents, the CIBC, to this day, advances antiracist and antisexist texts and educational climates facilitating their inclusion

(Banfield 1998). The CIBC publishes a list of ten ways to analyze children's books, encouraging parents and teachers to examine everything from the storyline to the illustrations to the author's background.[73]

Parallel Protests

Examining curriculum democratization efforts to promote Jewish and African American cultures and linguistic opportunities in public schools reveals not only similarities to each other, but also to resource equalization protests. Lacking a particular curricular resource, activists engaged in disruptive movements that obstructed routine activities at every level of the educational hierarchy. When the public schools did not change, Jewish and African American groups created courses and texts, trained teachers, and created parallel institutions on their own. Each effort engaged multiple segments of the community to accurately assess existing curriculum and to demand accountability from various levels of the educational establishment. Hebrew protests featured well-organized and longstanding groups within the Jewish community while African Americans' demands arose from a wide swath of organizations and individuals that lacked cohesion or a central organization. Yet each protest, because of similar board actions, unfolded in similar manners.[74]

Strong emotions about the future of each group precipitated activists' demands and informed their mobilizing frames. Movements then followed similar trajectories as activists addressed local curricular shortcomings by targeting, first, establishment insiders and then institutional outsiders. These object shifts allowed for tactical innovations as transgressive contention with new actors and tactics unfolded during each movement. Jews and African Americans capitalized on existing unified sites to deploy community-based agency and counter the board's inaction through curriculum creation. However, each group lacked the authority to persuade the board to adopt their curriculum and impose its citywide inclusion. With regard to demands for African American history curriculum, the wide variety of independently operating organizations and individuals resulted in divergent, rather than universal, curricular demands.[75]

Lacking support from educational authorities and influential allies, maximum success occurred at the most local levels, in individual schools and classrooms with students and teachers from their own communities where they, rather than the board, controlled curriculum. In each groups' repertoire of contention, these diversions represented a break from existing protest tactics, which had become routine, and a new cycle of autonomous inclusion of cultural forms. When board support for curricular revisions was not forthcoming, Jews and African Americans drew on ethnic cultures to mobilize support and develop extrascholastic organizations and institutions.[76]

In each case, activists capitalized on teachers' potential to be intellectual, political, and transformative figures by providing Jewish and African American students with the intellectual tools necessary to become critical agents through transgressive emancipatory curriculum (Foucault 1970; Freire 1976, 2000; Giroux 1988; hooks 1994). With personal knowledge as oppressed members of society, teachers validated and legitimized Jewish and African American children's experiences and promoted students' democratic engagement in national and international social justice movements. Creating their own curriculum allowed Jewish and African American activists to include culturally centered perspectives and transformative Judeo and Afro-centric knowledges rather than working their culture into existing curricular order. The board recognized the potential threat of teachers' curricular control by firing African American teachers developing Afrocentric curriculum and refusing to hire Jewish teachers for Hebrew classes.

Divergences and Differences

Although similarities existed between each curricular-related protest and those seeking resource equalization, so too did important differences. The media, particularly newspapers, played an important role in every protest with the exception of those seeking Hebrew. The African American press documented African American protest as it occurred, thereby facilitating the generation and expansion of networks of activism. The *Age* and *Amsterdam News* became active participants as they investigated texts, exposed them when contacted by parents, printed editorials demanding their removal and the inclusion of African American history, and solicited information about and notified the community of parallel institutions, Freedom Schools, community centers, local libraries, and private homes, where cultural knowledge could be acquired.

Mainstream media, the *New York Times* in particular, largely ignored these protests, thereby limiting potential allies' knowledge and sympathetic support. Not a single article documented Jews' protests to include Hebrew, only announcements of its inclusion. During African American's eighteen-year-long case, the *Times* only published twenty-two articles regarding demands for their history. The majority of *Times* articles highlighted white organizations' study of texts or the board's belated adoption of *The Negro in American History*. Instead, the paper criticized well-known progressive educational organizations, such as the Carnegie Foundation, for highlighting racist depictions of African Americans in elementary school books (that is, the evil animal always had black fur) and printed furious editorials when racist books were censored.

Another difference between the protests was the involvement of mothers. Within the African American community, similar to the Harlem 9 and Gary Plan cases, mothers played a critical role in demanding curriculum representative of their children's experiences and lives. Their role as cultural educators well-documented (Collins 2000; Kelley 1996), African American mothers in NYC took their faith in this knowledge to empower their children outside the private realm of the home in demanding the schools provide this cultural education to their children. Jewish mothers, on the other hand, were completely absent from demands to include Hebrew, revealing intracommunity tensions hindering Jewish activism.

Unresolved Intracommunity Constraints

Longstanding intracommunity cultural differences and tensions inhibited mobilization, organization, and, in the case of African American history, a singular demand which educational authorities could address. Though Hebrew curriculum sought to unify German and Russian Jews through a Zionist racial project, activists never addressed differences in each group's structural position and access to opportunities. As activists glossed over economic, ideological, and cultural differences, Hebrew lost its unifying potential. Within the African American community, activists failed to address different national and class backgrounds, instead pursuing curriculum focusing solely on descendents of African slaves. Failing to highlight multiple dimensions of their identities, activists missed an opportunity to challenge contemporary essentialist thinking regarding the "nature" of Jewish and African American identities and limited each movement's potential for success.[77]

Elite German Jews appeared as the face of the Hebrew movement. Russian Jews had a complicated and strained relationship with this group (Goren 1970; Jacobson 2002; Rischin 1978). Longstanding suspicion of elite activity within the Russian Jewish community resulted from experiences both in Russia and NYC. An attachment to Yiddish combined with skepticism of initiatives from the German-Jewish upper-class directed at the lower classes, particularly after their abandonment during protests against the Gary Plan, likely hindered support for this alternative Jewish language in the schools.

African American activists failed to address intraclass and community differences existing between African Americans and West Indian African Americans and cultures of Northern and Southern African Americans. Nor did they explicitly link African and African American cultures, instead only hinting at their connection. Activists also ignored the West's history of oppression in Africa, the impacts of global slavery, and its continued effects on national and international politics. Failure to account for diverse cultures and ideologies hindered communitywide mobilization, unification, and the generation of a consistent unifying narrative or umbrella organization with which to confront the Board of Education.

Loose networks of activism and knowledge inhibited large-scale public protest. Instead, activism occurred within the privacy of educational institutions and each community, compounding the lack of sympathetic support. However, the length of each protest, nearly two decades, testifies to these demands' importance and each groups' commitment to challenging dominant ideologies in the sites most conducive to change, local levels of the educational bureaucracy, individual classrooms, and community institutions, when the schools did not accede to their demands.

Institutional Evasion and Structural Constraints

Community-based differences intersected with educationally based constraints and racially based inequalities to inhibit Jewish and African American representation in the curriculum. The Board of Education perceived Jews and African Americans as non-experts and their demands for cultural curriculum as an illegitimate problem unworthy of attention. Contemporary political and economic phenomena also affected protest trajectories. Although Jews created all curriculum materials, the Depression economy alongside an expanding student population inhibited the board's willingness to embrace Hebrew. With increasing national attention to desegregation following *Brown*, the board had its hands full dealing with expanded protest tactics by the Harlem 9 and other groups seeking integration. As these publicity-generating protests spread through the city, they captured the board's attention and drew it away from less spectacular curricular reform demands. Though demands for resources and recognition intertwined, the board likely perceived them as competing interests and hoped that its symbolic adoption of one textbook would silence activists demanding curricular reform.[78]

Similar to resource-related protest trajectories, both Jews and African Americans lacked sufficient legitimate power and legal precedent to compel action in their favor in an educational bureaucracy diffused across multiple state and local offices. Only one Jew and one African American, respectively, sat on the Board of Education during these cases, which inhibited significant substantive changes to local curriculum. No law existed to promote cultural representation in public school curriculum. While intercultural education and other language programs existed, these voluntary programs lacked legal precedence and institutional structures upon which activists could lean to promote their interests.

During these cases, Jews and African Americans' demands directly opposed each era's dominant ideology and were confounded by these periods' economic duress. Anti-Semitic and nativist peaks in the 1930s and Cold War conformity in the 1950s had important consequences for protests. Any demands for cultural innovations perceived as anti-American would hinder activists' success. Therefore, dominant ideologies imposed acquiescence and minimized curricular reform within a state institution committed to conformist ideologies. These ideological constraints, combined with the media's lack of attention to their concerns, inhibited each group from generating anything more than symbolic and insufficiently sustained sympathetic support from groups outside their community.[79]

Real threat of economic survival on a daily level precluded widespread attention to curriculum not directly linked to economic mobility and profoundly affected protest trajectories and outcomes. Jewish protest occurred during the most devastating economic depression to ever hit America. For Jewish parents and children concerned with their daily social and economic livelihood, Hebrew's absence did not directly challenge Jewish students' academic and economic success and paled in comparison to the immediate threat of Depression-era poverty. Given these real concerns, and the existence of multiple institutions within the community to ensure cultural preservation, many Jewish parents may have simply felt these efforts extraneous. Another, smaller economic depression occurred in the immediate post–World War II era. Unemployment peaked as the nation transformed from a wartime industrial economy into a peace-time service economy. As in most periods of economic crisis, African Americans struggled to gain employment as they competed with thousands of returning white servicemen for scarce positions. Given the poverty experienced by many African Americans during this era, attention to curriculum reveals the relevance activists saw of curricular representation to social equality.

Symbolic and Substantive Success

Neither Jews' nor African Americans' efforts to transform the curriculum or acquire greater educational resources for their children succeeded. The reasons for this failure lie in the structure of racism against which these groups struggled for resources and cultural improvements. Perceiving Jews and African Americans as racial outsiders, the board maintained racial ideologies and existing educational structures, in the form of misrepresentation in the curriculum and unequal resources, inhibiting these groups from achieving social acceptance as full and equal American citizens. Any significant curricular revisions would have signaled a dramatic shift in the racial status of each group.

Educational authorities maintained a high level of power within each school. As a result, Jews and African Americans relied on high school principals, who then looked to the board's authority before implementing activists' demands. But activists could not enforce inclusion of accurate representations in curriculum encountered by African American and white children, a not insignificant problem for activists hoping for a more equal and interracial future.

Unlike their countertactics during the publicity-generating resource protests, the board banked on exhaustion and sectarianism within each community as it evaded activists' demands. As Jews and African Americans achieved small successes in local schools, educational authorities certified each groups' demands at the most symbolic, rather than substantive, level by validating claims just enough to accede to minimal curricular revisions. Although the schools expected acquiescence, these countertactics, which absorbed and co-opted Jewish and African American protests within the schools, pushed activists outside the hegemonic state's jurisdiction, forcing them to promote their goals within new and existing community-based institutions.[80]

Only after the very definitions of whiteness had broadened, as a result of larger structural and political events, to include Jews, was Hebrew granted full recognition through a Regents' exam. This highlights how the global political context greatly affected (and continues to affect) the content of public school curriculum. The schools, upon perceiving Jews as white, and their culture as similar to that of other white Europeans, certified Jews' whiteness and curriculum demands simultaneously. But by the time the Board of Regents created an exam in Hebrew, the majority of Jews had either moved, or were less than five years from moving, out of NYC's public schools and into the suburbs.

Although the board published *The Negro in American History*, public school curricular content never significantly changed. Nor did the book's use appear widespread. This board tactic satisfied activists' most basic demand without significantly altering school content or culture. In the years immediately following this case, African Americans' struggle to include culturally relevant curriculum lay at the heart of community control demands in the Ocean Hill–Brownsville district.

5

Multicultural Curriculum, Representation, and Group Identities

> At every historical juncture of the racialization of dominant educational institutions in the United States, African Americans and other racial minorities have contested and have sought to redefine hegemonic conceptions of racial differences in "intelligence" and "achievement" and the curriculum strategies of inclusion, exclusion, and selection that these commonsense racial theories have undergirded.
>
> —Cameron McCarthy, *The Uses of Culture*, 1998

Curriculum debates are, at their root, ideological debates about who belongs within the American populace. Textbooks written from a Eurocentric perspective, as they often are, exclude the (hi)stories of indigenous peoples and minorities and teach children that these groups are neither full members of the American citizenry nor equal contributors to American history. More than just ignoring minority student experiences, this curriculum, as part of a "civilizing mission" (Ladson-Billings 1999: 21), has, for centuries, attempted to strip minorities of their cultures and customs. Lacking power within the school system, especially curricular control, minorities also lack influence over the racial meanings and identities these books replicate. As a result, the books children read and the lessons children learn in schools perpetuate stereotypic racial meanings, identities, and therefore, inequalities and power relations.[1]

America's diversity has ensured hotly contested debates over the curriculum and the cultures promoted and valued in the public schools. As a result, culture wars, really racial projects, over public school curriculum are historic. Accurately perceiving this withholding of religious, linguistic, historical, and cultural recognition as oppression since public schools' inception, excluded groups engaged in multiculturalist efforts to disentangle America's history of inequality from the narrative of freedom and justice.[2]

With school culture privileging the majority, Protestant Anglos, minority groups, and progressive sympathetic supporters, for hundreds of years, have waged a "war of maneuver" in America's public schools to challenge whiteness's hegemonic hold on the curriculum. Minority groups and organizations such as the Intercultural Education Movement responded to anti-immigration legislature and the Americanization attempts sweeping the nation with movements to preserve immigrant groups' cultures and promote racial equality and social justice. Most ethnic groups' efforts to preserve their religious cultures, ethnic cultures, and languages in schools failed. Instead, Germans, Italians, Irish, Japanese, and Mexicans developed community-based parallel institutions, schools, cultural organizations, and familial traditions, to ensure cultural continuity.[3]

Like those of other marginalized groups, Jews' and African Americans' efforts to include Hebrew and African American history directly challenged the schools' Americanization efforts by amending the hegemonic, textbook-based metanarrative privileging white Europeans and replicating "otherness" among minority children. Jewish and African American activists deployed both politics of semblance emphasizing their similarities to other groups and politics of difference highlighting their unique contributions. Goals of each protest centered around full equality and social justice and demanded that schools, in a society infused with racism and anti-Semitism, acknowledge their citizenship and preserve their cultures to promote a transformative political agenda. To do so, Jews and African Americans articulated an alternative narrative highlighting their culture and contributions to global and American society, which was informed by an oppositional consciousness affording them agency to resist domination and promote full equality.[4]

Like contemporary multicultural protests, activists sought to establish respect for stigmatized and marginalized groups, discourage hostility, and remake the public sphere to include themselves through the extension of citizenship rights across cultural differences. As seen in previous chapters, schools stifled activists' efforts to hold a critical mirror up to society, gain access to citizenship and cultural rights within the schools, and maintained both racial inequality and the inextricable link between representation and resources.[5]

Politics of Semblance and Plural Visions of Citizenship

Jews and African Americans demanded equal curricular representation to achieve cultural citizenship and equal resource distribution by disseminating knowledge of their cultures and histories widely, removing disparaged identities, and promoting race relations. Narratives went beyond the national discourse of Americanization and integration to express a multicultural vision of America absent of racial nationalism and replete with equal dignity and "parity of esteem" with all Americans sharing a common identity. Jews' and African Americans' politics of semblance promoted schools that would allow every NYC public school student to "conceive of themselves as global citizens, people who can work with others of different races and ethnicities to counteract centuries of harm done to all children—black, white, and other." To do this, Jews vociferously argued for linguistic representation in the form of Hebrew language classes while African Americans demanded the replacement of stereotypical depictions of their group with full accounts of their role in the nation's and world history.[6]

Equal Linguistic Representation

Jews' central argument for teaching Hebrew rested on their belief in its equality to other languages (Latin, Greek, French, German, Spanish, and Italian) then taught in the public schools. Dismayed that it was "treated differently," the Hebrew Committee implored educational authorities to consider "Hebrew on an absolute parity with other foreign languages taught in the public schools of this State" since, "like every other modern language taught in our schools, Hebrew has a country to which it belongs, namely, Palestine." This was not just about the language; these Jews believed if the schools treated their language equally, society would treat their children equally.[7]

Jews claimed that teaching Hebrew would promote "sociological and democratic tendencies in education." Hebrew's inclusion would improve the religion's prestige "not only with Jewish students, but with their non-Jewish schoolmates as well" as they "acquire a greater appreciation of Jewish life and culture through contact with the students of Hebrew." Without these classes, Jewish students' peers would "remain ignorant of the history and literature of the Jews." Confirming Jews' perceptions, sociolinguists argue that knowledge of a speech community, even without participation, increases social acceptance of the group (Johnson 2000). Within the speech community, regular language use validates core personal and ethnic identities and elevates the sense of cultural vitality. Although the Board of Superintendents believed Hebrew would "be elected only by Jewish children" and would "accentuate race distinction," "students of all faiths and denominations," including African Americans, enrolled in Hebrew courses.[8]

In addition to altering others' perceptions of them, Jewish activists believed in the course's "moral value," since "Jewish children are filled with a just pride when they see Hebrew on a par today with the outstanding languages of mankind." Far more than just "a subject for passing examinations," Hebrew signified a "source of pride and moral strength" and improved Jewish students' morale while simultaneously promoting race relations and equality. Hebrew classes, and schools' validation of their culture, would therefore preclude the psychological confusion that arose after children encountered Hebrew in Jewish institutions. "Just as the child is emotionally and mentally prepared to continue his studies, he is thrown into an environment and atmosphere which totally ignores and disregards his history, language, and literature, in short, his entire cultural background. He finds out very soon that what in his childhood he was taught to consider sublime and or great importance, does not even take its place in the High School or College curriculum. . . . The Jewish child becomes cynical, if not hostile, to all that he has learned in his Hebrew elementary school, for he feels as though he has been deceived and fooled." Contrary to the board's claims that language cliques do "not promote the Americanizing of Americans," the HC argued that Hebrew classes would promote the "development of an integrated personality," facilitating Jewish children's existing double consciousness and academic success. The schools' validation of their language and culture would "remove a sense of inferiority and discrimination and will restore self-respect to many of these pupils" so that the language, and by proxy, the Jewish identity, did not have "some handicap attached to it."⁹

Ultimately, Hebrew language classes could preserve the religion, foster Jewish communal ties in America, and contribute to a nationalist movement to create an international imagined Jewish community and state. According to Jewish student groups, unless the board recognized their "existence and aspirations as a national and cultural entity," there was no future for the Hebrew language, and thus, no future for Jews in America.¹⁰

Equal Historical Representation

Texts denying groups a place in the nation's history, society, culture, also deny these groups' ability to be, and *be perceived as*, equal citizens. To correct this recognitional inequality, African Americans advocated for curriculum that promoted perceptions of their children as equal to other American children. While Jews argued that their own and other children would be psychologically damaged without Hebrew classes, African Americans believed the racist images and use of "nigger" in textbooks, readers, and songbooks would have psychological consequences for *white* children who, internalizing "the prejudice they devour daily," would then perpetuate racial inequality. This diverged from the psychological argument deployed in *Brown* and anticipated contemporary research finding that multiethnic readers improved white attitudes toward African American children.¹¹

Throughout their protests, African Americans denounced the use of "pickaninny," "darky," and "coon" in their children's texts. A letter to the editor exposed teachers' use of "insulting songs" such as "Swanee River" and "Dixie," castigated Superintendent John J. Theobald and his "equally prejudiced assistants" and called the Board of Education "Hitler's Mansion." These vivid, angry comments spoke to the frustration of hundreds of African American parents with children forced to endure disrespectful, inaccurate, and downright insulting images of themselves. Parents also denounced negative depictions of Africa. Protesting a teacher who described African Americans' physical characteristics as "greasy messes" and "dirty" during a film about Africa, Mrs. Muriel J. Paul argued that "white students in that class who are in the process of formulating their views on black people have been done a great disservice by hearing such degrading remarks *at a time like this.*" Mrs. Paul instead insisted on Africans' beauty nearly a half decade before "Black is Beautiful" rhetoric.[12]

African American activists, using logic similar to Jews' during attempts to remove the religious element of the Gary Plan, argued that negative images of African Americans would stir "attitudes of hate, suspicions and fear" as students encountered "prejudiced interpretations in so-called standard history texts" and "vicious propaganda, designed to smear the Negro and degrade him in the sight and opinion of his neighbors at home and abroad." Fannie P. Byrd, contact director of the Harlem YMCA and TU member, charged that books' and plays' stereotypical depictions of "the happy-go-lucky, trusting, child-like Negro nature, enjoying the sunshine and fearing the shadow . . . gives a distorted concept of the Negro and perpetuates racial stereotypes" and "widespread misconceptions about [African Americans'] culture and character."[13]

Removing these offensive books, according to parents and community organizations, would leave white students "free from prejudice" and allow them to perceive African Americans as "an integral part of American society, that despite obvious racial differences, [as] human beings, fundamentally live the same way in this vast country." The James Weldon Johnson Memorial Collection of Children's Books developed a list of "Books About Negro Life for Children" to "help white children gain a truer, more sympathetic picture of their fellow Americans." African American activists also hoped students would bring these lessons home to their parents. Myrtle Bates, chairman of the Committee for Democracy in Textbooks, writing to the *Amsterdam News* argued, "if children were taught to respect all groups and to recognize their value to our civilization, they would not as adults tolerate or condone the unfair treatment accorded members of these groups."[14]

In addition to textbook revision to remove negative stereotypes, African American activists demanded the schools integrate their history into American history lessons. A 1947 *Amsterdam* editorial scored the public schools for failing to include a "factual explanation of American history and the part played in the development of the nation by all people, who have come to this country from all parts of the earth and contributed their full share of blood, sweat, devotion, and tears, which have made America great, rich, prosperous and strong." Nearly fifteen years later, community groups studying their children's books found that 98 percent of "American school textbook publishers were guilty of holding Negroes and other minority groups up to ridicule in books they write and publish for school children to read." They condemned publishers for "not only presenting Negroes and others in derisive and derogatory lights, but deliberately, or ignorantly, misrepresenting them and their role in American history." Community-created curriculum explicitly addressed

African Americans'"contribution to the American way of life and life in America."[15]

Protests to end NHW also demanded the holistic and year-long presentation of African American history. The *Amsterdam News*' managing editor, S. W. Garlington, during his weekly Minority News Report on WEVD, demanded the end to the "Jim Crow history" "sideshow" as a "special segregated subject which a student may or may not take, or as the record of the life and experience of a people of so little importance as not to warrant inclusion into the full stream or body of the history of a white country." Garlington, like many others, believed, "what the Negro does is part of American history and must be fitted into the American historical pattern or it is not the nation's history." William James, in a letter to the editor, mirrored this sentiment, stating, "I don't think we should set aside one week of the year for reminding ourselves that Negroes actually do have a history." While NHW continued, its content became more radical between the postwar and pre–Black Power eras.[16]

Equal Social and Economic Opportunity

Jews' and African Americans' narratives reflected their preoccupation with economic integration for their children and the resource-related benefits of integrated curriculum materials. Multicultural scholars argue that resources and representation are critically linked—that representational marginalization, distortion, or absence perpetuates social, political, and economic inequality. Jews and African Americans recognized that without equal treatment in the curriculum, their children would not be treated equally. Hebrew and African American culture would make Jewish and African American children better Americans and facilitate upward mobility and full citizenship for the entire community.[17]

For Jews, this meant rejecting the "public school's control of the major time of the children," which had "been forced upon the American Jewish parents" and fostered a "one-sided adjustment" to American life that precluded societal cultural retention. Hebrew possessed "greater social, cultural and personality values than the study of some other foreign language" to the tens of thousands of Jewish youth in NYC, who as they became better Jews would be better Americans. A Jewish child enrolled in Hebrew would be better prepared to "contribute his knowledge and experience to the enrichment of the great American society and culture." He or she would also enjoy a shared American culture with other ethnics acquiring language skills in their local schools. But without a Hebrew Regents' exam, Jewish children experienced injustice in their inability to compete for college admissions. This inhibited their educational and occupational attainment and represented an additional educational burden for Jewish students interested in this culturally relevant language.[18]

African American children experienced similar assaults on their cultural identities and potential academic outcomes. An *Amsterdam News* editorial linked textual depictions with future race relations. "Of all the so-called minorities, the nation's largest segment, the Negro, is certainly the most sinned against from every point of view. . . . The Negro's place in American civilization will never be adequately achieved unless the history of the race is fully told to the children in every school in the country, from kindergarten to graduate college. Any other approach to the race problem will fail . . . because the education of the child will be warped, his human relationships out of balance, and his view of the world a muddled picture, stirring attitudes of hate, suspicion and fear, in their relations to other people." Seven years later, a letter to the *Age's* editor expressed dismay about college-bound African Americans' lack of knowledge regarding this history, believing it essential to their success.[19]

To amend these deficiencies, African American activists, including the Junior High School Coordinating Committee, to which many of the Harlem 9 belonged, demanded curricular revisions alongside resource-related improvements in local schools. A conference sponsored by the Forest Neighborhood House in 1951 regarding housing, employment, and civil rights issues, recommended a "program of intercultural education for the entire public school system," explicitly linking contemporary depictions with future economic success.[20]

Attacking vocational education that trained African Americans for lower-class jobs, activists critiqued pictures depicting them on different economic tiers than whites. Predicting these depictions' effect on children's perceptions of African Americans and the potential discriminatory effects later in life, a writer argued, "efforts should be made to integrate the illustrations. In the present books Negroes are portrayed only as inferior persons engaged in domestic work. Why can't they be used as models for doctors, nurses, teachers and scientists rather than as maids and porters? We will never achieve integration if our books only show . . . that Negroes scrub floors and that bosses should always be white. Since we know that children will never learn to respect all races until they have been oriented to their successes and capabilities." These efforts challenged visual images of African American inferiority that promoted a racial future replete with all the inequality of the present.[21]

Preserving Culture, Resisting Hegemony

Although Jews and African Americans demanded equality, but not at the cost of their culture. Their racial projects of cultural projection (Omi & Winant 1994; Merelman 1995) conscientiously challenged the schools,' and society's, silencing of their voices and cultural disenfranchisement by legitimizing their community's knowledge and traditions. This politics of difference articulated their cultures' distinction and relevance to their children (Collins 2000; Harding

1991). To counteract the schools' Americanization and assimilation efforts, these protests reframed the hegemonic interpretations of American culture as monolithic and ideologically singular in the privileging of white Western knowledge. Jews' and African Americans' challenges to curriculum that maintained ideologies of racial differences, hierarchies, and power relations within a culture of conformity (Apple & Christian-Smith 1991; Banks 1996) represented radical departures from the national metanarratives. These efforts resemble modern Afrocentric curriculum that integrates personal, cultural, and popular knowledge into the public schools.

To preserve their cultural traditions, Jews called on the schools to recognize the city's large Jewish student population and their language. They asked, "Why should Jewish children in a cosmopolitan city like New York be forced to acquire a knowledge of other people and of other languages but not for their own?" Demanding African American history and culture, activists argued that their children *were* different from white children and entitled to curriculum acknowledging and validating their differences. A 1961 conference of African American and Jewish parents examining texts' treatment of minorities explicitly rejected the melting pot model, stating, "'Americanization' of people not only fosters conformity but also disparages the cultural strains within the community."[22]

For many Jews, the loss of Hebrew language knowledge was "one of the most heartbreaking phenomena in Jewish life in America." In the face of rising assimilation and anti-Semitism, Jewish education, particularly Hebrew language skills, was "of vital importance to the Jewish community in New York" and essential to the "future of [the Jewish] people in America." This curriculum would afford Jewish children pride in their "race and know what it means to belong to it." With the "power to form and shape personal identities" and maintain communal boundaries and solidarities, mother-tongue language knowledge transmits cultures and provides its adherents with frameworks to create and sustain particular worldviews, ideologies, and consciousnesses. As a tangible link to the homeland, language knowledge creates and extends mental links to real and imagined ancestral nations as it knits together people who speak it. Without it, according to Richard Alba (1990), "knowledge of large portions of an ethnic culture is lost" (10) since, as noted Chicana theorist Gloria Anzaldúa (1987) states, "ethnic identity is twin skin to linguistic identity—I am my language" (59).[23]

Jews' racial project to enhance language differences challenged America's historical destruction of linguistic diversity and homogenization of group cultures through English-only polices. "Awake[ning] the Jewish public to an interest in Hebrew," the "language of the Jews," would counteract high school students who were "completely drawn away from Jewish scholarship." This preventative measure would create "schooled ethnics," knowledgeable about their heritage and tied to both religious worship and a Zionist state. The HC was on to something. Contemporary researchers find that Jewish Education heightens both cultural retention and Zionist sentiment.[24]

Used in synagogues and proposed as the official language of a future Zionist state, Hebrew became a contestable but nonreligious symbolic cultural attribute that could be bargained for in schools. With curriculum derived from Hebrew's cultural, rather than religious, elements, Jewish activists rejuvenated the "renascent modern language" alongside Hebrew culture and literature. Its inclusion marked "another step along the highroad of the restoration of this ancient language." During this movement, within the community's elites, Hebrew stood as "not only the symbol of Jewish nationality in its new form; it was both a value and a goal" of the global effort to revitalize an international Jewish community and revive its centuries-old language (Ben-Bassat 1999: 146; Haramati 1972; Harshav 1993; Shohamy 1999).[25]

Like Jewish activists seeking cultural recognition from the Board of Education, African American parents insisted the public schools preserve their history and heritage. To ensure African American students "know that they had a proud history," parents requested mandatory, year-round inclusion of African American history in "all Negro High Schools" since "Negroes actually do have a history."[26]

Allusions to an inferiority complex used to argue against segregation in *Brown* were conspicuously absent from African Americans' discourse regarding the instruction of African American history and culture in the schools. Contrary to America's metanarrative of African American inferiority, local residents saw "dignity in being a Negro" and demanded "that Negro history be taught to him and his children." As Jonathan Zimmerman (1999) finds, these efforts at prejudice reduction targeted white students, not African Americans. Although perhaps not representative of the entire population, a contemporary study examining African American students' attitudes prior to attending Freedom Schools found, "at the first interview—before attending Freedom School—these boys and girls *did not* harbor such negative attitudes." Instead, they knew of and expressed pride in African American accomplishments.[27]

NYC's African American community, ahead of the contemporary integration discourse, charted a course toward pan-Africanism. Conferences discussed the common heritage between "Afro-Americans" and Africans, thereby shifting away from the term "Negro" while simultaneously attempting to foster cultural unity between people of African descent. A letter to the editor championed a pan-African identity since there was "no such thing as the West Indian Negro, Spanish Negro, French Negro and so forth, but Africans all." The author preferred African American history over integration since "a change in the curriculum would be of greater benefit to the African American child rather than sitting in the same classroom with the white children. The teaching of African American history, not to be confused with Negro history, would give character, pride and dignity."[28]

Jews and African Americans believed presenting and preserving group cultures in schools would also positively affect their communities' families. Parents needed schools to corroborate and validate, rather than discredit, their cultures to ensure consonance between school- and community-based knowledge. Both Jews and African Americans referenced the centrality of the family with seeking cultural inclusion. Parents play a critical role in perpetuating group cultures, values, traditions, and consciousnesses of the community to their children. For Jews and African Americans, both with histories of broken family ties, maintenance of familial bonds was vital.

Russian conscription laws tore Jewish families asunder by removing men and young boys from the home and community, often for decades. First-generation Jewish children's acculturation to America, which expanded the cultural distance between Jewish parents and their children, distressed many in the Jewish community. As a communicative form different from that of the dominant group, Hebrew had the potential to unite Jewish parents and children in culture and prayer, diminish familial breakdown, and bridge the gap between New and Old World traditions. Courses in Hebrew could mitigate the "heartbreaking phenomena" of Jewish children's alienation from their parents that occurred when the schools inhibited the "tens of thousands of children who acquire a fair knowledge of Hebrew in elementary Hebrew schools" to build on existing knowledge. Instead, Hebrew language classes would generate "mutual bonds of appreciation and respect . . . between pupils and their parents on the basis of cultural achievement and understanding."[29]

Throughout American history, whites have subjected the African American family to trauma. Enforced separations during slavery yielded to migratory separation and family destruction by lynching. As a result, African American mothers, "othermothers," and real and constructed family ties became vital to both individual families and the entire community (Foley 1997: 123; Collins 2000). Seeking changes to the curriculum, African American activists sought to preserve the "virtues and solidarity in [the] African American community and family traditions . . . passed from generation to generation." Emphasizing the problematic dissonance between messages at school and at home, an African American mother asked, "How can I teach my child to be proud of his heritage when he is being taught things like this in school?"[30]

Moving Past Multiculturalism

Jewish and African American curricular revisions moved beyond superficial exercises that emphasized heroes, holidays, and food to include deeper knowledges of each group's history and culture and encourage students to enact radical politics. Activists rejected assimilationist ideologies and rejected America's dominant historical narrative, positioning European technology and intellect at the center of modern history. Activists in these cases, articulating both celebratory and proletarian versions of Judeo- and Afrocentricity, placed Jewish and African contributions and experiences at the center of America's and world civilization's development. This knowledge prepared Jewish and African American children to participate in social action-oriented and transformational national and international liberatory movements. In this way, Jews' and African Americans' efforts resemble contemporary Afrocentric curriculum that challenges Eurocentric models by studying "African peoples from an Africa-centered prism" (Oyebade 1990: 233).[31]

Hebrew's and Africa's Role in Western Civilization

Hebrew maintained the unique distinction of melding the ancient, biblical, mythical, and historical with the modern world to contribute to art, literature, and music. Mark Eisner, in a speech delivered at a rally sponsored by Ivriah, the Women's Division of the Jewish Education Association, declared

> Many of us have not realized that in Palestine the Hebrew language is the means of communication of the man in the street. Its rich accents and picturesque expressions are no longer confined to Synagogue and Student Hall but are heard everywhere. With this, of course, have come the modifications and enrichments due to the absorption of modern names, ideas and expressions wich necessarily characterize every living tongue and result in idoms which indicate the virility of the language. Modern Hebrew, having lost none of the granduer of old, is today the living, vibrant, forceful yet graceful expression of the scholar, the poet and the artisan and the merchant as well. The Golden Age which produced the poetry or the philosophy of Ibn Gabirol, Judah Halevi, and Maimonides seems likely to be reborn. Hebrew can express as well the joys of social, political and economic freedom, as the tears and suffering of oppression and despair; it can equally be the language of music and the dance, and the voice of denunciation and retribution.

Supporting these and other activists' sentiments, a well-known Semitic scholar at Johns Hopkins University, W. F. Albright, wrote to Wise of Hebrew's status as a "repository of an exceedingly rich tradition, both in literature, history and thought." This influence spanned "the importance of the bible in the history of mankind since the Hellenistic age" to the "choicest elements in the accumulated cultural tradition of the Ancient East and best in the religious and literary culture" safeguarding knowledge through the Dark Ages and spurring knowledge accumulation of the Renaissance.[32]

The Hebrew Committee championed Hebrew's role in Western civilization's development and its literature, culture, and religion by placing it at the zenith of classical languages. Eliminating Hebrew and preserving the language of "Romans and Greeks, although those languages had died and lost their practical value," was an "anomaly and paradox." Since modern authors wrote Hebrew "novels, plays and books of philosophy and other contemporary thought," Jewish activists argued that Hebrew was "the language of the greatest literary treasure of the human race." It "includes the experiences, thoughts and sentiments reflected in vicissitudes of a people which has lived through many ages and countries. It has influenced the thoughts and sentiments of the Christian and Mohammedan world" from which philosophical concepts of ethics derived. Hebrew recorded the "customs, traditions and culture of a people as old as history itself," as one of the "great civilizations in history," and "increasingly a living tongue."[33]

Alongside its "tremendous influence upon Western civilization," Hebrew had important underpinnings for American ideology. The language linked "the ideas that dominate the historic consciousness of the Jew" to America's democratic roots. Taught, and required for graduation, in American universities during the colonial era, activists noted that many of America's founding fathers studied Hebrew prior to taking the nation's helm. Placing Hebrew at the center of American and world civilization linked Jewish children to both America's and the Jewish community's past and future.[34]

African Americans, though seeking equal citizenship during the civil rights movement unfolding simultaneously, did not downplay their cultural identities while demanding curricular revisions. Instead, protests during an era of cultural conformity reveal African Americans' belief in their culture's centrality to America's cultural and economic development. Newspaper articles, features, and editorials lauded their unique history as a source of pride. An editorial in the *Amsterdam News* speaking in honor of Negro History Week in 1948 declared, "World peace will be impossible unless there is inculcated in the minds of our youth of all countries that there is no such thing as a pure, superior, or inferior race; that the Africans and Asiatics possess older civilizations and cultures than those of the peoples of Europe; and that ancient African history constitutes one of the brightest pages in the whole story of the evolution of man. The mis-education of the Western peoples is largely responsible for the false notions and beliefs so religiously held by thousands of well meaning and honest but mis-informed men and women." Thirteen years later, in 1961, a cartoon featured an African American man, "traveling too light," as he stepped over the line from segregation to integration without his clothes, labeled "racial heritage." Without pride in the accomplishments of the race, African Americans would be naked in an integrated society.[35]

African Americans lobbied hard to promote their contributions to American and global history. Members of the Harlem 9 demanded American and "Attican" history in the curriculum of every NYC high school. They countered the curriculum's absence in local schools by installing it in Freedom Schools held during the boycotts. School hallways in African American neighborhoods, such as those in P.S. 119 in Harlem, featured "pre-European history and culture of the African people, the heights to which Negroes in the United States have ascended."[36]

Autonomously created curriculum depicted African Americans as capable and competent individuals who contributed prominently to American history. Curriculum developed by P.S. 63's PTA in 1959 allowed students in grades four through six, whether studying "history, literature, music, science, or art," to "know of the role Negroes have played in these fields." Four years later, in 1963, the Interborough Negro History Committee's fourteen-page *Revised Negro History Guide* for children in kindergarten through sixth grade, emphasized Afrocentric themes through African Americans' role in American history, science, and culture. Zenith Books, released by Doubleday and approved by the board in 1964, gave "minorities a fair deal in the study of America and world history and literature."[37]

The board-released *The Negro in American History* included African and African American history "from early Egyptian slavery . . . to the recent passage of the Civil Rights Bill." This book, documenting African American autonomy, agency, and culture, represented a significant departure from earlier schoolbooks neglecting African Americans' efforts to acquire more rights. After the book's release, James L. Hicks, of the *Amsterdam News*, noted the length of time it had taken for African Americans "to bring the power structure in our schools to the point where it [was] willing to admit that the Negro has a great history and that that great history should be taught to all our children in all our schools."[38]

African American Heroes: From Moral Hard Men to Radical Cultural Activists

Examining the heroes presented in schools between 1946 and 1964, particularly during Negro History Week, provides a case study in the shift away from African Americans' politics of semblance to a politics of difference, past multiculturalism to Afrocentricity. At the beginning of this period, curriculum often featured Booker T. Washington, Jackie Robinson, Matthew Henson, and George Washington Carver, moral hard men who succeeded economically within the tight confines of American racism. They broke through white stereotypes and expectations to succeed in spite of oppressive and hostile social conditions, but did not challenge the assimilatory themes underlying America's racist system. Instead, they succeeded by either aiding prominent white men or improving technology from which they would benefit in a two-tier agrarian economy. For whites, these nostalgic figures represented "good Blacks" who fulfilled subservient roles in American society without challenging the racial hierarchy that kept African Americans confined to second-class citizenship (Levine 1997: 420). But African Americans perceived these figures differently. These were men who somehow achieved success in a society with all the cards stacked against them. Since their success brought material rewards to the larger community, this figure of "exceptional Blackness" (Van Deburg 1997) challenged dominant ideologies regarding African American potential. These alternative meanings reveal the subversive possibilities of curriculum, even when chosen by the dominant racial group.[39]

As militant precursors of Black Power replaced integrationist rhetoric of the 1950s, activists supplanted extraordinary men and moral hard men with international figures contributing to politics, culture, and emancipation. These included Langston Hughes, Countee Cullen, Marion Anderson, Ralphe Bunche, Adam Clayton Powell Jr., Congresswoman Bessie Buchanan, Kwame Nkrumah, and Toussaint L'Ouverture. These men and women directly challenged America's racist society by both their very existence and their willingness to attack the national and international racial and economic orders.

By the end of the era, African American freedom fighters, represented well in the NAACP's *Negro Heroes of Emancipation* pamphlet highlighting activists from the American Revolution to the present, challenged America's structural racism as they struggled for "identity and achievement." These self-consciously racially oriented radical, and often nationalist, cultural activists championed African American group pride and mobility as they worked to improved the material, social, and political conditions of the national and global African community. Preceding the more prolific, controversial, and militant African American heroes that emerged during the 1960s' Black Power movement, these radical cultural activists enacted their race-consciousness and enthusiasm to challenge mainstream society's values, policies, and culture. They included, and were sensitive to, the social, political, economic, and spiritual needs of the African American community. Many of these activists lived in, worked in, and represented NYC's African American community, who encountered these figures on the streets and in the stores, bars, and churches. These men and women, to African American students and adults, signified the possibility of both individual success and widespread social change that could dramatically alter American society.[40]

Enacting Plural Citizenship: Transformative, Nationalist, and Participatory Curriculum

A quarter of a century apart, in extracurricular Hebrew Culture Clubs and Freedom Schools, Jewish and African American students encountered similar opportunities to experience participatory cultural nationalism. In doing so, they joined an imagined community of global Zionists and freedom fighters in the American South and encountered national and international celebrities and cultural heroes.

Like contemporary scholars promoting critical race theory in education, Jews and African Americans injected cultural and experiential knowledge, "skills, abilities, and contacts possessed by marginalized groups that often go unrecognized and unacknowledged" (Yosso 2005: 69). Rejecting schooling to the dominant racial norms that replicated racial inequalities and power relations, Jewish and African American activists injected transformative knowledge to alter America's racial terrain by promoting upward mobility and active participation in contemporary social change abroad, at home, and in school. Activists' nationalist curriculum featured global struggles for independence and equality to re-invent national identities, promote autonomous nationhood, and challenge global oppression.[41]

Group solidarity and the development of political communities were essential to this curriculum. The mental connection to a global Jewish community became vital to the American-based anti-Nazi movement as violence against Jews in Europe increased and the Holocaust became a reality. African American participation in anticolonialist movements abroad and at home allowed for the development a of global diasporic consciousness and, viewed alongside Jewish efforts, reveals both groups' opposition to international oppression and racism. This curriculum not only critiqued knowledge presented in schools but confronted school's authority, power, and Jews' and African Americans' position in the city's educational arena and within the racial hierarchy as constructors of new cultural meanings of their group identities.

International Zionism

Zionist student groups, Avukah (the student branch of the Zionist Organization of America), Young Judaea, and Histadruth Ivrith, initiated Hebrew demands and remained engaged throughout the duration of the protests. During the Annual Hebrew Week and National Hebrew Day, sponsored by Histadruth, *The Young Judaean* advised, "Young Judaeans especially should realize the importance of Hebrew in developing a love for the Jewish people and the Jewish land. It should be considered a duty of every Young Judaea member to learn to speak Hebrew. Even though we may not intend to live in Palestine, we can, perhaps, in this country, best get the spirit of the new Jewish homeland by being able to read the language in which everything Jewish in Palestine is written." Later that year, the magazine encouraged members to "help to spread the knowledge of Hebrew so that it will not only be an ancient language to use, but one which we can use just as feely as it is used in Eretz Israel [the land of Israel] today." Students also encountered international Jewish celebrities, such as Albert Einstein, who offered symbolic support.[42]

Alluding to Hitler's rise in Germany, Jewish activists claimed that Hebrew language acquisition was an international issue for "Jews who still have faith in their national and cultural heritage, and who are vitally interested in the preservation of this heritage, no matter where they are, whether in Russia, Lithuania, Germany or America." In May 1933, the HC's primary spokesperson, Stephen Wise, "put everything aside in order to give [himself] without reservation to the work for our brother-Jews in Germany." During this pivotal year Hitler established himself as Germany's chancellor, consolidated state power within the Nazi party, and opened Dachau, the first concentration camp. Contrary to board claims that because "Jews are under fire in various parts of the world, the moment is ill advised for the introduction to Hebrew," activists believed that *now* was the most important time to introduce Hebrew.[43]

Hebrew coursework went beyond language, introducing the Jewish literature of Hayyim Bialik, David Frishman, and Saul Tchernichovsky. A member of Hovevei Zion, a Zionist group, Bialik was later named Israel's national poet whose work, in Hebrew, is often credited to the revival of the language. Like Bialik, Frishman hoped to revive Hebrew and wrote his stories about mitigating conflict between traditional Jewish and modern western culture entirely in Hebrew. Tchernikovsky's Hebrew poetry featured similar emphases on the experiences of Jews in the Diaspora.[44]

Frequent references to and depictions of Palestine appeared in the Hebrew coursework. The textbook for third- and fourth-year Hebrew students was "handsomely illustrated with pictures of Jewish life in Palestine." Teachers of advanced courses kept students "abreast of the growth of the language in modern Palestine" and taught about the nation's landscape, Hebrew songs, dances, folklore and literature. Building on this knowledge, students completed art projects and showcased works by Jewish artists, read and discussed Palestinian newspapers, produced literary works, and, at some schools, entire newspapers written in Hebrew. Pageants and assembly programs featured skits about Palestine, Hebrew songs, and plays depicting Jewish holidays. At Thomas Jefferson High School, students watched as sixty students sang Hebrew songs alongside a forty-piece orchestra while sixteen students danced the hora (a traditional Jewish dance). After school, students and teachers from high schools across the city held a weekly radio program, "Dawn Over Palestine," describing cities and places in Palestine.[45]

Global Pan-Africanism in NYC Schools

Conceptualized by Du Bois and cemented in African American consciousness with Marcus Garvey's United Negro Improvement Association, pan-Africanism sought to erase the international racist color line. Rather than a uniquely American phenomena, white racism, exploitation, and domination left a global stain on humanity. By facilitating African American economic and ideological freedom, global consciousness, and the ascension of African leaders challenging Western colonial imperialism, pan-Africanism generated a global front of antiracism. In post–World War II NYC, African American children read of African leaders in the African American press and encountered representative figures and cultures. Discussions of literature, art, and global historical innovations addressed the role of Western hegemony in the creation of global segregation and the shared fates of Africans both on the continent and in the Diaspora.[46]

Guest speakers and assemblies at African American schools allowed students to witness, firsthand, Africans' removal of their colonial chains and the establishment of independent nations. An African exchange student attending Long Island University spoke with students at JHS 25 on "progress being made hourly in his country, Kenya, in education, self-government and economic growth." He received "barrages of questions" from students interested in Africa. At Wingate High School, Vusumzi Maki, an alternate delegate to the United Nations from Ghana, "attacked the apartheid policy of the present government of the Union of South Africa and described the position of the African in that country. . . . [He] charged that the government was trying to force the African back into a tribal society and thus it was using the hated 'pass laws' to supply white farmers with free labor. . . . [T]he African seldom left the farms at all after they were sentenced, unless they escaped." Maki closed his presentation with a critique of the lack of global initiative to intervene in the situation and the West's general attitude toward Africa.[47]

While high school students spoke with consciousness-raising speakers, younger students encountered African culture through visits from African dancers and musicians. In June 1961, 1,500 children from Harlem attended a program featuring Dinizulu dancers practicing African rituals, music, dances, and songs. At the junior high school level, guest speakers, such as African dancer Pearl Primus, connected politics with art through an exchange of cultural artifacts between school children in Brooklyn and Nigeria and Liberia.[48]

Jewish demands for Zionist curriculum were echoed in African Americans' similar conceptions of the Pan-African movement. In 1919, Du Bois linked pan-Africanism with Zionism's emphasis on cultural cooperation among diasporic group members: "the African movement means to us what the Zionist movement must mean to Jews, the centralization of race effort and the recognition of a racial front" (Du Bois cited in Marable 1996: 1999). Alain Locke (1992 [1925]) declared Harlem, "the home of the Negro's 'Zionism,'" the epicenter of a movement to understand white privilege and its effect on global African identities and consciousness (14). Like Zionism, pan-Africanism sought to provide mental connections and a source of pride for Africa's diasporic descendents.

Bringing the Southern Civil Rights Movement
into Northern Classrooms

African Americans promoted an oppositional consciousness among students with activities directly linked to and which allowed them to participate in the civil rights movement. For example, P.S. 125 in Harlem sponsored a Freedom Bake to raise money for SCLC's voter registration efforts in Alabama. They also sent a "letter to President Kennedy protesting the arrest in Birmingham of the courageous boys and girls who were jailed because of their participation in a freedom demonstration." To memorialize African American children killed in the Birmingham church bombing, eight- and nine-year-old students, "budding rights fighters," at P.S. 119 (Harlem) sang freedom songs from memory and recited Langston Hughes' poetry. At an assembly honoring Medgar Evers after his assassination, children appeared "sad with their hearts in their eyes when they noted and sang Evers' favorite song 'We Shall Overcome.'"[49]

Bringing the movement into the classroom, "with an eye on training more teenage Negro youths to be well versed on all phases of the Negro's struggle for equal opportunities in this nation," the director of the JHS 139 Community Center introduced students to sixteen-year-old Lawrence Cumberbatch (whose mother participated in the Harlem 9 protests). Cumberbatch walked, with a group of students, from Brooklyn to Washington, D.C., for sit-ins and the March on Washington that featured Martin Luther King Jr.'s "I Have a Dream" speech.[50]

For NYC children to be involved in these efforts, their teacher, and likely, their parents had to teach them of unfolding civil rights movement events and their relevance to themselves, as African American children in the North. During these events, students demonstrated this transformative curriculum's efficacy as they critiqued America's racist structures that denied them opportunities as African Americans and demanded equality.[51]

Not only did students encounter the civil rights movement, so too did local teachers. Lecturing teachers at Harlem's P.S. 180, civil rights activist and author James Baldwin critiqued the schools' failure to provide students with the knowledge necessary to survive in a racist society and denounced the false image of the African American child in texts and propagated by teachers. He declared,

> If I were a teacher in any Negro school teaching a Negro child a few hours a day and have an apprehension of his future, with every hour growing grimmer and darker, I would try to make that child know that the dangers by which he is surrounded are a result of a criminal conspiracy to destroy him. . . . The black man was brought here in chains for labor and that he believes that he is an animal because he's told that he's an animal and he's treated like an animal. . . . If this animal should ever suspect his own worth and believe that he is a man, he will begin to attack the power structure. It is a deliberate policy, hammered in place to make money off the backs of Black fellows.

Baldwin concluded his fiery speech with demands for education to "liberate" African American youth.[52]

In-school participation in the contemporary civil rights movement through rituals re-created throughout the nation allowed children to enact deeply rooted oppositional consciousness and cultures. The appearance of revolutionary cultural figures such as Langston Hughes and James Baldwin highlights the community's rich literary tradition and cultural figures' role as beacons of freedom. Students as young as ten could internalize these struggles and, not only identify with participants in a national movement fighting for racial solidarity and equality, but challenge the racial metanarrative of white hegemony promoted in school texts and across society (Goldberg 1993; Pride 2002).

By returning "the gaze of the discriminated back on the eye of power" (Bhabha 1994: 112), Jewish and African American activists not only provided the intellectual tools to empower their children to resist the hegemonic ideologies of the dominant society, but to act on this information. In each case, Jewish and African American participation in citizen action projects, "*meaningful* experiences," allowed students to develop a sense of political efficacy and enact "the practice of freedom" (Banks 1996: 345, emphasis in original; Dewey 1954, 1997; Freire 2005; hooks 1994).

Extrascholastic Parallel Institutions

Because the public schools rejected their cultures, Jews and African Americans developed community-based institutions to preserve them. These institutions provided children with unique cultural frameworks to interpret the biased knowledge presented to them in the public schools. As teachers within these institutions, Jews and African Americans controlled the critical multicultural knowledge to address power differences and the roots of oppression, generate oppositional consciousnesses, and promote social justice.

Facing increased assimilation, Americanization, and a loss of cultural heritage, Jews championed Hebrew schools. Like those of Indians, Vietnamese, and Chinese today, these parallel institutions ensured that Jewish children, accommodating to dominant beliefs in public schools, retained cultural traditions. These educational efforts intended to continue the culture and religion through marriage sought to mitigate a loss of religious identity, behavior, and ethnic attachments. Enrollment in Hebrew schools peaked in 1950 with close to half a million students nationwide.[53]

In the African American community, Freedom Schools and extracurricular practices allowed parents to familiarize their children with knowledge of their culture and history. In January 1954, a letter to the *Age* suggested, "a private school supported by awakened Afro-Americans to teach African history, our past greatness, and the future possibilities of our people here in the Western world."

Four years later, in 1958, Thedra Dixon, a Brooklyn mother, sought out a school to teach her children "the history of the African American race. I've been unable to find such a school. But I do deem that it is important toward development of status elevation—thus better adjusted citizens of tomorrow. . . . I have taught them all that I know but feel that this [is] not enough. They have such a thirst for knowledge and show so much interest, I feel it is my obligation to seek aid." The *Amsterdam News* responded with an editor's note informing members of the African American community that, "The Parent Teacher Association at [P.S.] 133, 2121 Fifth Ave., headed by Mrs. Ruby Sims [held] classes in Negro history three times a week in their homes." Other African American activists encouraged parents to boycott the public schools' annual Brotherhood Week programs and, instead, "sit down with your children and teach Negro history which the Board of Education refuses to add to the curriculum." However, institutionalizing the delivery of this historical knowledge outside of school did not diminish protest for the official recognition of this curriculum in local schools. Rather, parents continued their struggle through both overt demands to the board and inclusion of contemporary events relevant to the African American community in local classrooms.[54]

During boycotts, Freedom School courses featured African American history and culture to bestow "the kids in Harlem [who] have never had Negro history in school . . . [with] some pride in their heritage." During a 1964 boycott, Siloam Presbyterian Church's Freedom School featured comedian and activist Dick Gregory. His lecture, "We Negroes," described his participation in the civil rights movement and argued that African Americans, though they lacked financial resources, exercised considerable power:

> Do you young people know that in the south we've closed up restaurants and didn't have a penny in our pockets? Some didn't have a penny to their names. If the man had said that he'd serve them, they wouldn't have been able to pay for a meal. But they got out there and marched in this civil rights fight that you're taking part in today. They have power. They closed many, many restaurants, and will close many more. The Negro controls the fate and destiny of this country. We're the number one strong man in this nation. You have so much strength and power, even the cops are afraid of you. Trying to arrest us when we get out there today is like trying to put a tornado in jail. How did we get this power? Nature gave it to us. In the history of the world nature reaches out and gets her underdog and says—"Let's go!" No one can stand in the way of nature.

At the Kennedy Community Center's Freedom School, fourth grade boys discussed "the meaning of the boycott and how it related to the Birmingham bus boycott. The idea of choice as a means of freedom was fostered throughout the discussion." These citywide Freedom Schools represent important precursors to the development of community-controlled schools in the Brownsville–Ocean Hill district beginning in 1968 in which activists explicitly inserted culturally relevant education into the curriculum to subvert schooling based on white standards (Shujaa 1994).[55]

Alongside parallel institutions, community-based organizations arose to promote "a period of intensive study and teaching of the history of the race." In 1961, local activists, including some former Harlem 9 members, formed Sterling Artist, Inc., to distribute films about African American history and culture. Local African American fraternities and CORE chapters sponsored African history courses to introduce school children to Africa's contributions to world history. A session held by the Delta Sigma Theta sorority in Brooklyn "made the kids feel differently about the history of the last 300 years and gave them a glimpse of the brilliant corridor beyond that."[56]

Many organizations focused on African, rather than African American, history. Community school coordinator Dr. James E. Allen's first adult African History course, held at the NAACP's request, found forty-nine adults crowded into a classroom at P.S. 5 in December 1958 learning about Africa's contributions to world civilization. Allen began his lecture with a quote from Arnold J. Toynbee's widely used book, *A Study of History*: "the Negro race has not made any contributions to world civilizations." The course would refute that perception through "endless data proving Toynbee to be grossly in error." Allen went on, "Africa must be viewed in a new light and kingdoms which prospered under African American kings must be made known. . . . We find so many distortions of the Negro's life and contributions to world civilization in books, films and stage presentations. We will study these commissions and omissions but we will compile accurate information about the African American man's history." Other centers in and around Harlem offered African American adult learners classes about their roots. The African Theological Center held classes in "West African history, language, arts, and philosophy." As direct ancestors of many African American New Yorkers, this course exposed them to knowledge of their cultural roots. This adult education, argue Antonio Gramsci (1971; 1978; 1985; 1995) and Paulo Freire (1970; 1976; 1985; 1993; 1995), is central to transformative political change. For those adults interested in passing the information on to the next generation, the Afro Arts Cultural Center's teacher course, "Africa and World Affairs," featured fifteen sessions, each about a different African nation, the first of which was Ghana.[57]

Critical transformative education in the form of pan-African culture and history signifies an attempt to revolutionarily transform an oppressive society. To educate students of all ages, activists moved outside of the classroom and into the larger community to champion a pan-African political consciousness. Courses presenting African independence movements linked global anti-imperialist efforts to the civil rights movement unfolding in America. This instruction, focusing on African nations and their culture, were particularly radical given the contemporary hegemonic discourse that focused on the exotification and civilizing of Africans.

Unlike during the 1968 Brownsville–Ocean Hill crisis, parents did not seek a complete overhaul of the educational process. During the Brownsville–Ocean Hill episode, and in later Afrocentric public schools, African American educators developed "an alternative system of values that, unlike those of whites, would 'emphasize that which is private and ethnic as against that which is public and culture-blind,' and which would redefine the public education market to reward resources found in the Black community" (Podair 2002: 66). This curriculum questioned the legitimacy of the institutionalized white power structure emphasizing individualism and Western cultural superiority, and sought to replace it with one based on "black 'normative values'" such as group cohesion, color consciousness, and respect for "Afro-American culture" (Podair 2002: 62; Hamilton 1968). However, this heightened emphasis on transformative and liberatory curriculum laid the groundwork for the critique of educational values that erupted during the 1968 Ocean Hill–Brownsville strikes.

Multicultural and Judeo- and Afrocentric Citizenship and Cultural Visions

Like demands for improved resources, Jews' and African Americans' politics of semblance and difference sought both inclusion in American public life and history and retention of cultural differences. Directly linked to national and international social, political, and economic issues, Jews' and African Americans' logic for the preservation of their culture shifted over time. Beginning each movement with politics of semblance, activists then moved beyond dominant integrationist and inclusionist rhetoric to promote transformative Judeo- and Afrocentric curriculum that would not only preserve their culture but empower community youth to enact change.

Jewish and African American activists' initial politics of semblance highlighted the intellectual and civic value of Hebrew and African American history due to their contributions to world civilization and modern American history and culture. Arguing that cultural artifacts were significant for their own and the entire American community, activists sought an affirmative version of recognition that sought redress for "disrespect by revaluing unjustly devalued group identities, while leaving intact both the content of those identities and the group differentiation that underlie them" (Fraser 1998: 32; Taylor 1994). Communities seeking respect for their identities desire more than tolerance; they sought recognition through policies to amend identity-based inequalities.

Activists believed, during these eras of racism, anti-Semitism, and xeno-phobia, that when other children learned of their similarities to Jewish and African American children and these groups' role in American and world history, they would perceive them as no different from themselves. This cross-cultural knowledge contact would therefore diminish stereotypes, enhance American race relations, and symbolize a large step toward social, and then economic, equality. More than just tangible benefits of new curriculum in classrooms, the board's inclusion of Hebrew and African American history would have signified society's "symbolic recognition of [Jews' and] African Americans' worth, status, [and] existence . . . within the larger state community" (Kymlicka & Norman 2000: 129). Jewish and African American children could then reap the academic benefits of being perceived as equal to other American children. Without this recognition, each continued to be subject to social, economic, and political oppression both within and outside of the educational arena.

Jews' and African Americans' politics of difference sought a "new and more democratic mode of civil integration" (Alexander 2001: 238) in an America that accepted into the public realm, rather then relegated to the private realm, their stigmatized ethnic traditions. Engaging cultures and traditions of resistance embedded within each community, Jews and African Americans demanded the city and Board of Education furnish them the curricular rights and resources entitled to them as American citizens. This war of maneuver inside the schools attempted to preserve particular cultural attributes, language, and familial bonds while strengthening their children's knowledge of group history, contributions of each group to American and world civilization, and contemporary nationalist efforts. When that failed, a war of position created parallel institutions outside the schools. These efforts challenged the racialist ideology of the United States and the hegemonic monoculture that dominated public school curriculum. Explicitly transformative curriculum rooted in contemporary social movements allowed students both the knowledge and opportunities to contribute to social justice causes.[58]

Though perhaps limited from today's standpoint, at the time of each case, Jewish and African American curricular challenges represent efforts to dismantle the foundational ideologies of America's racist system and power distribution that marginalized each community's youth. By petitioning for the inclusion of Hebrew and African and African American history in the Western canon, Jews and African Americans challenged the very definition of what this canon is and who belongs to it. During these racial projects, Jewish and African American activists attempted to rearticulate their identities by challenging the minority status assigned to them. They claimed epistemic privilege to reconstruct the meanings of their experiences as oppressed groups lacking equal access to curricular representation in the context of an American institution expressing an ideology of equality. These movements to construct identities building upon, but not sublimating themselves to, an American identity signified radical departures from assimilationist and integrationist doctrines, discourses, and rhetoric.[59]

Self-consciously acting to preserve and strengthen their cultures, rather than submit to the dominant assimilatory American cultural force, Jews' and African Americans' narratives offer significant insights into activists' subjective orientation toward their ethnic origins (Alba 1990). Hebrew and African American history sought to mediate the differences between curricular portrayals and the realities of lived experiences of each group and to promote a more consistent presentation of each group's culture in the public schools. If this occurred, the educational system, rather than being a culturally distinct and colonizing space, would become an incubator for group-based cultural difference. When these demands were not forthcoming, both groups maintained parallel institutions to ensure that, while accommodating to American values in school, children retained their cultural traditions and oppositional outlooks.

Jewish and African American efforts to remake NYC's curriculum challenged not unintentional oversights but a curriculum that maintained a racial and religious hegemony in the schools and in the nation. Through measures of differing intensity and severity, schools countered activists' efforts by absorbing protests through subversion, silence, and selective inclusion of cultural artifacts to ensure that relations of competition, exploitation, domination, and cultural selection remained fixed. New York City, a diverse city of immigrants, had no place for Jews and African Americans in the curricular canon or within its opportunity structures.

6

Racism, Resistance, and Racial Formation in the Public Schools

For students of America's public school history, New York City's rejection of activists' claims may not be a surprise. Throughout American history, public schools, often touted as a universally available institution, have operated as central mechanisms maintaining America's *herrenvolk* democracy, with democratic citizenship rights reserved for whites and denied to subordinate groups. At their inception, public schools established whiteness as the true American identity by excluding African Americans, maintaining racial boundaries and ensuring a rigid racial hierarchy. This perpetuated African Americans' inferior status as uneducated workers, facilitated the equation of whiteness with intelligence, and relegated them (and later, Native Americans, Latinos, Asians, and Southern and Eastern Europeans) to second-class citizenship. Therefore, public education has historically been, and remains, a homogenizing, Americanizing, and assimilatory force that conscientiously sorts different groups according to their initial position in the racial and class hierarchies and replicates existing stratification.[1]

In NYC's public schools, Jewish and African American youth received schooling that replicated the racial hierarchy, rather than an education of culturally relevant curriculum alongside academic material necessary for social, political, and economic success in America. Jewish and African American activists faithfully believed the schools would grant their demands to enhance education and improve their material conditions and racial position. But a public school system steeped in America's racial inequalities and ideologies, and therefore resilient in resisting their demands, shattered their optimism. NYC's schools, when faced with pressure from racial minorities, dug in their heels to restabilize the racial hierarchy and reinscribe racial difference. As they did so, they championed policies by claiming they benefited minority groups when they actually either maintained the status quo or worsened their problems. These protests illuminate the central, and often hidden, role of schools and their mechanisms in maintaining inequality and oppressive conditions.

The specific constraints and opportunities found in the social, political, and economic context of the racialized society in which each group struggled to achieve their goals affected movement outcomes and reaffirmed links between group-based identities, cultures, and resources. Culturally rooted narratives and resources, although critical to mobilization, strategies, and tactics, failed to persuade the city and Board of Education to enact anything but symbolic changes. By rejecting Jews' and African American's claims for equal distribution of resources and curricular representation, NYC's antimulticulturalist school system denied each group educational rights and resources. Above all, race, particularly the power invested in whiteness, structured movement trajectories, opportunities, and outcomes.

What Happened: Racialized Multicultural Movements

The use of multiculturalist rhetoric to extend citizenship rights to particular aggrieved groups who desire to maintain their cultural traditions is relatively new. Efforts to achieve these goals are not. During these cases, Jews and African Americans acknowledged and contested the privileges of whiteness embedded as citizenship rights in the educational realm by demanding the schools decouple these phenomenon in, what I call, critical multicultural social movements. Activists linked the inequality and power differentials they experienced in schools and in larger society to the perceived differences between themselves and other Americans. They then used group-based cultures to demand access to the American Dream without dissociating from cultural communities of origin. Given that the nation, and therefore the nation's school system, did not perceive Jews and African Americans as equal to other American citizens, NYC's public schools refused demands for strategic reallocation of mobility-generating resources and curriculum reform. This rejection dismissed their claims to American citizenship and reaffirmed their cultural differences.[2]

During these protests, activists struck at what they believed to be the heart of American inequality—the educational system—to deconstruct America's racial hierarchy. Jews and African Americans demanded that the school system recognize its role in affecting each groups' social subordination and begin promoting the material goals of equal protection and opportunity, economic and social equality, and freedom. This was not just about better schools or group cultures in the curriculum. Jews and African Americans yearned for a holistic reconstruction of American social relations through an enforced equality of status within the inextricably linked economic, political, social, and cultural spheres alongside the ability to retain cultural differences in public.

These groups' demands for respect for, not just tolerance of, their American and cultural identities challenged the underlying structural inequalities manifesting in everyday educational patterns and practices that inhibited their children's ability to participate in America's social, cultural, political, and economic institutions. Campaigns for democratic education offered an alternative vision of the existing collective "we" in American society and in the schools. These racial projects, like critical multiculturalism, used a politics of recognition to "name, interpret, and make visible histories of discrimination and disrespect" (Hobson 2003: 5). Had they succeeded, they would have altered America's racial hierarchy, constructed new conceptions of belonging within American society, and rearticulated the meanings of race in America.[3]

Jewish and African American activists demands' reflected their desires for educational rights then available only to white students; but they were not seeking a white identity, as other groups have done. These efforts to expand the curriculum to include both academic and culturally relevant curriculum resemble what activists like Du Bois had sought for decades. Du Bois (1973) argued that minority youth, particularly African Americans, needed both classical studies to enhance their reasoning capacity and material supporting the value of their own cultures, which whites encountered in the regular glorification of European Americans. Addressing educational inequalities in a nation that often fails to acknowledge white privilege, Jews and African Americans contested the political and social power of white institutions that perpetuated links between resource inequality and devalued identities.[4]

Waging challenges against institutional power, Jews and African Americans aimed their discourse at establishment insiders and a mobilizable public. Ideological shifts in the larger political discourse allowed for the deployment of different frames over the course of the movement, suggesting the critical role political opportunities play for identity-related demands. Ultimately, activists could not convince the Board of Education of their demands' legitimacy. This denial was particularly striking in the case of the Harlem 9—given that these events occurred after *Brown*, when the nation was in the midst of civil rights turmoil and the board might have been amenable to desegregation demands. The difficulty Jews and African Americans experienced in achieving these goals reveals the centrality of rejecting recognition claims to maintaining unequal citizenship. By ignoring race-based educational inequality, the schools perpetuated unequal outcomes inhibiting full participation in American social life.

America's Racial Structures and Racist Schools

In early- and mid-twentieth-century NYC, schools accomplished what they have done for centuries; they institutionalized interconnected power relations, resource inequalities, class differences, and racial identities and meanings. Rather than a Golden Door to mobility and social, political, and economic success, NYC's schools locked out Jews and African Americans. This was not a laissez-faire process, with schools, embedded in a larger racial structure, acting as an "invisible hand" to promote inequality. Rather, in the face of protests by hundreds of thousands of Jewish and African American parents, teachers, community leaders, students, and citizens, NYC's public schools stolidly opposed any changes promoting even the possibility of Jewish and African American equality.

Racially based inequalities structured the logic for, the opportunities and constraints experienced, and the outcome of each protest. Jews' and African Americans' historically specific and socially constructed racial differences were embedded in the particular social, political, and cultural contexts of these eras. "Common sense" perceptions of physical and cultural differences justified discriminatory policies and practices that reified power relations and hierarchical racial structures of opportunity. When confronted by activists, NYC's Board of Education not only opposed change but used countertactics to absorb protests, entrench differences, and restabilize the racial terrain upon which Jews and African Americans waged their battles. The school system affected each groups' racial subordination by impeding Jews and African Americans from rearticulating their devalued ascribed racial identities that excluded them from the American mainstream.[5]

As racial outsiders, Jewish and African American students experienced overt discrimination that denied their ability to participate as equal citizens in the American democracy, and their identity remained disparaged. Lacking membership to this exclusive category—whiteness—each group encountered exclusionary practices by the Board of Education, which systematically denied them resources and enhanced each groups' racialization as nonwhites. Each group truly believed that altering America's educational structure and opportunities would provide their children with the tools necessary to correct America's entire racial system of inequality. The schools' fierce resistance to their efforts reveals both the system's power to inhibit racial progress, and the fundamental role of education in structuring larger social inequality. However, this system operates in concert with other institutions, such that without changing larger social structures, the educational system cannot be changed to accommodate the demands of racial minorities seeking enhanced opportunities and rights in American society.

Critical race theorists argue that whiteness exists as a form of property, and, in addition to the psychological wages theorized by Du Bois, enhances the opportunities of those who have it. Manifested and deployed in a variety of ways, whiteness, normalized in classrooms, allows school administrators and staff to exclude nonmembers from quality education. In classrooms, texts and teachers ignore or marginalize different cultures while celebrating and legitimizing the dominant culture (Ladson-Billings & Tate 1995). White teachers exhibit subconscious biases that privilege white students, even as they often preach a colorblindness that ignores structural inequalities and barriers to success. During these protests, white privilege restricted Jewish and African American students' access to school property by relegating minority students to crowded classrooms lacking quality equipment, teachers, and healthy learning environments, and curriculum that perpetuated reputation and status property (that is, that African American schools were "difficult"). In doing so, the schools protected and re-inscribed the value of a white identity.[6]

Lacking whiteness, and the power necessary to change their social conditions, Jewish and African American children encountered hidden curriculum that reinscribed racial identities by teaching children their place in the racial order. NYC's schools resigned Jewish and African American students to the most overcrowded, underfunded, and crumbling schools staffed with racist teachers and administrators who treated children like animals and failed to provide them with anything but the most basic academic knowledge. Insufficient academic resources and vocational curriculum trained Jewish and African American students for the lower rungs of the economic ladder while whites gained knowledge to achieve economic success. Textbooks excluding and stereotyping Jewish and African American histories implicitly instructed students and teachers of each groups' racial difference and lack of contributions and value to NYC's and America's history. The exclusion of the Hebrew language and African American history from a curriculum that included other European immigrants' languages and white history, highlighted Jews' and African Americans' difference from white children. Each practice instructed Jewish and African American children of their subordination to other groups while whites learned of their superiority, thereby instilling in young children knowledge of, and legitimizing, America's racial hierarchy.[7]

Jewish and African American activists attempted to throw a wrench in this machine to end the schools' role in assigning differential resources and inferior identities to each group. Neither group claimed whiteness, but instead demanded that the schools decouple the links between citizenship and whiteness to provide them with quality education equal to that of whites while retaining their group cultures. In doing so, they critiqued America's system of racial nationalism and capitalism. But these longstanding racial ideologies and the racial ascription machine proved too resilient to allow for change, particularly in the context of NYC's public schools, a bureaucratic institution historically resistant to change.

Activists encountered systemic and institutional racism that fostered racist practices. The foundation of educational resource inequalities undergirded white political and economic power and ideologies. Within this system, power differences between Jewish and African American activists and the white city and educational establishment allowed whites to retain formal and informal control over minorities' access to education, which impeded their access to critical social, political, and economic rights and resources. Products of power relations and historical forces rather than neutral negotiations among actors of equal social status, the continued racialized meanings of each group's identity maintained the racial order, hegemonic power, and meanings of whiteness (Cornel & Hartmann 2007; Fredrickson 1998; Gould 1996; Omi & Winant 1994), even as each group sought to subvert it.[8]

Rejecting or ignoring activists' claims, the schools remained antimulticulturalist as they engaged a colorblind logic in their staunch defense of the racial order. Schools' deep investment in dynamically resisting Jewish and African American efforts were reflected in countertactics to publicly evade and structurally promote educational inequality and racialized identities. By failing to address the ways in which they disadvantaged Jewish and African American youth, the Board of Education promoted and disseminated racial meanings, denied Jews and African Americans citizenship rights, and reinstitutionalized a society structured by racial difference. Contrary to popular belief, schools did not facilitate Jews' ascension up America's social or economic ladder. Instead, they held them in a similar position as African Americans. Rather than allowing either group to transcend structural inequalities, schools deployed a variety of mechanisms to entrench racial and class differences between these groups and the dominant majority.[9]

Scholastic and Extrascholastic Racialization Mechanisms

America's public schools do not operate in a vacuum. Racial master narratives erected around Jews and African Americans ideological and political barriers that inhibited their abilities to transcend America's racial structures (McCarthy 1998; West 2002; Winant 1994).

Any board action to improve Jews' or African Americans' schools and provide them with academic curriculum would have represented a dramatic departure from existing educational thought and society's racial narratives and attitudes regarding each group. Given the embedded racial hierarchy during the resource-based protests, this was highly unlikely. During the Gary Plan, these ideologies and constraints inhibited Mayor Hylan, even after committing to improving schools during his campaign and pursuing these goals after the election, from moving the wheels of the educational bureaucracy toward greater equality. The board, had it instigated a citywide school desegregation program, an influx of money to schools in predominantly African American neighborhoods, or both, would have garnered national attention and set a precedent in urban educational reform. Instead, the board argued that vocational education was best for disadvantaged groups. In truth, these policies cemented the racial and economic order. Small alterations to public school curriculum symbolically assuaged disparaged groups but failed to alter the racial hierarchy. Instead, board policies established racially based difference as the basis for economic inequality.

With schools structured to reject their demands, activists quickly found that only when they operated autonomously and at the most local levels of education could they inject Hebrew and African American culture into the curriculum. When seeking change, Jews needed the principals' support to teach Hebrew. Where this did not exist, the course was not taught. Ultimate success, a Regents exam, occurred only after society embraced Jews within the family of white ethnic groups as a result of larger structural changes in American society in the years after World War II. African American success was incremental and, like Jews,' dependent upon local support. Where principals supported their efforts, African American history appeared in classrooms, on school walls, and during school assemblies. Where principals did not support the curriculum, it was not taught, and those creating the curriculum faced severe consequences, such as termination. In both cases, curriculum creation and comprehensive dissemination occurred outside, not inside, the schools.

Having only token members on the Board of Education and in the city and state bureaucracy, Jews and African Americans lacked not only political power, but "access to non-discursive power-brokering arenas" (Hobson 2003: 11–12). The board marginalized decisions of its sole African American member (Rev. John M. Coleman and, later, Rev. Gardner C. Taylor) during each case. During the Gary Plan, Jews alleged that the manufacturing industry's investment in education trapped their children in the racially based economic hierarchy of sweatshop labor. The two Jewish Board of Education members, who maintained ties to the Rockefeller conglomeration, vocally supported the Gary Plan. The Hebrew Committee's strategic reorganization included educational insiders, but they too lacked sufficient authority to produce change. The disproportionately small Jewish and African American teacher population represented not establishment insiders but outsiders beholden to the Board of Education for their jobs. Since the board dismissed teachers during these eras for their real and imagined political ties and work on culturally relevant curriculum, they had even less power than during progressive eras. Clearly, "political power in school systems often does not translate to bureaucratic power in that same organization" (Binder 2002: 228). In local government, Jews and African Americans were similarly sparsely represented and retained little real control over local politics, particularly in terms of education.[10]

School policy regulation, left largely to individual states, allows them to maintain inequalities until particular groups challenge the status quo, which often occurs in the form of lawsuits against the schools. The judicial system represents a site of contested terrain where actors challenge racial identities and access to educational privileges. While the Harlem 9 initiated lawsuits to change legal precedent regarding segregated schools in NYC, all of which failed, this option never surfaced during the Gary Plan. Groups rarely targeted the schools through lawsuits during the 1910s, and immigrants' lack of knowledge of the system precluded this possibility. While the Board of Education affirmed *Brown* in 1954, it did not believe it applied to Northern schools. Until 1960, when Paul B. Zuber contested segregated schools in New Rochelle, New York, Northern states were largely immune from challenges to the legality of de facto segregated schools. Today, a number of European nations and Canada mandate multicultural curriculum to ensure equal dignity among different cultures. But in early- and mid-twentieth-century America, no law existed to facilitate the representation of group cultures in the schools.[11]

The mainstream press published disparate, but largely derogatory, depictions of Jewish and African American activists during resource-based protests and virtually ignored efforts to include culture in the curriculum. Stereotypical images of minorities in the mass media contribute to racist ideologies and diminished support for policies to adjudicate past and present discrimination. Negative depictions of Jews and African Americans during these protests had a conscious and subconsciously persuasive effect on individual members of the state apparatus even as African Americans and Jews attempted to appeal to them as rights-bearing citizens of the same political community. The media's silence regarding the Board of Education's often openly discriminatory policies further galvanized whites, who benefited from these policies, to hinder sympathetic support from potential movement allies.[12]

Unintended Consequences: Reifying Racial Structures

Unintended consequences (Pail, Mahler & Schwartz 1997), rather than allowing for change, institutionalized inequality and reinscribed negative conceptions of racialized identities by providing the city and Board of Education with new ways to maintain inequality. Responding only symbolically to demands, the state insulated ideological elements of the protests, maintained the racial order, and absorbed the movements. As such, future movements required new rhetorical strategies, tactics, and frames. The movements, though they laid groundwork for later mobilization by each group, also provided state authorities with rhetoric useful to maintaining racial hierarchies and ideologies for generations to come.

Neither Jews nor African Americans could reverse resource inequalities or remove curriculum that predominantly trained each group for jobs inhibiting social and economic mobility. Jews succeeded at their most basic and literal demands, the removal of Mayor Mitchel from office and the halting of the Gary Plan's introduction into additional schools. But decimated budgets inhibited both the reconversion of Gary schools to those employing academic curriculum and the construction of new school buildings in overcrowded Jewish neighborhoods. Attempting to enroll their children in schools outside their neighborhoods (in current rhetoric, enact "school choice"), African American activists increasingly encountered the board's commitment to "neighborhood" schools. The board reasoned that their proximate location to children's homes and potential for maintaining neighborhood ties actually benefited African American children. In reality, this policy maintained segregation for both African American and white children. This language became an attractive and powerful frame that continues to justify residentially and racially segregated schools.

Small symbolic, but nonmandatory, revisions to the curriculum perpetuated existing understandings of racial differences and alleviated the board of responsibility for future, more substantial, changes to an overtly discriminatory curriculum. Lingering racist texts on school bookroom shelves perpetuated ignorance of minority groups by members of the dominant group since the accurate, yet optional, texts rarely reached entire student populations and failed to engage understandings of group similarities and differences in any meaningful way. Existing texts' failure to critically examine structures and ideologies underlying contemporary racial hierarchies only maintained the status quo.

Ethnic Resources and Culturally Rooted Movement Tactics

While hampered by ascribed racial identities within NYC's racial structure of subordination, Jewish and African American agency produced and informed extensive efforts to enact change. Jews' and African Americans' identities and group cultures played critical roles as stores of networks, tactics, logic for demands, and oppositional knowledge during each protest trajectory. During each movement, both groups enacted culturally rooted tactics and repertoires of action and mobilized group-specific political culture and cultural objects, many of which their peers used simultaneously. These displays represent a progression of translating group-based oppositional consciousness and political cultures into action. Activists' racialized understandings of inequality embedded in each community as oppositional cultures and consciousnesses allowed them to attack America's contemporary racial narratives "explaining" inequalities between themselves and whites. Challenging the educational mechanisms of this inequality, activists revealed the social realities of marginalized groups often rendered invisible to those imbued with white privilege.[13]

Jewish and African American ethnic cultures provided activists with both the rhetoric and resources necessary for mobilization. These cultures endowed groups with a "basis for solidarity among the potential members of the group; mobilize[d] the group to defend its cultural values and to advance its claims to power and status, and resources" (Conzen et al. 1992: 5–6). They also provided them with the ideological tools necessary, particularly in these cases, to craft demands emphasizing the "compatibility of the sidestream ethnoculture with American principles and ideals." More than just agency, ethnic cultures supplied each group with the tangible resources necessary to demand change—ethnic niches and political networks with resources and information essential to protest.[14]

During each protest, activists transformed their ethnic cultures "from an insular tradition into an armory for purposes of political contestation and as a tool for appropriating political power" (Kosak 2000: 108). Jewish ethnic culture manifested as beliefs and practices embedded in religious traditions and as a collective memory of cultural trauma due to centuries of oppression alongside efforts to combat American anti-Semitism to establish a nascent mobilization framework. As a tool to contemplate and ameliorate the harsh realities of life in America, African American culture, rooted in West African traditions and continuously reconstructed in America, is rich with symbolic meanings. In NYC, the nation's African American capital, their culture had been passed down through generations and reinvigorated during the Harlem Renaissance. By the mid-twentieth century, this cumulatively developed culture, activism, and resistance manifested in politically motivated working-class oppositional consciousnesses designed to withstand structural oppression and demand changes when confronted with inequality. As a result, at the onset of Jews' and African Americans' protests against NYC's educational bureaucracy, community activists drew on multiple tools from their cultural repertoires to generate activism, develop mobilizing frames, and carry out protest events.[15]

Drawing on these cultural toolkits, boycotts and mass protests, high in ritual solidarity, became dominant symbols. They provided activists with opportunities to use culturally rooted and American symbols to "legitimize the demand for power and rights" (Kosak 2000: 108), revealing that "opposition and democratic values can go hand in hand" (Harris 2001: 61). During the Gary Plan and efforts to institutionalize Hebrew courses, Jews drew on knowledge gained during earlier efforts to assuage discrimination, unionize the garment industry, boycott price-fixing kosher butchers, challenge quotas and "gentlemen's agreements" that kept Jews out of universities, places of employment, and social clubs, and strike against the schools to ensure Jewish teachers' rights (Hyman 1986: Goren 1999). In addition, they engaged in tactics used during concurrent protests against America's involvement in World War I and seeking women's suffrage in New York (Sterba 2003). African Americans drew on both late and early civil rights movement tactics by utilizing, first, state-sponsored channels of protests such as the courts and regulatory agencies and then increasingly turning to noninstituional, nonviolent tactics such as strikes, boycotts, and Freedom Schools. Marching into City Hall and the Board of Education, activists transformed *themselves* into cultural objects. Their presence in these halls of authority challenged the very cultural hegemony they sought to overcome.

Religious culture provided activists with additional mobilization tools. Both Jews and African Americans have a long history of challenging and withstanding oppression through religious frames and cultures. Jews, fleeing pogroms in

Russia, and African Americans, during both slavery and resistance leading up to and during the civil rights movement, used similar Old Testament rhetoric describing their delivery out of bondage to the Promised Land. Religion provided each group with powerful mobilizing rhetoric, networks of support, tangible resources in the form of money, volunteers, supplies, and freedom to autonomously design and enact mobilization strategies. Activists turned churches and synagogues into loci of protest. Religious clergy supported and extended resources to both anti–Gary Plan activists and the Harlem 9.[16]

Although unable to translate their demands into improved opportunities for their children, Jews' and African Americans' deep reliance upon cultural scripts reveals the unlikelihood of protest occurring without drawing on these identity-based resources. Cultural narratives shaped activists' demands and leant themselves to short-term coalition building and long-term movement potential. Protests created foundations of activism for racially and socioeconomically oppressed parents who were extremely alienated from NYC's power structures, particularly the Board of Education, to become politically active and leaders in their communities—which many did. Jews' and African Americans' increasing reliance on their ethnic and cultural identities during the resource-related Harlem 9 and Gary Plan cases suggests the high salience of these identities.[17]

Multicultural Identity Work: Preserving, Enacting, and Struggling with Multiple Identities

These struggles for improved educational quality represented more than attempts to acquire citizenship-based entitlements in the educational domain. Affirming their status as citizens and maintaining cultural pride became means of achieving economic justice and social equality for Jews and African Americans. Results occurred not in schools but within their own communities as Jews' and African Americans' identities underwent shifts to accommodate their new conceptions of their place in American society, the rights to which they believed they were entitled, and the importance of their cultural identities. Activists' articulation of links between identity, resources, and race-based inequality promoted a particular type of multicultural identity work—they mobilized culturally rooted plural consciousnesses while simultaneously attempting to diminish the larger public's negative stigmas attached to Jews and African Americans. Challenging the schools, Jews and African Americans disputed white society's hegemonic claims to quality education and drew a boundary between the white power structure and their own ethnic communities.[18]

During these historical junctures, Jews and African Americans contended with discrimination as liminal citizens and desires for full inclusion in American society even as they continued practicing vibrant and deeply rooted cultures.

Living in segregated ethnic and racial worlds, and vulnerable to racism and anti-Semitism within the larger society, Jews and African Americans began these protests demanding two goals—that the schools provide their children with the same resources to which nonstigmatized racial groups had access, and that the schools allow each group to preserve elements of their culture. These demands departed from existing master narratives within the dominant society that emphasized ethnic-group detachment, Americanization, and assimilation to white norms. To achieve their goals, Jewish and African American activists mobilized both politics of difference and semblance using collective action frames that resonated with the larger community but contained hidden transcripts related to their own particular group history and status in NYC. As they did so, they found themselves attempting to rearticulate society's subjective understandings of being Jewish and African American, resulting in new conceptions of their identities within their own communities.

Throughout their protests, Jews and African Americans interwove group-specific desires with broader definitions of citizenship and freedom to reconstruct national definitions of citizenship so that members of their groups were included therein. Jewish and African American activists utilized a citizenship-based identity to confront "the values, categories, and practice of the dominant culture." Claiming rights and deploying actions to acquire educational equality as American citizens, each group attempted to redefine what it meant to be Jewish and African American by removing the stigmas attached to their group identities so that they could be conceived of as equal citizens even as they retained cultural differences. As these groups acted as, sought membership in, and enacted participatory practices and civic cultures of the larger American society, activists embedded hidden transcripts featuring culturally nationalist sentiments and collective memories of historical oppression. In doing so, they reconstructed their collective identities to include both cultural and American-based elements.[19]

Although deploying a master frame of rights referencing injustices Jewish and African American children experienced in the schools, activists' shifting use of mobilizing frames, depending on whether efforts occurred in public or private, reveal the dual nature of each group's identity. Never relinquishing their claim to an American identity, activists wove together group-specific frames featuring a changing rhetoric that integrated specific cultural histories of collective trauma, symbols and stories related to their distant and recent past, and contemporary economic, political, and social conditions. In private, activists replaced vague terms of history, hidden transcripts, inclusive, and universalist elaborated codes (Ansell 1997: 362) used in public settings with boundary stories highlighting their separate and distinct cultures and customs.[20]

Negotiating multiple knowledges and alternately celebrating and suppressing differences between their own and American cultures, activists intertwined identity narratives featuring both group cultures and experiences alongside American values of democratic participation and equality of opportunity. This allowed each group, as they took on, heard, and enacted these identities, to "grow into" and then disseminate conceptions of their identities alongside existing rhetoric, discourses, and understandings of race. As they did so, both identities, an American identity and either a Jewish or African American identity, became inextricably bound together in the collective memory of the group. Neither Jews nor African Americans could relinquish the dualities of their identity as this duality *became* their identity.[21]

Jews' and African Americans' narratives featuring desires to, and the compatibility of, maintaining ethnic cultures while embracing and enacting an American identity reveals important similarities between these groups' identities and Du Bois's (1995 [1903]) double consciousness, Kallen's (1924) pluralistic identity, Anzaldúa's (1987) mestizaje consciousness, and identities described by scholars addressing segmented assimilation. The existence of multiple consciousnesses and activists' use of politics of semblance and difference highlighting particular group histories, culture, and current conditions in America and similarities to other Americans, respectively, reveals rarely addressed similarities in both identity conceptions and processes of racial formation experienced by different racial groups, irrespective of schools' efforts to constrain group agency. These new identities, tactics, and narratives would have important consequences for the future of the relationship between Jews and African Americans, both in NYC and nationally.[22]

Desiring full membership in the American citizenry, Jews and African Americans challenged the public schools to improve educational resources and institutionalize culturally relevant curriculum. Schools rejected Jews' and African Americans' efforts to achieve radical democracy, the initiation of society-wide discourse on race that included a political agenda devoted to the reallocation of resources, and left the underlying structures, cultures, and ideologies unaltered. Using rhetorical flourishes to justify low-quality education for racial minorities, the Board of Education retrenched stigmatized racial identities and long-term social, political, and economic inequality. Although they failed to achieve their stated demands, by the end of each protest, Jews and African Americans had reconstructed their identities in ways that would dramatically impact both their relationship and future endeavors. These protests therefore reveal the power of social movements, even when goals are largely unmet, to change groups' conceptions of their own identities and lay the groundwork for future events and movements.

7

The Foreseeable Split

Ocean Hill–Brownsville and Jewish and African American Relations Today

When most people think about Jewish and African American struggles in NYC's public schools, they instantly recall the Ocean Hill–Brownsville (Brooklyn) conflict of 1968–1971. In this conflict, Jews and African Americans faced off against each other as they battled for control of the schools. However, they did so with conceptions of the schools that had been diverging for decades, beginning with the conclusion of the Hebrew case in the immediate post–World War II era and continuing through both African American cases. Therefore, the story presented here would be incomplete without connecting these cases to both the 1968 conflict and contemporary differences in Jews' and African Americans' integration into American society; especially since the protests, and identities and concurrent ideologies developed therein, laid the groundwork for the 1968 strike's outbreak and outcomes. Close examination of these protests reveals that this split, though it surprised many, was foreseeable.

Jewish Advancement and African American Stagnation

Between these protests and the 1968 Ocean Hill–Brownsville strike, Jewish and African American educational and occupational trajectories diverged dramatically, beginning with America's entry into World War II. Anti-Semitism during the Depression led to higher unemployment rates among Jews, but kept them in school longer. This resulted in sufficiently high levels of educational attainment to launch them into the middle class in the postwar period, and with it the belief that hard work would eventually lead to economic success in America. However, African Americans' material position, between the end of their protests and the 1968 strike, not only failed to improve but actually got worse. Simultaneously, African Americans' ideologies shifted away from assimilation and toward Black Power, leading to increased demands for community control and transformative curriculum to change NYC's educational structure. These diverging class positions and ideologies, even as Jews and African Americans colluded to eradicate racism during the height of the civil rights movement, provided the groundwork for perhaps the most symbolic racial and ideological break between these two groups in American history. But the story is not as simple as Jews moving up and away from African Americans. Changing structures of whiteness accompanied shifting ideologies, identities, and economic conditions within each community.

American society, and all of its structures, slowly opened up privileges of whiteness to Jews during World War II. During the war, Americans confronted the shocking consequences of Nazi Germany's delineation of Jews as a racial other, and this led to revulsion with, and Western rejection of, anti-Semitism. This occurred simultaneously with government policies promoting Jews' equal treatment. The U.S. Army institutionalized Jewish equality with other Europeans with the provision of Jewish rabbis alongside Catholic priests and Protestant ministers. Although Jewish soldiers experienced anti-Semitism from their peers and superiors, their symbolic inclusion allowed them to unite and perceive each other as equals when it mattered most, under fire in foxholes. Government recognition of Jewish equality paved the way for "integrated" troops as European Americans of all nationalities and religions fought alongside each other against a common enemy and therefore identified as Americans rather than separate nationalities. This, however, also facilitated European ethnics' ability to perceive themselves as different from the segregated African American troops, in opposition to whom they had already spent decades defining themselves as they struggled for scarce resources in American ghettos. By the war's end, Jews' position as equal to other whites, and America's commitment to a "triple melting pot" (Herberg 1983) among European Protestants, Catholics, and Jews had been cemented.

When these Jewish soldiers came home, the government granted European American veterans access to the greatest affirmative action program in American history, the G.I. Bill. Veterans' housing and education benefits allowed them to purchase a piece of the American Dream—a home in the suburbs with access to high-quality public services, education, and jobs in the newly expanding service sector that increasingly fled the cities and established itself in the suburbs. Although restrictive covenants kept Jews out of many suburban communities, as a whole, unprecedented access to social resources promoted their rapid mobility into the American mainstream. Capitalizing on educational gains made during the Depression, Jews quickly became a "model minority," surpassing other groups' educational and economic success, and facilitating their movement into the middle class. In these suburbs, Jews gained access to the quality of schools their parents and grandparents had demanded during the Gary Plan. These schools propelled them to prestigious universities, particularly as colleges removed quotas barring Jews—another signal of their acceptance by social elites into white society. For Jews, this enhanced access occurred without changing the structure of education, as they had demanded during their protests. Instead, the nature and structure of race in American changed to include them. This not only allowed their children opportunities unforeseen only a generation before, but also further distanced Jews from African Americans, socially, economically, and ideologically.[1]

Within the Jewish community, ideas about the racial nature of Judaism shifted between the onset of the Depression and World War II. For much of American history, Jews considered themselves a separate race, different from non-Jews, or "goyim." However, during their demands for Hebrew courses and opposing the Gary Plan, they articulated a Jewish identity that was thoroughly compatible with being American and highlighted similarities between themselves and the larger American society. Jews, as they took on a Du Boisian identity, which included their both Jewishness and their Americanness, shifted away from racial rhetoric that separated themselves from other Americans.[2]

As Jews moved out of the urban ghettos and tenuously held onto their middle-class status, conditions within the African American community worsened. By the early 1960s, African American children desperately needed higher quality schools to improve their social conditions. Decades of protest to improve resources and curricular representation for African American children, had changed nothing. In fact, things had gotten worse. Exclusion from veterans' loan programs and educational benefits reinscribed African Americans' status on the bottom of the racial ladder as previously racialized groups moved up. The government's redlining policy trapped African Americans in disintegrating neighborhoods and packed them into overcrowded housing projects abandoned by whites after the war. Exacerbating government-initiated inequalities, NYC's rapidly deindustrializing economy cast thousands of African Americans into poverty. Concentrated poverty, unemployment, and segregation, combined with an insufficient tax base to sustain the increasingly segregated and resource-poor schools, found African American children trapped in schools that necessitated dramatic changes to improve their social and economic conditions (Clark 1989; Stevens 1971).

A 1964 State Education Commission report legitimized parents' fears. Not only had segregation worsened, so too had conditions in these schools and, the report warned, if the board did not act, segregation rates would double in another five years. In only four years, between 1959 and 1963, segregation in elementary and junior high schools had doubled. With African Americans dramatically overrepresented in vocational high schools and "special" or "600" schools designed for "problem students" whose function remained "vague" as a result of "*no* clear statement of the present curriculum" (5, 24) their drop-out rate soared. The board could have used its power to prevent this by changing feeder patterns, redistricting schools, constructing comprehensive high schools outside of ghetto areas, increasing teacher training, and creating educational complexes with both elementary and middle schools. Yet it chose not to do so. Consequently, African American parents continued to demand change using both protest tactics and ideologies developed by the Harlem 9 and during demands for African American history curriculum.

As protests continued, former members of the Harlem 9 remained active as leaders of educational and community-based social action organizations. Bernice Skipwith, Carmen Aviles, Luree Brown, Shirley Rector, and Frankie Wimbush went on to be Parents Association presidents. Leolive Tucker went on to become president of the NAACP Metropolitan Education Council. Isaiah Robinson became president of the Harlem Parents Committee. Activists' transition from outsiders begging the school board for concessions to community leaders suggests the capacity of social movements to foist grassroots level activists into powerful positions in their communities.[3]

Shirley Rector became the education chairman for the New York Branch of the NAACP and featured prominently in a later lawsuit, with the aid of Paul B. Zuber, against the NYC schools. She claimed the board maintained "a racial quota system in assigning Negro students to the city's public high schools." Rector's son boycotted the schools after being assigned to an all–African American vocational high school in spite of his high grades. A month later, John J. Theobald agreed to Open Enrollment for high school students (previously reserved for students in elementary and junior high schools). However, educational equality eluded the majority of African American children unable to transfer.[4]

Many members of the PAAED continued their activism with the Harlem Parents Committee (HPC) and drew national attention in their efforts to improve the schools. Drawing on the Harlem 9's tactics, the HPC declared their intentions to boycott the schools and conduct sit-ins and stand-ins at the board and local schools in August 1963 to call attention to segregation. Leolive Tucker drew on her own experiences with the Harlem 9 in describing her reasons for action: "After more than 10 years of meetings with the Board of Education on this question of education, there have been no improvements. We still have heavy teacher turnover, bad attitudes by the teachers and watered-down curriculums in our schools. Negro and Puerto Rican children aren't learning." The HPC demanded an expedited integration deadline for all of NYC's schools after state education commissioner Dr. James E. Allen Jr. placed responsibility for desegregating the schools on the NYC Board of Education.[5]

Paul Zuber's aid to the Harlem 9 began a new era of school protest in NYC and northern school systems nationally. In 1961, he argued the landmark New Rochelle desegregation suit, which, for the first time in American history, found that de facto segregation in the North resembled de jure segregation in the South, which had been declared unconstitutional by *Brown* and subject to similar remedies. He continued litigation to desegregate schools in Newark, New Jersey, Englewood, New Jersey, and Chicago, and won the A. Philip Randolph Award for "Man of the Year" until hired as the director of the Center for Urban Environmental Studies at Rensselaer Polytechnic Institute, where he worked until he died at age sixty in 1987.[6]

The Parents' Workshop for Equality picked up where the Harlem 9 left off and created a large-scale organized protest that garnered national attention in 1964. Milton Galamison and grassroots African American and Puerto Rican activists from Brooklyn and Harlem (including the HPC) used the Harlem 9's tactics to challenge ongoing inequality. During the boycott, the PWE established citywide Freedom Schools to teach African American and Puerto Rican children academic and culturally relevant subjects. On February 3, 464,361 out of 1,037,757 students (45 percent) and over 3,500 teachers (about 8 percent of the workforce) boycotted. Demands for community control and autonomy that surfaced during the Harlem 9's protests took on new urgency during these protests. By 1968, community control represented the single most important issue for African American educators and a dramatic departure from ideologies of integration and racial liberalism (used in later events by whites) to a master frame of empowerment in the form of Black Power.[7]

Ideological Alignment and Divergence

As a result of different class positions and experiences in America, by 1968, Jews and African Americans had developed divergent ideologies with regard to race and opportunity in America. These ideological differences developed over a relatively short period of time and differed sharply from historical similarities between these two groups that found them collaborating on centuries-old efforts to confront American racism and anti-Semitism. More so than any other group, Jews acknowledged the similarities between racism and other forms of oppression, such as anti-Semitism. Facing similar plights, Jews and African Americans disproportionately collaborated on civil rights issues to improve individual opportunity, a key tenet of liberalism. Allied in the larger fight against American social injustice, Jews and African Americans saw discrimination's effects in hotels, restaurants, jobs, high-quality housing, and schools. Each community's newspapers regularly reported on racism and anti-Semitism. Editorials decrying the evils of anti-Semitism in the African American press expressed just as much outrage as anti-lynching editorials in the Jewish press. Overrepresented in social justice organizations, Jews aided African Americans accused of the most audacious crimes, such as the nine young men, known as the "Scottsboro Boys," accused of raping two white women on a train, and supported often-unpopular antilynching legislation. In this atmosphere, and often working together in Communist, socialist, and labor organizations, Jews and African Americans forged the ties leading to their collaboration during the civil rights movements.[8]

But this relationship was fraught with conflict. Ethnic rivalries existed alongside of genuine sympathy for each other's plight. Jews, though experiencing discrimination, also experienced financial success. Patterns of urban ecology found Jews moving into neighborhoods abandoned by previously upwardly mobile immigrants and establishing businesses. There, they capitalized on economic opportunities and fulfilled their historic position as middlemen by selling to African Americans, but not hiring them in their stores. As they did so, they developed personal relationships with their clients and neighbors. Some of these assuaged the development of potential prejudices as families and children got to know each other. But because these relationships did not occur on an equal footing (Allport 1954), antagonisms developed on both sides as each adopted society's existing stereotypical conceptions of the other (Baldwin 1967; Goldstein 2006; Marx 1967; Rieder 1985).

As the 1960s came to a close, ideological differences stemming from each group's contemporary economic position met daylight. Big changes in Jews' social, political, and economic opportunities occurred alongside African American stagnation in these areas. This resulted in shifting conceptions of American society's openness and possibilities among Jews (Rieder 1985). Although always on guard against anti-Semitism, they truly saw America as a place where everyone could succeed with hard work. This bootstrap liberalism obscured the reality of the privileges granted to them as whites, which facilitated their success. Instead, Jews believed that African Americans, since the passage of the Civil Rights and Voting Rights Acts, had access to the same opportunities as themselves. Failing to recognize the deep structures and affect of racist ideologies, Jews adopted values that posited individual shortcomings, rather than structural inequality, as the cause of social and economic failure. As a result, many Jews perceived African Americans' persistent poverty as their own fault and, given their belief in America's equal opportunity, felt that if they only worked harder, they too would succeed.

These beliefs left their deepest imprint on the city's lower-income Jews, who confronted low-income African Americans and saw their plight as personal, rather than structural. As African Americans moved into their previously all-white enclaves, Jews saw crime, drugs, and youth "hanging out" (much as they themselves had done only a generation before) increase but attributed these problems to African Americans' inferior values and culture. Themselves in a precarious racial and economic position, these Jews felt deeply threatened by African Americans. Jews feared their own racial and economic position would deteriorate—in terms of social resources, personal safety, and, potentially, their racial status (as had historically occurred to other groups living proximate to African Americans). For the first time, Jews voted with Catholics on racial issues. This shifting voting bloc signaled a new political and, eventually, a social realignment with Jews behaving like, and demanding the privileges of, whites.

While Jews embraced liberalism as the American credo, African Americans saw things differently. Not only did they blame America's racist structure for their poverty and oppression but they saw Jews an embodiment of this system, even if they were not wholly a part of it. As owners of their homes, sellers of their household goods, and employers paying their wages, Jews were often the only whites African Americans encountered. Existing stereotypes of Jews as greedy and shiftless intertwined with their existing economic position as middlemen who handled nearly every penny African Americans earned and spent. This retrenched anti-Semitic ideologies alongside accurate perceptions of the closed system that kept African Americans subordinate to white racial groups on the lower rung of the racial ladder. Simultaneously, Jewish secularization, assimilation, declining ethnic attachments, and heightened symbolic ethnicity occurred alongside open displays of African American pride during which they celebrated, and demanded others recognize, their identities and culture. After centuries of jostling for position, sometimes arm-in-arm, in America's racial hierarchy, Jews and African Americans had begun walking on divergent ideological and experiential pathways into America's future.

In this precarious and quickly crumbling relationship, Jews misunderstood African Americans' desires for their schools and their multiculturalist demands for Black Power. This, combined with Jews' inability to remove their newly acquired spectacles of whiteness and look at the world through the lenses of oppression worn by African Americans, tore asunder these longstanding, though conflict-rife, bonds. More than this, it cemented Jews' racial status as whites. African Americans viewed Jews' success and diminished sympathy for racial equality as proof that they had become both racially and ideologically white. So too would the rest of America.

The Big Split: Ocean Hill–Brownsville

African Americans in Ocean Hill–Brownsville, after years of demanding improvements in, demanded autonomous control *over* their neighborhood schools. In a surprising move, the board granted it. African Americans, to ensure control, dismissed white teachers, inserted culturally relevant curriculum, and engaged culturally embedded learning styles to promote self-esteem, self-determination, and communitywide advancement to challenge the racist system of American schooling. African Americans wanted their children in a school system completely different from the one that Jews held in such high regard. And Jews' individualist meritocratic beliefs could not reconcile these competing ideologies.[9]

Many Jews considered African Americans' decision to fire Jewish teachers a particular affront given their historical alliance. With Jews overrepresented as teachers and administrators, African Americans perceived them as an embodiment of an educational system that kept their children locked in low-wage jobs and a destructive cycle of poverty. When Jews refused to support, or even attempt to understand, African American demands, although disappointed after years of support, African Americans recognized this as evidence of Jews' whiteness.

Unable to recognize the logic for African Americans' actions, Jewish members of the American Federation of Teachers (AFT) faced off against their neighbors and former allies. During a series of strikes, charges of anti-Semitism and anti-Americanism flew as some decidedly anti-Jewish fliers circulated through the borough. The entire city took sides. Jews and Catholics aligned, as whites, against African Americans. No longer did Jews and African Americans march alongside each other demanding equal rights. Instead, Jews accused African Americans of teaching racism and could not understand that a few books about African American culture were insufficient to challenge the structure of racism embedded in the schools.

These strikes, and the community control experiment, unalterably reconstructed NYC's racial terrain. A newer, deeper divide existed between Jews and African Americans and a Jewish-Catholic alliance against African Americans on social and political issues had been forged. Perhaps most important, Jewish ambivalence toward whiteness had been replaced with conscious appropriation of this identity. Jews' actions signaled not only that they were white, but that the rest of society perceived them as such. African Americans, on the other hand, experienced few gains. A disproportionate percentage of the community continued to experience persistent poverty alongside a small African American upper class competing with the same whites against whom they had squared off during the strikes for scarce social resources, jobs, housing, and high-quality schools. This set the stage for decades of ethnic competition and diminished collaboration.[10]

Jewish–African American Relations in Post–Brownsville–Ocean Hill, NYC, and America

Over forty years after these strikes, Jews' and African Americans' relationship remains deeply affected by the Ocean Hill–Brownsville strikes. The very mention of these two groups in the same sentence often elicits comments about this historical breakpoint—and for good reason. This episode looms large in the American collective conscious because it solidified the national splintering and collapse of generations of collaboration.

After the peak of collaboration during the civil rights movement, Jews and African Americans today appear to have settled into a more representative period of these groups' complex history of collaboration and conflict. With Jews overrepresented among the social elite and African Americans overrepresented in the lower classes, class differences and their subsequent different day-to-day realities keep Jews and African Americans in largely different worlds. Continuing tensions erupt between these groups over neighborhood "turf" in Crown Heights, Brooklyn, and international issues that find African Americans aligning themselves with oppressed Palestinians against the Jewish State of Israel. On an ideological level, African Americans no longer consign Jews to a fellow-victim status. Instead, they see them as whites and, due to their history of ethnic conflict and a collective history of cultural trauma, have higher rates of anti-Semitic attitudes than other groups. On the other hand, Jews vote alongside African Americans and support liberal social and racial policies and continue to work together in social justice organizations.[11]

Although similar, these divergent histories reveal the historically dependent contrast between racism and anti-Semitism. Anti-Semitism continues to exist, but processes and structures of racialization no longer limit Jews' opportunities or restrict them to a particular social location. On the other hand, Americans perceive Jews as different from other groups, less loyal to America (and more loyal to a foreign nation—Israel) than others, with different values, to whom many are not sure they want their children marrying (King & Weiner 2007). Nearly 1,000 anti-Jewish hate crimes every year in America testify to the nation's ongoing perception of Jewish difference. Although Jews have access to privileges of whiteness that allow them to achieve success in America without the same stigma or inequalities to which African Americans, Latinos, and Asians are subject, they embody a different type of white racial group. This suggests that whiteness, with all of its malleability, could, at some point, again exclude Jews, as it did at the turn of the twentieth century, to the dismay of assimilated Jews who believed their place in America's racial status was secure. The effects of racism appear far less likely to disappear. Deeply institutionalized racism continues to structure the lives and opportunities of African Americans, as it has done since the nation's inception. Stark differences in income, wealth, education, and health find African Americans securely at the bottom of America's racial hierarchy, with diminished life chances in every social realm.[12]

The potential exists now, perhaps more so than at any other time in recent memory, for the relationship to be repaired if Jews use their positions of power and influence to change racial realities in America for the better with policies to truly aid racial disparities in education, employment, health, housing, and other social realms. Some have pointed to the many Jews in President Barack Obama's cabinet and in advisory positions as the groundwork for significant future collaboration. President Obama also hosted the White House's first Passover seder. This event, commemorating Jews' flight from slavery and into Israel, is the historic root of Jewish and African American rhetoric regarding

America as the Promised Land. Celebrating this holiday together captures the historic links between these two groups. However, symbolic gestures alone will neither repair this relationship nor promote social equality for African Americans. Addressing both of these issues will require Jews, and other whites, to move past sympathy to recognize the structures of whiteness that allowed their parents and grandparents to move through the racial hierarchy to the position of privilege in which they exist today. Without explicit attention to racial differences and the structural mechanisms that maintain them, America, and therefore the relationship between Jews and African Americans, will remain a racially splintered community.

Conclusion

The Future of Minority Education
and Related Scholarship

These historical struggles and their results offer contemporary scholars, activists, and theorists new insights into processes of education, identity formation, and movement trajectories. Jews' and African Americans' inability to promote change by attacking the mechanisms perpetuating and ideologies underlying deeply rooted racial inequalities raises large questions regarding the potential role of schools today to alleviate racial inequality. This is particularly true when we consider that Jews did not achieve their demands until they became white, which many new immigrant groups appear to have no interest in doing. Lacking the privileges imbued in whiteness, these groups also lack sufficient political power to change their social and educational circumstances. Children of contemporary nonwhite immigrant groups, now roughly 20 percent of the population, continue to lack access to high-quality schools promoting upward mobility or featuring culturally relevant curriculum, suggesting activists will protest on behalf of their children. They, like Jewish and African American children described here, remain locked outside America's Golden Door of education. To study these school-based protests, sociologists must examine similarities between different racial groups' identity formation processes and the specific role of race in shaping social movements.

Today's minority groups operate in the same racist society and confront the same racist ideologies inhibiting minority advancement, as did Jews and African Americans described here. Decades of civil rights legislation has improved African Americans' educational and occupational attainment, but a variety of social inequalities find nearly every indicator of social, political, and economic success sharply divided along racial lines. In schools, the segregation clock has been turned backward. African American and Latino students attend schools *more* segregated and resource poor than prior to *Brown* and comparable to the apartheid-era education in South Africa. Curriculum, though it no longer contains the worst stereotypes of minorities, continues to ignore histories and cultures of nonwhite groups.

Overcrowded classrooms, racially biased and insensitive teachers, curriculum tracking only into vocational classes, a lack of advanced placement and college preparatory courses and material, outdated textbooks, and history and literature classes that perpetuate stereotypes and remand minority youth to the lower rungs of the economic and racial ladder exist today, as in years past. Compared to whites, racial minorities, particularly immigrants, have lower grades and test scores, are less likely to graduate from high school, attend college, and graduate from college, and are more likely to be incarcerated and become pregnant as teens. Their average incomes and occupational attainment are lower than that of whites, resulting in less wealth and opportunity to pass onto the next generation. These problems are particularly profound for low-income immigrant groups such as Mexicans, Cambodians, Vietnamese, and some Africans who segmentally assimilate into a lower socioeconomic position.[1]

Religious minorities, particularly Muslim students in the post-9/11 era, experience cultural dissonance and oppression in the schools similar to that of Jews early in the twentieth century. Although America offers more freedom and opportunities for these groups than other Western nations, most American public schools do not accept, much less provide sanctuary for, Islamic practices. Instead, Muslim students face social stigma when seeking to pray during designated times, wear headscarves, wear pants during gym class, or eat cafeteria food that conforms to their dietary habits. In multicultural New York City, teachers lack knowledge of Muslim culture and perpetuate negative stereotypes of these students, as they did to African American students in the mid-twentieth century. Nor does Muslim culture or Arabic history appear in most multicultural curriculum. Affected students believe these factors negatively impact upon their educational opportunities.[2] As a result, resistance has developed in cities with large Muslim populations. Activists have both attempted to inject knowledge of Islam into multicultural curriculum and establish Muslim charter schools, similar to what Catholics did in the mid-1800s when public schools infringed on their religious beliefs. Young Muslims' experiences reveal that as well-meaning as teachers may be, students do not need overtly racist teachers to encounter a racist educational experience.

Most legislative and policy initiatives targeting minority youth have only exacerbated ongoing racial inequality. Policies promoting school choice, vouchers, and charter schools privilege parents with the most social capital. These initiatives divert crucial public funds and parent-based social capital from the initial schools and relegates those children with the least family-based resources and power to public schools with the least resources. Charter schools, run with little oversight by individuals or corporations, have a spotty record of achievement. Some schools provide excellent alternatives to local public schools while others diminish students' academic achievement compared to their public school counterparts. In the worst cases, state officials have shuttered these schools after misusing public funds by not providing children with any educational instruction. None of these programs amend the larger structure or content of public education to provide minority children with the same quality education as white students.[3]

The most prominent piece of education legislature in decades, No Child Left Behind, has, by 2009, been almost universally derided by education experts as a policy failure (Darling-Hammond 2007). With this policy in place, test score gaps between minority and white children have grown. Science, history, art, music, and other "non-essential" classes have been completely removed from urban schools so that teachers can focus solely on preparing students to pass math and reading tests (Kozol 2005). Once the tests have been completed, teachers are unable to teach an entire year's worth of actual curriculum in the two months of school remaining. Like vouchers and school choice, these policies *diminish*, rather than enhance, minority students' academic success, and reinscribe racial identities and race-based social inequalities.

As this book was written, recently inaugurated President Barack Obama signed into law a monumentally large stimulus package including at least $100 billion over two years for education (consider that the entire 2007 education budget was $59 million). Of this, $39 billion must be used in elementary through high schools and an additional $9 billion could be used to improve school infrastructure. Simultaneously, an economic recession finds many parents withdrawing their children from elite private schools and enrolling them in local public schools (Hoffman 2009; Harper, Fabbre & Rado 2009; Yan 2009). These resource-rich parents, imbued with power and privileges of whiteness, have the potential to demand, and achieve, real changes to the structure of every American public school. Therefore, tremendous potential exists to holistically improve minority education such that it parallels that of white students. Or, parents and policies could create a larger divide with some schools, those attended by whites, getting more and better resources and leaving resource-poor schools further behind. However, as shown by policies implemented during these cases, particularly the Gary Plan, educational strategies directed at minority youth tend to retrench, rather than alleviate, racial inequalities. Educational experts and policymakers must be cognizant of these possibilities if they want to truly improve the quality of minority education in America.[4]

Jews' and African Americans' inability to affect change by improving access to educational and curricular resources for their children raises large questions regarding the utility of legislature such as No Child Left Behind for producing educational equity for minority children. Given the many groups that remain educationally marginalized, it is questionable that schools will allow for upward mobility and social equality. Large populations of Latino, Asian, African, and Muslim immigrants hope that the schools will improve their children's opportunities. However, I find that until immigrant groups are accepted as social equals to whites and not subject to racially based discrimination in other social milieu, their children and other marginalized groups will remain educationally, socially, economically, and politically disenfranchised.

Therefore, those looking to America's schools to promote change may need to seek solutions elsewhere. In a racist society, in which children bring with them to school racist ideologies and conceptions (Hatcher & Troyna 1993; Rizvi 1993), schools maintain inequalities and compound and legitimize the existing racial hierarchy. Larger structural changes within society may need to occur before the schools are willing to provide sufficient funds to alleviate existing resource inequalities and promote minority mobility, and explicitly antiracist curriculum will be necessary to counteract these forces. Seeking these changes, and addressing persistent resource- and identity-based inequality, parents and other concerned citizens will continue to protest. Recent research finds that immigrants identifying as both American and as a member of an ethnic identity promotes social action (Klandermans, van der Toorn & van Stekelenberg 2008), suggesting the possibility for increased mobilization among racial and religious immigrant communities in the future.

To study these all but certain protests, scholars of race, education, and social movements must address two key issues. First, scholars must attune to the pivotal role of race in a racially structured and stratified society and the connections between differentially allocated resources and racialized identities. During social movements, not all actors are imbued with equal power, as a result of devalued identities. Race, as system of meanings and power relationships, and ethnicity, as an enabling source of group culture, play critical roles during social movements and illuminate the relationship between resources and identity in social movements. These multicultural social movements linked identity and resources by actors constrained by racial identities but enabled by group identities and cultures.

During Jews' and African Americans' protests, racial differences shaped broad social, historical, and institutional contexts, characteristics of the group (such as networks of solidarity, access to various forms of resources, communities of support, oppositional consciousness, and traditions of activism), and decisions and reactions of state agencies. Racialized inequalities, access to resources, power, and opportunities shaped macro-processes, such as trajectories of activism and outcomes, and movement-specific orienting frames, narratives, opportunities, and constraints.

Although resulting in considerable constraints, group-based identities and culture allowed two of America's most marginalized groups to mobilize group-specific demands against the educational system during decades of extreme racial and ideological oppression. While African Americans faced severe repression and threat during the Cold War, when any challenges to the system were suspected as a threat to the American way of life, similar fears of communism existed during the 1910s for Jews, especially since many Jews were believed to be, and were, socialists. That these groups protested at all during these eras is a testament to the strength provided by group-based oppositional consciousness and cultures to produce defiant displays of perceptions of rights and entitlements. In the long term, these efforts increased group cohesion, networks of solidarity, and diasporic consciousnesses within the Jewish and African American communities and displayed the potential for political power that would become useful later in the century as Jews and African Americans continued to protest, and eventually, gained successes in terms of fair wages, voting rights, and community control of public education.

The second issue scholars examining future protests must address are similarities between white and nonwhite groups' identity formation processes. Sociologists currently rely on two different traditions to explain the identity formation of African Americans on the one hand and white ethnics and new immigrants on the other. Similarly, few sociologists have embraced theories that argue for cultural maintenance within minority communities. Instead they conflate desires for equal opportunity and access to resources, such as citizenship and rights, with desires to lose their own cultural traditions. These protests find both Jews and African Americans capitalizing on, and demanding the protection of, existing cultural resources as they encountered racially based structural, political, and organizational constraints.[5]

During Jews' and African Americans' protests, three key similarities emerged. First, all groups, even if based only on their physical presence in this country, desire some form of incorporation into American social, cultural, political, and economic life. Second, tension exists between desires to assimilate into American culture and to retain elements of one's group culture due to the pressure to conform to dominant cultures in order to be accepted as fully "American." Alexander (2001) argues that when individuals assimilate, only the person is accepted, not the traditions of the person and group. Qualities considered "foreign" remain stigmatized, such that people desiring to adhere to them must do so in private. This suggests that assimilation, or pressure to assimilate, reproduces rather than dissolves stereotypes. Third, both groups experience duality in their identity such that they exhibit and identify themselves as American and participate in American life but also identify with elements of a natal culture, reworked and reconstructed since the group first arrived in America.[6]

While these similarities exist, social scientists rarely compare racial formation processes of different European and non-European groups to determine whether and why identities are similar or different. These findings suggest the potential for examining identity formation and mobilization of different voluntary and involuntary groups using similar terms, conceptions, and theories. This will allow scholars to grapple with the complexities of the interaction of multiple identities in different contexts and historical locations. In addition to considering different racial and ethnic groups' identities similarly, sociologists must address the dialectical process of structure and agency by taking seriously the role of history and culture of each group in shaping both their conceptions of their own racial identity and agents' role in the process of "group-making" (Wacquant 1997: 225).[7]

Schools in America, although almost universally posited as pathways to mobility, have proven, throughout American history and in the face of thousands of justifiably angry parents and citizens, resilient in resisting any change promoting minority mobility. With American youth falling further and further behind academic proficiency of other industrialized nations, largely as a result of racially based inequalities, the future of American education may well depend on the system's ability to give these parents what they have been demanding for generations—culturally relevant curriculum that provides youth with the knowledge necessary to compete in a global economy.

METHODOLOGICAL APPENDIX

At the center of this study are the stories of African Americans, "swarthy Jews," immigrants, single mothers, and the poor, all of whom have been historically marginalized, delegitimized, and silenced in much sociological research. This project engages an antiracist standpoint theory and critical race methods to "present group voices in a manner that [does] not pathologize or reify them" and privilege the daily lives of "invisibilized" groups (Mirza 1998: 90). These bottom-up historical explorations use marginalized groups' desires and demands to understand how schools shape racial inequalities and identities and how activists mobilize to confront both these inequalities and effects of mobilization on group identities.[1]

Research Design: Data Sources and Considerations

For all cases, primary archival data sources were used to, first, construct a theoretically informed chronological account of each protest case, and then determine and analyze activists' conceptions and interpretations of their racial, ethnic, and American identities *at the time*. I triangulated all information using sources from a variety of ideologies within each community to ensure that descriptions of both cases and demands are accurate.

Actors' narratives often differ in public, when among people who consider them inferior, and in private, when free to speak their minds without fear of further subordination (Alexander 2001: Kelley 1996; Scott 1990; Taylor & Whittier 1992). To explore these public and private articulations of identity, I collected data from public and private protest accounts. Data from the public sphere included newspapers, trial transcripts, and local and state government and educational officials and organizations. I used newspapers to identify individuals and protest locations, and create timelines of protests and master name and organization lists to guide collection of archival data. I obtained information from the private sphere from manuscript collections originating within each community.

Data Sources

GARY PLAN AND HEBREW PROTESTS. Contemporary newspaper accounts of the protests against the Gary Plan and for Hebrew included mainstream and Jewish newspapers. Mainstream papers included the *New York Times*, the *New York Daily Globe*, the *Brooklyn Daily Eagle*, and the *New York Sun*. English-language Jewish newspapers included the *American Hebrew, Jewish Tribune and Hebrew Standard*, and *Jewish Daily Bulletin*. The *American Hebrew*, founded in 1879, was the "major Jewish weekly with a Reform inclination" (More 1981: 116), to which many Jews were quickly turning. The editorial staff, members of the German-Jewish upper-class, condescended toward Russian Jews but vigilantly opposed American anti-Semitism. On the other hand, the *Jewish Tribune and Hebrew Standard* reflected the ideas of recent Jewish migrants, many of whom were Orthodox. The *Jewish Daily Bulletin* is frequently cited in studies examining Jews' sentiments toward the schools (Moore 1981; Brumberg 1986). I chose these papers for three reasons: each was published continuously throughout the Gary Plan era, reflected the concerns of different segments of the Jewish community, and has been relied upon by previous researchers of these eras.

Documents from the manuscript collections of NYC's Board of Education, mayoral papers, and at the American Jewish Historical Society provided additional insights into these protests. New York City's Municipal Archives house both New York City's Board of Education and mayoral paper collections. Board of Education records detailing the Gary Plan and subsequent Jewish concerns can be found in Series IV.H.3.c. Data regarding Hebrew cases was primarily located in Series 755: Bureau of Reference, Research and Statistics, Reference Collection, and Vertical Files 409, 409.1, and 412. Mayoral papers examined for the Gary Plan included those of John Purroy Mitchel (1914–1917) and John F. Hylan (1918–1925). A small folder regarding the Gary Plan can also be found in Mitchel's papers at the Library of Congress. During the Hebrew case, NYC's mayors included James Walker (1926–1932), John L. O'Brian (1933), Fiorello LaGuardia (1934–1945), and William O'Dwyer (1945–1950).

Documentation of activism for Hebrew classes at NYC's American Jewish Historical Society appear in the records of the Jewish Board of Education, the Kehillah, the Educational Alliance, and the Society for the Advancement of Judaism. The papers of Stephen S. Wise, the acting chair of the Hebrew Committee, offer the most valuable record of these efforts. His papers exist on microfilm both at the American Jewish Historical Society and Brandeis University. James P. Rosenbloom, the head librarian at Brandeis, graciously lent these papers. Also at the AJHS are papers of Jewish organizations supporting the Hebrew Committee's efforts and working autonomously to promote Hebrew language classes. These include the Educational Alliance, the Society for the Advancement of Judaism, the Board of Jewish Education, the United Jewish

Appeal's Oral History Collection, and Zionist student organizations Young Judaea and Avukah.[2] Additional information about Zionist student groups appears in the papers of Zionist activist and adult Avukah member, Judah Pilch, at the YIVO Institute for Jewish Research. Finally, Israel S. Chipkin's papers are available at The Joseph and Miriam Ratner Center for the Study of Conservative Judaism at the Jewish Theological Center.

THE HARLEM 9 AND AFRICAN AMERICAN HISTORY. Newspapers, manuscript collections of neighborhood and parent organizations, mayoral records, records of the judicial system and the Board of Education of NYC provided a spectrum of views regarding these extensive protests for resource equality and identity recognition.

In addition to the *New York Times*, I examined the two citywide African American newspapers, the *New York Amsterdam News* and the *New York Age*. Seen by some as a radical paper for not employing whites, the *Amsterdam News* was founded by James Henry Anderson in 1909 and, for years, represented the nation's largest African American verified-circulation paper with a reputed circulation of 375,000 during the 1950s (LaBrie 1973). Under the guidance of C. B. Powell and Phillip M. H. Savory, two physicians who purchased the paper in 1935, the *Amsterdam News* "grew into a nationally prominent voice for African Americans" (Wilson 2001). The *New York Age*, founded in 1880 by T. Thomas Fortune, "probably the best known African American newspaper of the late nineteenth century," maintained a militant stance to fight America's systemic racism (Painter 1971: 40). The Chicago-based *Defender* acquired the *Age* in 1952, and it became the *New York Age-Defender*, but never regained its militant stance. The final edition was published on February 27, 1960. Following the *Defender*'s acquisition, until the late 1950s, the *Age*'s national focus resulted in less coverage of issues endemic to NYC.

At NYC's Municipal Library, the Board of Education and mayoral records include extensive documentation of educational inequality in African American schools and parents' subsequent concerns. The Board of Education's records contain material related to educational discrimination, inequality, and minorities, particularly documents in the Board of Education's Commission on Integration (Series 261), and Series IV.A.3, Educational Administration Records. The Harlem 9 protested extensively to Mayor Robert F. Wagner (1954–1965), resulting in data related to the African American community, discrimination, and education. The mayoral papers of William O'Dwyer (1946–1950), Vincent Impellitteri (1950–1953), and Robert F. Wagner (1954–1965) contain documentation of parents' concerns regarding curriculum.

NYC's Schomburg Center for Research in Black Culture holds papers of the Harlem Neighborhoods Association and the Harlem Parents Committee, of which the Harlem 9 were members, and of Ella Baker and Robert Parrish, both of whom worked extensively with the Harlem 9. These collections, with the exception of the Parrish papers' conspicuously missing information regarding the Harlem 9 protests, include transcripts of meetings, advertising fliers, and reports of school conditions. The papers of the HNA and HPC supplemented data for the African American history case found in the Council of Interracial Books. Additional documentation of parents' protest of curricular concerns can be found in the papers of the Congress of Racial Equality (CORE), available at the Library of Congress.

Court records outside of those available in the mayors' files included that of *Mallory v. Jansen*, filed in New York's State Supreme Court, available in this building's basement, and *City of New York vs. Skipwith in re*, available in Justice Justine Wise Polier's papers at Radcliff College's Schlesinger Library in Cambridge, Massachusetts. The transcripts available in Polier's papers were particularly important since this trial took place in Manhattan's Children's Court, for which records are sealed to the public.

Data Considerations

NEWSPAPERS. Although newspaper data can be biased, many researchers have documented newspapers' utility for social research when examining protests since factual aspects of these events are reliable and newspapers may be the only documentation of their occurrences (Franzosi 198; Olzak 1989; Ryan 1991; Tuchman 1972). With regard to protest events, newspapers are more likely to report large, local events involving conflict in central locations, particularly planned rallies, related to the papers' intended audience and ideological stance, which involve public figures, consequential actors or actions, and reflect the current political climate or represent a message event seeking to influence public opinion or action (Danzger 1975; Hocke, 1998; McCarthy, McPhail & Smith 1996; Oliver & Myers 1999; Snyder & Kelly 1977). As a result, potential bias in each paper likely benefited this project. No single, consistent line of thinking existed within either the Jewish or African American communities of NYC. To decrease bias, I used at least two different newspapers from each community. I read each available edition of each newspaper to avoid bias, accounted for protest events, and created master name and organization lists to facilitate research using archival manuscript collections (Hill 1993).

The ethnic press in America "offered a reflection of a group experience" and functioned as a "principal agent by which the identity, cohesiveness, and structure of an ethnic community are preserved and perpetuated" and a "vehicle through which the common concerns and purposes within ethnic communities [were] defined" (Wynar & Wynar 1976: 18). African American newspapers offered an essential medium of expression and communication within the community's public arena in the age immediately prior to the large-scale purchasing of televisions. The African American press maintained a racial orientation, which rendered it, "almost by definition, one of protest," and a supranational racial identity, which preserved ties among a national African American community through a popular media form (Painter 1971: 32). Each of these elements makes the African American press invaluable as a tool to understand African American sentiment. Jewish newspapers provided new immigrants with news from their countries of origin, served as vehicles for Americanization by teaching Jews how to read and understand English, and nurtured ethnic cultures and reinforced separation from the dominant culture. Jewish newspapers written in English "assumed a crucial role as it linked a dispersed . . . population to the local network of Jewish associational" life, fostering "a feeling of unity and consensus" throughout Jewish communities with disparate beliefs and practices (Wolseley 1971: 92).

MANUSCRIPTS. Archival manuscript data necessitates its own unique considerations due to the nature of the acquisition, storage and organization of records (Brooks 1969; Clemens & Hughes 2002). Manuscript collections for this project included both personal and organizational papers. Prior to collecting data I completed an "ethnography" of the archives (Dirks 2002) during which I researched their mission and purposes and, whenever possible, interviewed archivists to gain knowledge of the collections available and their organization, sedimentation, and authenticity. Manuscript data in general can be problematic due to file selection in each collection and potential erosion over time. This is especially true for collections of individuals who achieved fame within their communities or who believed their lives would be examined upon retirement or death (Milligan 1979; Platt 1981). Data triangulation ensured accurate accounting of protest trajectories and activists' sentiments. This was particularly important for this research given the greater potential for bias when examining racial groups due to a lack of accurate information regarding individuals, organizations, and events resulting from historical racism (Stanfield 1987).

Analytic Techniques

Using the sources described above, I first outlined the trajectory of protests, counterprotests, and tactics. I then engaged in a close examination of demands and identity narratives articulated by Jewish and African American activists. I used a strategic narrative approach to construct a theoretically informed chronological account of collective identity formation processes, changes over time and in relation to the demands articulated, historical contexts, and responses from the Board of Education. This comparative case/narrative approach enabled me to reconstruct each case's plot(s) and events with a clear focus on activists' identities and enhance analytic leverage in determining the causal mechanisms to explain the outcomes of school-based mobilization within the Jewish and African American communities.

This timeline of events allowed me to trace identity formation processes over time and across groups. I paid particular attention to explicit references to their own identities to explore changing conceptions of racial and national identities. Re-creating the narrative sequence of activists' testimonies regarding their collective identities, specific demands, and general conditions in the public schools and in their communities promoted the use of narrative and discourse analysis. Process tracing and strategic narrative concurrently allowed for the determination of whether "in different historical circumstances actors nonetheless were faced with situations that, in certain respects, were similar, and hence acted in certain respects, in similar ways" (Goldstone 1990: 289). I also noted historical sequentiality between cases to account for effects of previous mobilization on subsequent protests and identities.[3]

I used discourse analysis to identify activists' contentious identities and boundary stories (Tilly 2002; Whitebrook 2001) and racial narratives (Pride 2002) deployed by the Board of Education. Activists' narratives, articulated in public and private, allowed me to assess negotiation of identity boundaries, the impact of external forces, the development of cultures of solidarity, and challenges to dominant meanings of a particular identity. Boundary stories describing similarities and differences between Jews and African Americans in the larger society (often described in terms of "us" versus "them) revealed activists' interpretations of their own identities.[4]

This research also explored the role of group culture and agency during mobilization to answer Poletta's (1997) call for "more empirical work, especially comparative, on the circumstances in which cultures inspires, impedes and shapes collective action" (445). To understand each groups' mobilization of systems of meanings, I examined activists'"tool kit" or "backpack" of symbols, practices, and meanings mobilized during each protest (Hays 1994; Nagel 1994; Sewell 1999; Swidler 1986). I engaged Wuthnow's (1989) subjective, structural, and dramaturgic approaches for the study of culture, particularly ethnic cultures, to identify the meanings of narratives, beliefs, attitudes, opinions, and values of group members, the patterns and relationships among cultural elements that produce boundaries and categories within group consciousness, and the expressive and communicative symbols used to structure the social relations of the groups (10–14). This interpretive approach also attended to culturally embedded institutions of the individuals and groups under consideration (Skocpol 1988).

NOTES

INTRODUCTION

1. *New York Daily Globe*, Oct. 17, 1917, 17 [hereafter *Globe*]; *New York Amsterdam News*, July 20, 1957, 1, 32 [hereafter *Amsterdam News*].
2. While not a uniform practice, based on Richard B. Moore's (1992) argument, and an apparent preference among African Americans (Wilkerson 1989; though considerable debate continues), I refer to Blacks throughout the book as African Americans (see also Collier-Thomas & Turner 1994). However, I transcribe verbatim the words African Americans used ("Negroes," "Afro-Americans," "African Americans," etc.) during social protests. AJHS, BJE, Box 1, Folder 1, *Jewish Education to the Fore* (1937); *Amsterdam News*, Oct.10, 1959, 38.
3. Upon arriving in America, each group encounters a racialized social system embedded in social institutions that either facilitates or inhibits their opportunities (Bonilla-Silva 1995; Feagin 2005). Scholars often highlight European immigrants' constructed and adaptable nature of ethnic identities (Conzen et al. 1992; Sollors 1989; Vecoli 1964, 1990; Zunz 1985). Segmented assimilation among post-1965 immigrant groups results in a variety of self-identification that varies depending on social, political, and economic conditions encountered in America (Alba 1999; Alba & Nee 1997; Portes & Zhou 1993; Rumbaut 1994, 1997). Though debates persist (Barkan 1995; Brubaker 2001; Gans 1997; Glazer 1993), scholars continue to frame contemporary and historical immigrant incorporation experiences as assimilation studies wherein groups seek to enter mainstream American society and leave behind their group cultures (Kazal 1995). These theories often ignore the deeply embedded racial meanings and relationships that shape racial minorities' ability to access important social resources (Steinberg 2007).
4. Ongoing debates over bilingual, multicultural, and other curricula- and personnel-related issues highlight the degree to which control over the content of education is highly contested on multiple sides of each issue (Alexander 2001; Taylor 1994; Willett 1998).
5. Hall (1996) and Hartmann (2000) describe subordinated groups' use of different social institutions to challenge identities and meanings.
6. These methods are informed by Connolly and Troyna's (1998), and Parker, Deyle and Villenas's (1999) edited volumes exploring marginalized groups' racialization in the context of education.
7. Multicultural rhetoric has become so common that, in 1997, Nathan Glazer argued, "We are All Multiculturalists Now." Banks (2002), Bush (1999), Collins (2000), Kelley (1996), Kosak (2000), and Morris and Mansbridge (2001) document oppositional

consciousness and transformative knowledge in Jewish and African American social movements.

8. Critical education theorists such as Apple (1979, 1995), Bourdieu (1977), Freire (2000), Giroux (1980, 1988), Morrow & Torres (1995), Popkewitz & Fendler (1999), and Trend (1995) document how structural racism plays out in the educational arena.

CHAPTER 1   NEW YORK CITY'S RACIAL AND EDUCATIONAL TERRAIN

1. Scott (1990) discusses these dual perceptions of African Americans' success and failure in America and its effect on racial attitudes and policies.

2. In 1644, twenty years after they had been brought to Manhattan, eleven African American slaves brought from the West Indies successfully petitioned the Dutch government for their freedom. For race relations in colonial NYC see Foote (2004), Gronowicz (1998), Harris (2003), Hodges (1999), Scheiner (1965), and Wilder (2001). For broad Jewish history from 1654 until World War I, see Dwork (1986), Goren (1999), Grinstein (1947), Howe (1976), Kosak (2000), and Rischin (1978).

3. Longstanding tensions between working-class Irish and African Americans erupted in NYC during the Draft Riots, which were precipitated by Lincoln's declaration of the Conscription Act, exempting from military service citizens rich enough to pay $300. As the perceived cause of the war, African Americans bore the brunt of Irish workers' resentment, particularly prevalent in the dock districts where African Americans and whites fiercely competed for jobs. For days, flames engulfed NYC as the Irish set fire first to the fully occupied Colored Orphan Asylum, then African Americans' homes, businesses, and, finally, bodies, after they had been lynched from lampposts. Rioters assaulted African Americans in the streets and dragged them from their homes at night. Much of the remaining population fled NYC. "With these actions," according to Harris (2003), "white workers enacted their desires to eradicate the working-class black male from the city" (284).

4. Jews arriving from Germany prior to this were often skilled but poor (Rohrbacher 1997).

5. Welcomed by Polish King Stephen Batory, Jews arrived in Eastern Europe during the "golden age" of the 1500s. As moneylenders and traders, Jews found their social position plummet with the decline of the feudal system. After Russia annexed Poland in the 1700s, laws confined Jews to the Pale. The 1874 military reform, requiring all men, at the age of twenty-one, to serve in Russia's army, destroyed Jewish communities. The May Laws forbade Jews from owning or renting land inside towns, cities, and villages and imposed Jewish quotas in universities. Russians enacted violent pogroms, beginning in Odessa in 1871, and massacred thousands of Jews over a thirty-five-year period. Pogroms continued and, by 1907, nearly half of the Pale's Jews had left for America.

6. For African American education see Anderson (1988), Barnhouse Walters (1999), Cecelski (1994), Dunn (1993), Kluger (1977), Walker (1996, 2000), Watkins (2001), and Watkins, Lewis & Chou (2001).

7. For links between citizenship and education see ibid. and Barnhouse Walters, James & McCammon (1997), Clift (1966), Erickson (1997), Mills (1997), Nasaw (1979), and Tyack (1974). Northern philanthropists, supportive of Booker T. Washington's racial accommodationism, financed most of African Americans' post–Civil War Southern schools. These vocational schools reinforced "the lasting image of the

African American Worker as a 'Super Masculine Menial'" (Dunn 1993: 28; Cleaver 1968). For African Americans' reactions to low-quality education see Cecelski (1994) and Morris & Morris (2002).

8. Cf. Ellison (1992) for African American invisibility.

9. See Katznelson (2005), Lipsitz (1998), Massey & Denton (1993), and Pritchett (2002) for the critical role that post–World War II federal policies, such as the GI Bill, FHA housing subsidies, and highway development, played in shaping economic disparities between African Americans and whites, heightened residential and urban apartheid; and see Podair (2003) for NYC in particular.

10. See Fuchs (1956), Goren (1999), Howe (1976), and Rischin (1978) for Jewish voting patterns and Reid (1927) and Scheiner (1965) for that of African Americans. Russian Jews tended to vote Socialist but also voted Democrat and Republican. In the largely Jewish Lower East Side 9th District, with 450,000 Jews, only 13,614 cast ballots in the 1906 congressional election. Citywide, in 1910, only 110,000 of NYC's 1.5 million Jews registered to vote. In the 1920s, Manhattan's African American population of 109,133 counted only 22,000 registered voters and, of these, only 10,000 cast ballots. In 1932, 29 percent of those registered voted. This increased to 52 percent by 1940. Jewish political figures included U.S. Representative Meyer London and Manhattan Borough President Samuel M. Levy. By World War II, many of NYC's African Americans voted Democrat but maintained deep reservations given Southern Democrats' repressive racist policies. Not until 1944 did NYC send its first African American representative, Adam Clayton Powell, to Congress. These politicians lacked substantive control in local politics, particularly in terms of education.

11. See Biondi (2006), Bush (1999), Capeci (1977), Kelley (1996), McDowell (1984), McKay (1940), Naison (1983), Ottley (1943), Robinson (1997, 1983), and Weiner (2008) for African Americans' socioeconomic position and collective consciousnesses and action during this era, particularly Brandt (1993), Greenberg (1991), and Trotter (2000) for the riots.

12. See Sterba (2003) for NYC's Jews in World War I and Duker (1939) and Szajkowski (1972) for Jews' perceptions of and activities during World War I related to their former home countries. For African Americans' pro-Japanese sentiment see Brandt (1993), Ottley & Weatherby (1967), and Wynn (1993).

13. For African Americans' participation in, and ideologies during World War II, see above, Motley (1987), and Silvera (1969).

14. Not until Truman's Executive Order of 1948, desegregating the armed forces, did African Americans serve as equals with whites.

15. See Goldstein (2006) for the Jewish community's perceptions of itself vis-à-vis race.

16. While Glazer & Moynihan (1965) argue that Jews' relative success compared to the Irish, Italians, Puerto Ricans, and African Americans is due to their unique proclivity toward education, Gorelick (1981) and Steinberg (1989) provide evidence to the contrary by distinguishing between class, cultural, and national backgrounds within the Jewish community.

17. *Amsterdam News*, Apr. 28, 1951, 10; Oct. 17, 1953, 14; Oct. 31, 1953, 18, 34.

18. *Amsterdam News*, May 1, 1954, 1, 15.

19. *Amsterdam News*, June 5, 1954, 1, 3; NYCMA, BoE, COI, Box 4, Folder 37, "Minority Dispersion into the Total Housing Supply: Prospectus of an Action-Study Project," City of New York, Commission on Intergroup Relations, n.d.

20. *Age*, September 28, 1957, 6; June 28, 1958, 5, 24; July 19, 1958, 8.

21. NYCMA, BoE, Series 261: Commission on Integration (COI), Box 3, Folder 28, *Report*

on Integration (Report #1) by William Jansen, Superintendent of Schools, Sept. 19, 1957; Box 4, Folder 32, *Report to the Commission on Integration, Board of Education, City of New York by Sub-Commission on Educational Standards and Curriculum, May 14, 1956* (the Commission knew of discriminatory texts. The archives contained numerous reports and lists of them from parents' groups); Folder 36, *Report to the Commission on Integration, Board of Education, City of New York, by Sub-Commission on Community Relations and Information, May 3, 1957*; Box 5, Folder 39, *Report to the Commission on Integration, Board of Education, City of New York, by Sub-Commission on Guidance, Educational Stimulation and Placement Reports, March 2, 1956*; Folder 40, *Report to the Commission on Integration, Board of Education, City of New York by the Sub-Commission on Physical Plant and Maintenance, June 15, 1956*; *Report to the Commission on Integration, Board of Education, City of New York by the Sub-Commission on Teachers Assignments and Personnel, Dec. 7, 1956*.

CHAPTER 2   RESOURCES, RIOTS, AND RACE

1. For overviews of the Gary Plan see Bonner (1978), Bourne (1970), Cohen (1964), Lewisohn (1965), Mohl (1974, 1975), Ravitch (1968), and Szajkowski (1970).
2. In 1914, the Board of Education, located on East 59th Street in Manhattan, contained forty-six representatives hailing from all five boroughs. The mayor appointed each member to the board, including the superintendent of schools. The board then elected its president. Contention existed over the board's lack of control over school spending. Since the Board of Estimate allotted the Board of Education's funds, the Board of Education had to appeal to it, rather than the state or mayor, for funding. In other words, bankers and accountants, rather than educational experts, determined how much money the schools needed.
3. *Globe*, Sept. 11, 1914, 11; Wirt 1916.
4. Gaventa's (1982) treatment of the media in maintaining acquiescence integrates Lukes's (1974) theories of power.
5. For hidden curriculum and its relationship to social class, see Bernstein (1970), Boykin (2001), Cornbleth (1984), Gillborn (1992), Jackson (1968), and Vallance (1974). Schools historically placed girls in home economics and humanities, rather than math and science, classes (Fennema & Leder 1990; Tyack 1974). For race-based tracking and class- and race-based curriculum see Oakes (2005), Cusick (1983), Dreeben (1984), Featherstone (1987), Page (1987), and Rist (1970). Schools place poor and minority students in lower tracks and middle-class whites and Asians in college preparatory or AP classes. In lower tracks, below-grade-level curriculum teaches African Americans to passively follow rules rather than actively learn or challenge dominant thinking inside or outside of the classroom.
6. For example, Mayer C. Goldman was president of P.S. 46's PA, and founder of the FPA and PSBL while Mrs. Meyer Frankel led the School Welfare Association. Goldman appointed Seymour Rosedale to secretary of the FPA. David Rothschild acted as chairman of P.S. 93's PA's Legislative Committee and as president of the 18th District PA and appointed Frederick A. Pruchen of P.S. 54's P.A. as secretary. Sofia Loebinger was vice-president of the Federation of Public School Neighborhood Associations. *Brooklyn Daily Eagle* (hereafter, *BDE*), Apr. 7, 1916, 5, Apr. 6, 1917, 9; *Globe*, Oct. 8, 1915, school page, Dec. 6, 1915, school page, Dec. 16, 1915, school page, Apr. 6, 1917, 15, July 16, 1917, 12. See Tarrow (1998) for diffusion of movement tactics.
7. *American Hebrew* (hereafter *AH*), Jan. 23, 1914, 383, Feb. 19, 1915, 434, Oct. 22, 1915,

680–1, Dec. 17, 1915, 168; *Globe*, Oct. 4, 1915, school page; Nov. 20, 1915, 1; Nov. 30, 1915, 17; *New York Times* (hereafter *NY Times*) Oct. 4, 1915, 18, Nov. 5, 1915, 12, Nov. 7, 1915, 6, Nov. 10, 1915, 7, Nov. 25, 1915, 15; NYCMA, Mitchel Papers, Departmental Correspondence Sent, Box 7, Folder 152, Nov. 23, 1914; Box 7, Folder 153, Jan. 6, 1915, Jan. 19, 1915, Feb. 20, 1915; Subject Files, Box 100, Folder 155, Oct. 15, 1915.

8. *Globe*, Nov. 20, 1915, 1; NYCMA, Mitchel Papers, Oct. 15, 1915, Oct. 30, 1915; NYPL, Barondess Papers, Letterbook 48, Nov. 4, 1915.

9. *AH*, Jan. 23, 1914, 383, Feb. 19, 1915, 434, Mar. 19, 1915, 535, Oct. 22, 1915, 680–1, Dec. 24, 1915, 207; *BDE*, Jan. 17, 1916, 6; *Globe*, Oct. 6, 1915, school page, Nov. 8, 1915, school page, Dec. 13, 1915, school page; *Hebrew Standard* (hereafter, *HS*), Nov. 12, 1915, 11, Nov. 19, 1915, 5; *NY Times*, Nov. 7, 1915, 6.

10. In addition to the Kehillah, the International Order of B'nai B'rith, Council of Jewish Women, Union of Orthodox Rabbis of the United States, Union of Orthodox Congregations, Organization of Local Rabbis, Mizrachi, Hebrew Teachers' Organization, Chairman and Principals of Talmud Torah, and International Order of the Free Sons of Israel opposed the Gary Plan. *AH*, Dec. 3, 1915, 100–1, Dec. 17, 1915, 168; *Globe*, Nov. 22, 1915, school page, Jan. 18, 1916, school page, Apr. 10, 1916, school page; *HS*, Nov. 26, 1915, 2, Dec. 17, 1915, 4, Nov. 12, 1915, 10-B; *NY Times*, Nov. 25, 1915, 15, Dec. 1, 1915, 14.

11. *AH*, Mar. 3, 1915, 100–1; *Globe*, Oct. 15, 1915, 19.

12. *BDE*, Jan. 5, 1916, 3, Jan. 12, 1916, 4, Jan. 19, 1916, 4, Jan. 18, 1917, 10, Aug. 16, 1917, 12, Oct. 22, 1917, 2; *Globe*, Oct. 1, 1915, school page, Oct. 4, 1915, school page, Nov. 12, 1915, school page, Nov. 23, 1915, 17, Jan. 21, 1916, school page, Jan. 24, 1916, school page, Mar. 28 1916, school page, Mar. 31, 1916, school page, Dec. 1, 1916, 17, Aug. 14, 1917, 13, Aug. 11, 1917, 11, Aug. 27, 1917, 11, Sept. 7, 1917, 13, Oct. 12, 1917, 15, Oct. 23, 1917, 15, Nov. 8, 1917, 17; NYCMA, Mitchel Papers, Correspondence Sent, Box 7, Folder 152, Nov. 23, 1914; Folder 153, Jan. 18, 1915, Feb. 20, 1915; Box 8, Folder 160, Dec. 7, 1916; Box 8, Folder 162, June 28, 1917; Box 8, Folder 167, Sept. 6, 1917, Sept. 17, 1917, Sept. 18, 1917, Sept. 19, 1917, Sept. 24, 1917, Sept. 26, 1917; Box 100, Folder 155, Oct. 15, 1915; Departmental Correspondence Received, Box 24, Folder 251, Oct. 30, 1915; Box 24, Folder 260, Dec. 6, 1916; Box 24, Folder 261, May 20, 1916, Dec. 3, 1916.

13. *BDE*, Jan. 11, 1916, 10; *Globe*, Nov. 5, 1915, school page, Jan. 6, 1916, school page.

14. *BDE*, Jan. 8, 1916, 3, Jan. 22, 1916, 3, Jan. 31, 1916, 6, Feb. 11, 1916, 5; *Globe*, May 29, 1917, 11, Oct. 23, 1917, 15; *NY Times*, Nov. 20, 1915, 15.

15. *Globe*, Oct. 15, 1915, 19, Nov. 12, 1915, school page, Oct. 21, 1915, 15, Nov. 17, 1915, 15, Nov. 19, 1915, 23, Nov. 23, 1915, 17, Dec. 1, 1915, 17, Dec. 6, 1915, school page, Mar. 28, 1916, school page, Apr. 18, 1916, 12; *NY Times* Dec. 6, 1915, 8.

16. *Globe*, Jan. 6, 1916, school page.

17. *BDE*, Jan. 12, 1914, 4, Jan. 15, 1916, 7; *Globe*, Jan. 12, 1916, school page, Jan. 13, 1916, school page, Jan. 15, 1915, school page, Jan. 18, 1916, school page.

18. *Globe*, Apr. 10, 1916, school page. Soyer (1997, especially 7, 141) highlights the centrality of Jewish *Landsmanshaftn* to structuring Jewish networks and later mobilization.

19. *Globe*, July 18, 1917, 13, July 19, 1917, 13, Oct. 17, 1917, 13. NYCMA, BoE, Series IV/H/3/c, Box 97, Folder: 200.11 Gary Schools—Duplicate, 1911–1916; Box 98, Folder: 200.11. Gary Schools—Duplicate, 1916–1924. Cassedy (1997), Kosak (2000), Shandler (2000), and Sinkoff (1990) document the Yiddish language as a particular marker of the working-class Jewish community.

20. *Globe*, Mar. 18, 1916, 13, Mar. 21, 1916, school page, Mar. 22, 1916, school page.

21. *Globe*, June 26, 1917, 13.

22. *Globe*, Mar. 26, 1916, school page, Mar. 28, 1916, school page.

23. *Globe*, Apr. 4, 1916, school page, Apr. 5, 1916, school page, Apr. 6, 1916, school page.

24. *BDE*, Apr. 8, 1916, 9, Apr. 12, 1916, 10; *Globe*, Apr. 8, 1916, 12.

25. *Globe*, Jan. 21, 1916, school page; Jan. 24, 1916, school page; NYCMA, Mitchel Papers, Correspondence Received, Box 25, Folder 261, May 20, 1916. For increased repression leading to increased resistance see Rasler (1996).

26. *AH*, Mar. 16, 1917, 599; *BDE*, Jan. 11, 1917, 22; Jan. 18, 1917, 10.

27. NYCMA, Mitchel Papers, Departmental Correspondence Sent, Box 8, Folder 160, Nov. 17, 1916, Dec. 7, 1916; Departmental Correspondence Received, Box 25, Folder 261, May 20, 1916, Dec. 3, 1916; NYPL, Barondess Papers, Box 3, Folder "1916—Unsorted," Feb. 28, 1916; Box 2, Folder "1916, C-D," Dec. 15, 1916.

28. LOC, Mitchel papers, Box 17, Folder 1, Oct. 10, 1917; Box 18, Folder 2, Oct. 25, 1917; NYMCA, Mitchel Papers, Correspondence Received, Box 7, Folder 152, Nov. 23, 1914; Box 24, Folder 251, Oct. 30, 1915; Box 25, Folder 261, May 20, 1916, Dec. 3, 1916; Correspondence Sent, Box 7, Folder 153, Jan. 6, 1915, Jan. 19, 1915, Feb. 20, 1915; Box 8, Folder 162, June 28, 1917; Box 8, Folder 163, Sept. 17, 1917, Sept. 18, 1917; Box 8, Folder 167, Sept. 6, 1917; BoE, Series 755, Folder 33, Mar. 26, 1917, Apr. 12, 1917, Apr. 23, 1917, June 28, 1917, Sept. 24, 1917.

29. *BDE*, Apr. 12, 1917, 5, May 1, 1917, 2, May 2, 1917, 3, May 7, 1917, 18, May 8, 1917, 18, May 9, 1917, 3, Sept. 13, 1917, 10, Sept. 22, 1917, 7; *Globe*, Apr. 6, 1917, 15, Apr. 26, 1917, 15, May 2, 1917, 15, May 3, 1917, 15, May 8, 1917, 15.

30. *Globe*, Mar. 10, 1917, school page, Apr. 6, 1917, 15.

31. *Globe*, June 21, 1917, 15, July 3, 1917, 9, July 5, 1917, 15.

32. *Globe*, July 13, 1917, 15.

33. *BDE*, Aug. 5, 1917, 7, Aug. 16, 1917, 5, 12; *Globe*, Sept. 29, 1917, 10.

34. *Globe*, May 18, 1917, 17, July 16, 1917, 12, July 18, 1917, 13, July 19, 1917, 13, July 23, 1917, 10, July 26, 1917, 15.

35. *Globe*, Mar. 25, 1916, 13, Apr. 10, 1916, school page, Apr. 11, 1916, school page, Apr. 12, 1916, school page; Apr. 21, 1916, school page; Apr. 24, 1916, 15, Apr. 26, 1916, school page; Apr. 28, 1916, school page.

36. LOC, Mitchel Papers, Box 18, Folder 3, Oct. 28, 1917.

37. LOC, Mitchel Papers, Box 14, Folder 2, Sept. 13, 1917; Box 18, Folder 4, Oct. 29, 1917.

38. LOC, Mitchel Papers, Box 16, Folder 1, Oct. 3, 1917; Box 18, Folder 2, Oct. 25, 1917.

39. LOC, Mitchel Papers, Box 47, Folder 3, October 1917.

40. *Globe*, Oct. 18, 1917, 17.

41. *Globe*, Aug. 13, 1917, 11; Sept. 13, 1917, 15, Sept. 19, 1917, 10, Oct. 2, 1917, 13, Oct. 3, 1917, 15, Oct. 6, 1917, 13.

42. *Globe*, Oct. 12, 1917, 15.

43. Media coverage of the strikes was widespread. *BDE*, Oct. 18, 1917, 2, Oct. 19, 1917, 1, Oct. 22, 1917, 2; *Globe*, Oct. 18, 1917, 1, Oct. 19, 1917, 1, Oct. 22, 1917, 1, 15; *NY Times*, Oct. 17, 1917, 6, Oct. 18, 1917, 13, Oct. 19, 1917, 16, Oct. 20, 1917, 8.

44. *Globe*, Oct. 17, 1917, 1, 13, Oct. 18, 1917, 1, 17.

45. *BDE*, Oct. 18, 1917, 2; *Globe*, Oct. 19, 1917, 1, 17; *NY Times*, Oct. 19, 1917, 16.

46. *BDE*, Oct. 19, 1917, 1; *Globe*, Oct. 19, 1917, 1.

47. *Globe*, Oct. 17, 1917, 13.

48. *BDE*, Oct. 23, 1917, 11; *Globe*, Oct. 22, 1917, 15, Oct. 23, 1917, 15.

49. *BDE*, Oct. 22, 1917, 2; *Globe*, Oct. 19, 1917, 17, Oct. 22, 1917, 1, 15.

50. *BDE*, Oct. 19, 1917, 1, Oct. 20, 1917, 22, Oct. 23, 1917, 3; *Globe*, Oct. 23, 1917, 15. Bergen was later acquitted (*BDE*, Nov. 1, 1917, 20).

51. *Globe*, Oct. 16, 1917, 15, Oct. 17, 1917, 13, Oct. 18, 1917, 17, Oct. 19, 1917, 17, Oct. 22, 1917, 15,

Oct. 23, 1917, 15, Oct. 26, 1917, 15, Oct. 27, 1917, 2, Oct. 30, 1917, 15, Nov. 2, 1917, 19. Mitchel died on July 6, 1918, when his army training plane crashed in Louisiana.

52. *BDE*, Oct. 19, 1917, 6; *Globe*, Nov. 8, 1917, 2, 17; *NY Times*, Oct. 18, 1917, 13, Oct. 22, 1917, 7, Nov. 7, 1917, 1.

53. *NY Times*, Oct. 22, 1917, 7.

54. *Globe*, Nov. 26, 1915, school page; *NY Times*, Nov. 8, 1917, 3; Nov. 27, 1917, 12.

55. *Amsterdam News*, May 1, 1954, 1, 15.

56. *Amsterdam News*, June 5, 1954, 1, 3.

57. Per news conventions of the time, reporters referred to most married women using their husband's name. Located at 2121 Fifth Avenue, P.S. 133, or the Frederick R. Moore School, was built in 1948 after significant parental protest regarding the lack of educational facilities in Harlem. It was named after a former editor of the *New York Age* (hereafter, *Age*, Nov. 8, 1947, 1, Dec. 20, 1947, 1). Locations for schools are as follows: P.S. 10—117th St. and St. Nicholas Ave; P.S. 197—2230 Fifth Ave.; JHS 120—18 E. 120th St. at Madison Ave.; JHS 136—136th St. and Edgecombe Ave.; JHS 139—140 W. 140th St. at Lenox Ave. The *Amsterdam News* first dubbed the parents "the Little Rock Nine of Harlem." In January 1958, parents called P.S. 133 "the Little Rock of New York City" (*Age*, May 31, 1958, 2). NYCMA, BoE, Box 1, Folder 8, 11 June 1956; COI, Box 4, Folder 37; Box 6, Folder 61 (Percentages in board records never appeared as or totaled 100 percent); *Age*, Oct. 18, 1958, 1; *Amsterdam News*, Oct. 18, 1958, 2.

58. *Age*, May 31, 1958, 2, Dec. 13, 1958, 2; *Amsterdam News*, May 31, 1958, 24, Sept. 20, 1958, 6, Nov. 8, 1958, 1. Mallory later moved to 212 W. 129th Street to enroll her children in a "whiter" school in Washington Heights. Zuber was born in Williamsport, Pennsylvania, in 1926. He moved to Harlem in 1934 and attended segregated P.S. 157 at St. Nicholas Avenue and 12th Street. Because there were no academic high schools in Harlem, he attended the predominantly Jewish Thomas Jefferson High School in Brownsville, Brooklyn. After graduating from Brown University, Zuber joined the war effort. Upon return, he became an active member of Harlem's 369th Veteran's Association and, living at 2816 8th Avenue, Harlem, attended Brooklyn Law School at night while working for the NYC Health Department. *NY Times*, May 4, 1957, 26, Feb. 26, 1962, 21.

59. NYCMA, BoE, Box 1, Folder 8, June 11, 1956, 4. Although NYC schools similarly segregated African American and Puerto Rican children, Puerto Rican parents appeared uninvolved in most protests. The NYC public schools, during these years, waged a large, but culturally biased, campaign to assimilate Puerto Ricans by forcing them to drop their native tongue and cultural traditions to improve their educational background to approximate whites.' Therefore, the board appeared to consider Puerto Ricans above African Americans on the racial hierarchy by at least attempting to integrate them into the mainstream student population while ignoring problems faced by African American students. (See the NYC Board of Education's 1958 report, *The Puerto Rican Study, 1953–1957: A Report on the Education and Adjustment of Puerto Rican Pupils in the Public Schools of the City of New York*.) Only *after* the schools gave up on assimilating Puerto Ricans and began equating them to African Americans, did Puerto Rican protest against the schools begin in earnest (Rogers 1968).

60. *Amsterdam News*, Nov. 24, 1956, 1.

61. NYCMA, BoE, Series 261, Box 2, Folder 13, Speakers # 31, 33, 38, 40, 57, and 59, Jan. 17, 1957. Most junior and senior high schools in NYC during the 1950s were sex segregated.

62. NYCMA, BoE, Series 261, Box 2, Folder 14, Speaker # 38, Jan. 17, 1957.

63. NYCMA, Wagner Papers, Box 60, Folder 691, June 16, 1957, June 24, 1957, July 4, 1957, Sept. 22, 1957; Sept. 19, 1957; Sept. 28, 1957, Sept. 29, 1957; SCRBC, Ella Baker Papers, Box 4, Folder 20, June 28, 1957.

64. SCRBC, Baker Papers, Box 4, Folder 19, July 1957, July 3, 1957, July 29, 1957, Aug. 1957.

65. *Amsterdam News*, July 20, 1957, 1, 32.

66. SCRBC, Ella Baker Papers, Box 4, Folder 20, July 1957; Aug. 30, 1957; NYCMA, Wagner Papers, Box 60, Folder 691, Sept. 19, 1957; *NY Times*, Sept. 20, 1957, 1, 15.

67. *Amsterdam News*, July 20, 1957, 1, 32; SCRBC, Baker Papers, Box 4, Folder 20, July 3, 1957; July 1957.

68. SCRBC, Baker Papers, Box 4, Folder 20, July 1957.

69. NYCMA, Wagner Papers, Box 60, Folder 691, June 24, 1957, July 1957, July 4, 1957; SCRBC, Baker Papers, Box 4, Folder 20, June 16, 1957, June 25, 1957, June 28, 1957, July 1957, July 3, 1957, July 9, 1957.

70. SCRBC, Baker Papers, Box 4, Folder 20, Aug. 1957, Sept. 1957.

71. SCRBC, Baker Papers, Box 4, Folder 20, Aug. 30, 1957.

72. NYCMA, Wagner Papers, Box 60, Folder 691, Sept. 19, 1957.

73. NYCMA, Wagner Papers, Box 60, Folder 691, Sept. 22, 1957, Sept. 23, 1957.

74. *Amsterdam News*, Aug. 31, 1957, 1, Nov. 22, 1957, 3. Patricia went to the Downtown Community School in Manhattan and William Robinson Jr. to Our Saviour Lutheran School in the Bronx.

75. State Supreme Court, *Mallory v. Jansen*, "Memorandum of Law, Statement of Facts," Aug. 6, 1958; *Age*, Nov. 28, 1958, 1.

76. *Amsterdam News*, Jan. 25, 1958, 1, Feb. 1, 1958, 9, Feb. 8, 1958, 25, Apr. 5, 1958, 1, 9, Apr. 12, 1958, 16.

77. *Age*, May 31, 1958, 2, July 19, 1958, 8; *Amsterdam News*, May 24, 1958, 1.

78. *Age*, Oct. 18, 1958, 1, 6; *Amsterdam News*, Nov. 8, 1958, 8; *NY Times*, Oct. 15, 1958, 28; Oct. 29, 1958, 69.

79. *Amsterdam News*, Oct. 18, 1958, 2.

80. Polier was the daughter of Stephen Wise, the Free Synagogue's prominent rabbi and the Hebrew Committee's chairman.

81. *Age*, Nov. 8, 1958, 3, 33, Nov. 22, 1958, 2, 36; *Amsterdam News*, Nov. 8, 1958, 1, 4, 33, Nov. 15, 1958, 1, 36, Nov. 22, 1958, 1, 11.

82. *Age*, Dec. 13, 1958, 2, Dec. 20, 1958, 1; *Amsterdam News*, Nov. 22, 1958, 9.

83. *Amsterdam News*, Dec. 6, 1958, 10, May 23, 1959, 1.

84. *Age*, Jan. 24, 1959, 1.

85. *Age*, Dec. 6, 1958, 6, Dec. 20, 1958, 1, Jan. 24, 1959, 1; *Amsterdam News News*, Dec. 13, 1958, 1, 24, Dec. 20, 1958, 1, 25, Jan. 24, 1959, 8, Feb. 7, 1959, 1.

86. *Age*, Nov. 28, 1959, 1; NYCMA, BoE, Series IV/A/3, Box 22, Folder 3, Jan. 28, 1959; Series 261, Box 6, Folder 62, "Supreme Court: New York County, Special & Trial Term Part VII," Nov. 20, 1959; *NY Times*, Feb. 11, 1959, 31.

87. *Amsterdam News*, Dec. 26, 1959, 1, Feb. 6, 1960, 8, Feb. 20, 1960, 1; *NY Times*, Nov. 21, 1959, 23, Mar. 3, 1960, 15, Mar. 4, 1960, 16.

88. *Age*, Nov. 15, 1958, 3, 6, June 13, 1959, 1, 6; *Amsterdam News*, May 23, 1959, 1.

89. *Age*, Dec. 12, 1959, 6, Dec. 19, 1959, 1.

90. *Age*, Sept. 12, 1959, 1, 6, Sept. 21, 1959, 1; *Amsterdam News*, Dec. 19, 1959, 1.

91. *Age*, Sept. 12, 1959, 1; *Amsterdam News*, May 24, 1958, 1, May 31, 1958, 24, Sept. 20, 1958, 6; Oct. 128, 1958, 2; *NY Times*, Sept. 9, 1958, 1, Sept. 17, 1958, 25, Sept. 22, 1959, 42.

92. *Age*, Dec. 26, 1959, 1, 3; *Amsterdam News*, Jan. 16, 1960, 1.

93. *Amsterdam News*, Sept. 19, 1959, 1, Feb. 6, 1960, 8. See Lukes (1974) and McAdam (1983) for institutional countertactics used to thwart activists' tactical innovations (Tarrow 1998).

94. *Amsterdam News*, Dec. 26, 1959, 1, Jan. 16, 1960, 1, Feb. 20, 1960, 1, May 21, 1960, 6.

95. *Amsterdam News*, Dec. 26, 1959, 1, Sept. 10, 1960, 1, 6, 32, Sept. 24, 1960, 34, Feb. 10, 1962, 1, 18; *NY Times*, Sept. 12, 1960, 1.

96. Harlem's median income in 1960 was $3,480 while NYC's was $5,103. More than half of Harlem's residents, many in low-skill jobs, made less than $4,000 a year while 75 percent of all New Yorkers made more than $4,000 (Clark 1989 [1965]; Stevens 1971). For rising school segregation, see the State Education Commissioner's Advisory Committee on Human Relations and Community Tensions Report (1964).

97. See McAdam, Tarrow, and Tilly's *Dynamics of Contention* (2001) for transgressive contentious politics and social movement mechanisms.

98. Piven and Cloward's (1977) seminal *Poor People's Movements* describes protest arising among workers, African Americans, and welfare activists after a lost sense of systemic legitimacy.

99. Blau (1976), Bush (1999), Collins (2000), Ellingson (1995), Evans and Boyte (1992), Fantasia (1988, 1995), Goren (1999), Howe (1976), Joselit (1994), Kelley (1996), Kosak (2000), Levine (1977), Mansbridge & Morris (2001), Rischin (1978), and Soyer (1997) describe the rise of cultures of solidarity in free spaces and their use by working-class members of these subordinated groups.

100. Kosak (2000), McAdam (1999), Morris (1984), and Tilly (1978) use McCarthy and Zald's (1973) concepts of mobilizing structures to document protest generation at the local, grassroots, and neighborhood levels. See also Tarrow (1998) and McAdam, Tarrow & Tilly (2001).

101. Collins (2000), Gilkes (1980, 1983), Howe (1976), Joselit (1994), Kelley (1996), Kosak (2000), and Naples (1996) document the central role of Jewish and African American mothers in perpetuating group cultures and advocating on behalf of their children's material welfare.

102. Tarrow's (1998) discussion of media in creating "communities in print" during social movements draws heavily on Anderson (1991).

103. For strikes, boycotts, and riots see McAdam (1983) and Tarrow (1998). For these tactics by Jews and African Americans see Bush (1999), Harris (2001), Kosak (2000), McAdam (1999), and Sterba (2003).

104. Aminzade & McAdam (2001), Gaventa (1982), Goodwin, Jasper & Polletta (2001), Gould (2003), Hercus (1999), and Jasper (1998) describe emotions' role in social movements.

105. Mahoney's (2000) discussions of path dependence featuring institutional resistance to change (see also McAdam 1983) during social movements relies heavily on Giddens's (1979) dualistic analysis of structure and agency.

CHAPTER 3   RESOURCE EQUALIZATION AND CITIZENSHIP RIGHTS

1. Anderson (1988), Barnhouse Walters, James & McCammon (1997), Shujaa (1994), Tyack (1974), Watkins (2001), Watkins, Lewis & Chou (2001), and Woodson (1933) describe resource-poor schools' role in denying citizenship to African Americans.

2. Throughout this chapter, I analyze activists' statements to interpret their identity conceptions. Therefore, definitions of key terms are useful. Activists often use both narratives and discourses to generate collective action frames. Narratives

are the stories people tell about themselves and their relationships to others that often involve elements of each group culture, history, practices, and memory to make sense of, and are necessary for them to act in, their lives. Therefore, narratives, particularly those articulated during social movements, allow us to identify different aspects of mobilizing groups' perceptions of their identities (Somers 1992, 1994; Taylor & Whittier 1992; Tilly 2002; Whitebrook 2001). Discourses are "relatively bounded set[s] of arguments organized around a specific diagnosis of and solution to some social problem . . . situated within a field of debate wherein speakers struggle with one another to establish meaning, earn legitimacy, and mobilize consensus on belief and action" (Taylor & Whittier 1992: 107).

Collective action frames are the cognitive understandings, meanings, and rhetoric mobilized, produced, and disseminated during the course of social movements to attract new participants and target individuals and institutions to enact change (Snow & Benford 1992; Tarrow 1992). Mobilizing frames are those used to mobilize participants, from both within and external to their communities. Collective action and mobilizing frames often engage existing master frames, more general organizing schemata that are relevant to a wide variety of social movements and can be used over a long period of time (e.g., minority rights frames used during multiple movements in the 1960s) (Snow & Benford 1992; Tarrow 1998).

3. NYCMA, BoE, Box 2, Folder 13, Speaker #40, Jan. 17, 1957; *NY Times*, Nov. 7, 1915, 6; Schlesinger Library, Radcliffe Institute for Advanced Study, Harvard University, Polier Papers, Box 21, Folder 247, "Respondents' Memorandum, Statement of Facts," n.d. Young (1990: 25) describes rights as "institutionally defined rules specifying what people can do in relation to one another . . . social relationships that enable or constrain action." See Young (1990: 26) for definitions of opportunities as they relate to oppressed groups.

4. For African Americans' use of civil rights frames to acquire citizenship-based rights and resources, particularly in education, see Anderson (1988), Branch (1989), Cecelski (1994), Dougherty (2004), Morris (1984), Taylor (1997), and Walker (1996, 2000). Politicization of taken-for-granted rights and resources is central to mobilization of oppressed minorities seeking redistribution of resources (Young 1990).

5. Gunnar Myrdal's (1944) classic *American Dilemma* describes the fundamental contradiction of a society founded on democracy and equality while maintaining racial distinctions. According to Galston (1991: 221–224) and Kymlicka and Norman (2000: 7), civic virtues include: "(i) *general* virtues: courage; law-abidingness; loyalty; (ii) *social* virtues: independence; open-mindedness; (iii) *economic* virtues: work ethic, capacity to delay self-gratification; adaptability to economic and technological change; and (iv) *political* virtues: capacity to discern and respect the rights of others; willingness to demand only what can be paid for; ability to evaluate the performance of those in office; willingness to engage in public discourse."

6. *Globe*, Aug. 14, 1917, 13; NYCMA, BoE, Series 261, Box 1, Folder 8, Letter from Paul B. Zuber to Charles Silver, June 25, 1956; Box 2, Folder 13, Speaker #31, Jan. 17, 1957.

7. *Globe*, Aug. 14, 1917, 13.

8. NYCMA, BoE, Series 261, Box 2, Folder 13, Speaker #40, Jan. 17, 1957.

9. *Age*, Sept. 12, 1959, 1; *Amsterdam News*, Nov. 24, 1956, 1, 24; Jan. 12, 1960, 14; NYCMA, BoE, Series 261, Box 1, Folder 8, Letter from Paul B. Zuber to Charles H. Silver, June 25, 1956; Wagner Papers, Box 60, Folder 691, "Statement presented by Gloria Carter, PAAED at the Parents Meeting with Mayor Robert F. Wagner," July 11, 1957.

10. NYCMA, Mitchel Papers, Subject File, Box 206, Letter to Mitchel, Oct. 10, 1915; LOC,

Mitchel Papers, Box 17, Folder 1, Letter to Mitchel from Abraham Joffe, Oct. 10, 1917; NYCMA, BoE, Box 1, Folder 8, Letter from Zuber to Wagner, June 11, 1956.

11. *Amsterdam News*, July 20, 1957, 1, 8, 32; *Globe*, Oct. 18, 1917, 17; NYCMA, BoE, Series 261, Box 1, Folder 8, Letter to Wagner from Zuber, June 11, 1956.

12. Kymlicka (1995), Modood (2007), Shapiro & Kymlicka (1997), Taylor (1994), and Young (1990) conceptualize ideologies and describe practical implications of enacting multiculturalism in Western societies.

13. *Globe*, Jan. 24, 1916, school page, Nov. 30, 1915, 17, Dec. 1, 1915, 17.

14. *Globe*, Aug. 14, 1917, 13.

15. New York State Supreme Court, *Mallory v. Jansen*, petition to court, July 1957; Memorandum of Law: Statement of Facts submitted by Zuber, Aug. 6, 1958.

16. *Age*, Mar. 7, 1959, 1, Jan. 24, 1959, 1.

17. NYCMA, BoE, Series 261, Box 1, Folder 8, Letter from Paul B. Zuber to Mayor Wagner, June 11, 1956; *Age*, Sept. 12, 1959, 1.

18. *AH*, Oct. 22, 1915, 680–681.

19. Ibid, *Globe*, Oct. 4, 1915, school page, Nov. 20, 1915, 1.

20. *Globe*, Apr. 10, 1916, school page; *NY Times*, Nov. 25, 1915, 15.

21. *Globe*, Oct. 6, 1915, school page, Nov. 19, 1915, school page, Nov. 20, 1915, 1, 17.

22. *AH*, Oct. 22, 1915, 680–681; *Globe*, Nov. 20, 1915, 1; *NY Times*, Nov. 10, 1915, 7.

23. New York State Supreme Court, *Mallory v. Jansen*, petition to court, July 1957; Memorandum of Law: Statement of Facts submitted by Zuber, Aug. 6, 1958.

24. NYCMA, BoE, Box 2, Folder 13, Speaker #31, Jan. 17, 1957.

25. *Globe*, Oct. 18, 1917, 17; NYCMA, BoE, Series 261, Box 2, Folder 14, Speakers #33 and #38, Jan. 17, 1957; Box 2, Folder 13, Speaker #31, Jan. 17, 1957.

26. *Globe*, Mar. 28, 1916, school page; *Age*, July 12, 1958, 8, Dec. 20, 1958, 1, Feb. 14, 1959, 8, Nov. 28, 1959, 1; *Amsterdam News*, Dec. 6, 1958, 10, Dec. 20, 1958, 1, 25, Jan. 10, 1959, 1.

27. *BDE*, May 8, 1917, 18; *Globe*, Sept. 21, 1917, 15, Oct. 18, 1917, 17; *NY Times*, Dec. 6, 1915, 8.

28. NYCMA, BoE, Box 2, Folder 13, Speaker #33, Jan. 17, 1957.

29. CORE Papers, "Race and the Schools," Council for Civic Unity, Sept. 5, 1962; *Amsterdam News*, Jan. 10, 1959, 1, 7, 16, Feb. 8, 1958, 25; *Crisis*, Apr. 1962.

30. *Amsterdam News*, July 20, 1957, 1, 32.

31. *Age*, May 31, 1958, 2; *Amsterdam News*, July 20, 1957, 1, 32; *NY Times*, July 12, 1957, 13.

32. *Age*, Dec. 26, 1959, 1; Schlesinger Library, Radcliffe Institute for Advanced Study, Harvard University, Polier Papers, Box 20, Folder 244, "Minutes in the Matter of Skipwith heard by Hon. Justine Wise Polier in Bronx Children's Court," Nov. 7, 1958.

33. *Amsterdam News*, Jan. 18, 1958, 23, Jan. 25, 1958, 23.

34. NYCMA, BoE, Box 2, Folder 13, Speaker #57, Jan. 17, 1957.

35. *Globe*, Jan. 15, 1916, school page, Jan. 21, 1916, school page, Mar. 22, 1916, school page.

36. *Globe*, Sept. 7, 1917, 13, Oct. 12, 1917, 15.

37. *BDE*, Jan. 11, 1917, 22.

38. *BDE*, Jan. 18, 1917, 10.

39. For Jewish and African American delinquency see Brumberg (1986), Greer (1972), Moore (1981), Ravitch (2000), Rogers (1968), Taylor (1997), and Tyack (1974). Many Jewish youth saw involvement with Jewish mafia as a path out of ghetto poverty and toward financial success. The same became true for African American youth forty years later when they joined gangs that ran the "numbers" and the drug trade.

40. *AH*, Sept. 3, 1915, 442.

41. *AH*, Oct. 22, 1915, 680–681, Dec. 3, 1915, 100–101.

42. *HS*, Nov. 12, 1915, 10-B, Dec. 10, 1915, 2, 14, 15.

43. *BDE*, Jan. 8, 1916, 3; *Globe*, Nov. 30, 1915, 17; Dec. 13, 1915, school page.

44. For the necessity of culturally engaged teachers for minority children see Foster (1994, 1995), Hale (2001), King (1991), and Ladson-Billings (1992, 1994). Dougherty (2004) provides wide-ranging descriptions of teachers in African American schools in northern cities while Taylor (1997) focuses on NYC.

45. NYCMA, BoE, Series 261, Box 2, Folder 13, Speaker #38, Jan. 17, 1957.

46. NYCMA, BoE, Box 1, Folder 8, Letter to Charles Sliver from Paul Zuber and PCBE, June 25, 1956.

47. "X" schools contained 90 percent or more African American and Puerto Rican students in the 1955 PEA Report. Domestic Relations Court of the City of New York, Children's Court Division, New York County, In the Matter of Charlene Skipwith and Another, 180 N.Y.S. 2d 852; NYCMA, BoE, Series 261, Box 4, Folder 31, *Report to the Commission on Integration, Board of Education, City of New York by the Sub-Commission on Teachers Assignments and Personnel*, Dec. 7, 1956; Schlesinger Library, Radcliffe Institute for Advanced Study, Harvard University Polier Papers, Box 20, Folder 244, "Minutes in the Matter of Skipwith heard by Hon. Justine Wise Polier in Bronx Children's Court," Nov. 7, 1958.

48. NYCMA, BoE, Series 261, Box 2, Folder 13, Speakers #31 and 38, Jan. 17, 1957; *Age*, May 31, 1958, 2, July 12, 1958, 8, Dec. 20, 1958, 1, 4; Sept. 12, 1959, 1, 5; Sept. 19, 1959, 1,15; *Amsterdam News*, July 20, 1957, 1, 32, Aug. 31, 1957, 1,15, Jan. 18, 1958, 23, Jan. 25, 1958, 1,4,7, Feb. 8, 1958, 25, Oct. 4, 1958, 2, Nov. 15, 1958, 1, 36, Nov. 22, 1958, 1, 11, Jan. 10, 1959, 1, 16, May 23, 1959, 1, 9, May 21, 1960, 6.

49. NYCMA, BoE, Box 2, Folder 14, Speaker #40, Jan. 17, 1957.

50. Advocates of multiculturalism (Kymlicka 1995; Modood 2007; Young 1990) agree that marginalized groups' representation in governmental bodies is essential to promoting equality.

51. *Globe*, Apr. 8, 1916, 12, Oct. 17, 1917, 17.

52. *Amsterdam News*, May 31 1958, 24; *Globe*, Mar. 22, 1916, school page; Aug. 14, 1917, 13.

53. *Globe*, Jan. 24, 1916, school page.

54. *Globe*, Aug. 14, 1917, 13, Aug. 16, 1917, 13; *AH*, Dec. 3, 1915, 100–101.

55. NYCMA, BoE, Series 261, Box 1, Folder 8, Letter from Zuber to Wagner, June 11, 1956; *Amsterdam News*, Feb. 8, 1958, 25.

56. Schooling "is a process *intended* to perpetuate and maintain the society's existing power relations and the institutional structures that support those arrangements" (Shujaa 1994: 15, emphasis in original).

57. Marshall (1965: 78) defines civil and social citizenship as, respectively, "the rights necessary—for individual freedom—liberty of the person, freedom of speech, thought, and faith, the right to own property and to conclude valid contracts, and the right to justice" and "the whole range from the right to a modicum of economic welfare and security to the right to share to the fill in the social heritage and to live the life of a civilized being according to the standards prevailing in the society." Political citizenship is "the right to participate in the exercise of political power, as a member of a body invested with political authority, or as an elector of the members of such a body."

58. Gerstle (2001), Goldberg (1993), and Feagin (2001) explicate the deeply rooted structures of racism in American society and culture. Racial nationalism is essential to reinforcing these ideologies.

59. Young (1990) describes these elements as critical to achieving social justice and equality for marginalized groups.

60. Alexander (2001), Gamson (1992), Kubal (1998), and Scott (1990) describe disadvantaged groups' use of culturally resonant frames to generate mobilization.

61. See Scott (1990) for marginalized groups' use of hidden transcripts and Somers (1995) regarding reconciling multiple identities during social movements.

62. Discursive resources are "the cultural narratives and metaphors that social actors exploit in their public representations as well as the contesting ideological stances that they take on themes and issues on the political agenda" (Hobson 1999, 159). See Feagin (2001), Fredrickson (1971), and Takaki (2000) for superior analyses of America's *herrenvolk* democracy's reservation of citizenship rights for whites.

63. *Globe*, Nov. 30, 1915, 17.

CHAPTER 4   CONTESTING CURRICULUM

1. *Amsterdam News*, Jan. 12, 1946, 1, Feb. 2, 1946, 1, Feb. 9, 1946, 10, Feb. 15, 1947, 5; *NY Times*, Feb. 18, 1946, 10.

2. Jewish students regularly encountered anti-Semitic images in English books and absence from history books during this period (cf. Brumberg 1986; Fitzgerald 1979).

3. *American Hebrew*, July 6, 1923, 155; Lapson 1941.

4. Note that Hebrew's former champion, Joseph Barondess, passed away this same year. YIVO, Judah Pilch Papers, Record Group 1145, Box 1, Folder 1, *Avukah Annual of 1928*, 11–12; *Jewish Daily Bulletin*, Jan. 11, 1929, 3; *JDB*, May 3, 1929, 5; organizations included Agudath Hamorim, Histadruth Ivrit, Intercollegiate Menorah Association, Jewish Institute of Religion, Jewish Teachers Association, Yeshiva School for Teachers and Young Judaea. Avukah, a student organization promoting Zionism, affiliated with the Intercollegiate Menorah Association, enrolled high school and college students (*Encyclopaedia Judaica* [vol. 15] 1971: 450). Histadruth Ivrit encouraged "the knowledge and use of the Hebrew language, the publication of Hebrew books and periodicals, and an interest in Hebrew culture" (*Encyclopaedia Judaica* [vol. 8] 1971: 543). Young Judaea, a national youth organization affiliated with the Zionist Organization of America, promoted Zionism and the "mental, moral, and physical development of Jewish youth" (*Encyclopaedia Judaica* [vol. 16] 1971: 861).

5. The committee to address educational authorities included Judge Otto Rosalsky (chair), Dr. Samson Benderly, Bernard Deautch, Judge Benjamin Marvin, Nathan D. Perlman, Nathan Straus Jr., and Rabbi Stephen S. Wise. The curriculum committee included Dr. Nisson Touroff, professor of Hebrew Literature at the Jewish Institute of Religion (chair); Dr. Mordecai Kaplan, principal of the Jewish Teacher's Institute; Dr. Ralph Marcus, instructor at Columbia University; Dr. Harry A. Wolfson, professor of Jewish Philosophy and Literature at Harvard; and Rabbi Morton Berman (secretary). Mordecai Kaplan, rabbi and graduate of the Jewish Theological Seminary, founded the Society for the Advancement of Judaism (SAJ) in 1922. Kaplan believed that "American Jews really lived in two worlds, one American and one Jewish. The two worlds had to fit together, which meant that Judaism had to adapt to American conditions." Kaplan and the SAJ sought to modernize Judaism through new rituals alongside traditional religious elements (Diner 2003: 82).

6. *AH*, June 2, 1930, 938, June 9, 1930, 962; AJHS, JSO, Box 1, Folder 48, "Hebrew in the High Schools," *The Young Judaean*, Vol. 20, No. 5, May 1930, Box 40, Young Judean Folder, *Young Judaean*, Vol. 20, No. 5, May 1930, 1, Box 2, Avukah Student Action Folder, *The Bulletin*, Vol. 2, No. 2, Nov. 1930, 6; *NY Times*, June 26, 1930, 31, Lapson 1941.

7. AJHS, SSW Papers, William R. Kelley, Letter to Israel S. Chipkin, Apr. 13, 1931; Chipkin, Letter to Stephen S. Wise, Apr. 20, 1931; Gabriel R. Mason, Letter to Wise, Nov. 20, 1931.

8. AJHS, SSW Papers, Chipkin, Letters to Wise, Nov. 11, 1931, Nov. 17, 1931; Gabriel R. Mason, Letter to Wise, Nov. 20, 1931, Robinson, Letter to Wise, Feb. 12, 1932.

9. AJHS, SSW Papers, "Minutes of Conference at Brooklyn College," Mar. 3, 1932; George M. Wiley, Letter to Wise, Aug. 24, 1932; Chipkin, Letter to Wise, Nov. 28, 1932.

10. AJHS, SSW Papers, Chipkin, Letters to Wise, June 27, 1932, Jan 24, 1933, Jan. 31, 1933; May 29, 1934; Joseph J. Klein, Letter to Frederick B. Robinson, Feb. 15, 1937; Joseph J. Klein, Letter to Chipkin, Feb. 18, 1937. See Gorelick 1981 for Jews in City College.

11. AJHS, SSW Papers, Wise, Letter to Robert B. Brodie, May 5, 1933.

12. AJHS, SSW Papers, Chipkin, Letters to Wise, Nov. 28, 1932, Dec. 27, 1932, Jan. 9, 1933.

13. AJHS, SSW Papers, Chipkin, Letter to Wise, June 21, 1932, Letters to Campbell, Dec. 1, 1933, Dec. 7, 1933; Lapson 1941.

14. AJHS, SSW Papers, "Minutes of Conference Held at the Office of Dr. George M. Wiley of the State Department of Education at Albany, N.Y. on Monday Afternoon, January 16th, at 2:15 p.m.," Jan. 16, 1933.

15. AJHS, SSW Papers, Frank P. Graves, Letter to Wise, Jan. 19, 1933.

16. AJHS, SSW Papers, "Memorandum Concerning the Reinstatement of Hebrew by the New York State Board of Examinations," Nov. 27, 1933; Campbell, Letter to Wiley, Dec. 1, 1933; Wiley, Letter to Wise, Dec. 4, 1933; Chipkin, Letters to Wise, Dec. 5, 1933, Dec. 7, 1933; Wise, Letter to Chipkin, Dec. 22, 1933.

17. AJHS, BJE, Box 2, Folder 18, "Hebrew in High Schools Makes Progress." *Jewish Education News,* Vol. 3, 1934, 2, SSW Papers, No Author, Letter to Wise, 5 Mar. 1934; Wise, Letter to Graves, Mar. 7, 1934.

18. AJHS, SSW Papers, Chipkin, Letter to Wise, Nov. 28, 1932; Benjamin Veit, Letter to Chipkin, Jan. 5, 1934, Chipkin, Letter to Veit, Jan. 9, 1934.

19. AJHS, BJE, Box 2, Folder 18, "Hebrew in High Schools Makes Progress." *Jewish Education News,* 1934, 2; "New Text for Hebrew in High School," *Jewish Education News,* Sept. 4, 1936, 3; Chipkin 1937; Jewish Theological Seminary (JTS), Record Group 12 (RG12), Series 1, Box 1, Folder 19, Registrar of the Israel S. Friedlander Classes, Letter to Arthur A. Gladstone, Nov. 7, 1935, Courtesy of The Joseph and Miriam Ratner Center for the Study of Conservative Judaism, The Library of The Jewish Theological Seminary.

20. AJHS, BJE, Box 2, Folder 18, "Progress of Hebrew in the Public High Schools and Colleges," *Jewish Education News,* 1935, 3; "Teachers of N.Y. Public Schools Cooperating with JEA," *Jewish Education News* 1936, 2; SSW Papers, Benderly, Letter to Wise, Feb. 12, 1935; Chipkin, Letter to Mordecai Kaplan, May 8, 1936; JTS, RG12, Series 1, Box 1, Folder 13, Charles Ozer, Letters to Chipkin, Jan. 8, 1937, Jan. 18, 1937; Chipkin, Letter to Ozer, Jan. 13, 1937, Courtesy of The Joseph and Miriam Ratner Center for the Study of Conservative Judaism, The Library of The Jewish Theological Seminary. The Jewish Teachers Association became the American Association of Teachers of Hebrew with thirty-three members in 1941 (Lapson 1941).

21. AJHS, SSW Papers, Gabriel Mason, Letter to Avery Skinner, Nov. 21, 1935; Avery Skinner, Letter to Mason, Nov. 26, 1935; Chipkin, Letter to Wise, Jan 6, 1936; Wise, Letter to Chipkin, Jan. 7, 1936.

22. AJHS, SSW Papers, Chipkin, Letter to Wise, Dec. 3, 1935; Wise, Letters to Chipkin, Dec. 10, 1935, Apr. 6, 1937; Wise, Letters to Susan Brandeis, Dec. 10, 1935, Mar. 23, 1937; Wise, Letters to Frank P. Graves, Nov. 14, 1938, Dec. 16, 1938; Graves, Letter to Wise, Nov. 19, 1938; Wise, Letter to Brandeis, Dec. 16, 1938; Chipkin, Notes Regarding

Conference with Dr. Harold G. Campbell at the Board of Education on Thursday Afternoon, June 17th, at 5:00 p.m.," June 16, 1937.

23. AJHS, SSW Papers, Benderly, Letter to Wise, Dec. 19, 1934; Wise, Letter to Ralph Marcus, Jan. 7, 1935; Chipkin, Letter to Wise, Apr. 20, 1934, Wise, Letter to Chipkin, Mar. 2, 1936; Wise, Letter to W. J. Albright, Mar. 26, 1936; Wise, Letter to Charles Torrey, Mar. 26, 1936; Wise, Letter to John Dewey, Mar. 27, 1936; Wise, Letter to William Heard Kilpatrick, Mar. 27, 1936; Kilpatrick, Letter to Wise, Apr. 2, 1936.

24. NYCMA, BoE, Series 755, VF 409, "Junior High School Division Circular No. 42, 1935–1936," Apr. 24, 1936; AJHS, JSO, Edward Horowitz, "Hebrew in the New York High Schools," *The Young Judaean*, Feb. 1938, 4, 14; SSW Papers, Benderly, Letters to Wise, Feb. 12, 1935, Apr. 9, 1935; Chipkin, Letters to Wise, May 29, 1934, Oct. 23, 1935, Apr. 7, 1937, May 26, 1937; Mary Beldon James Lehn, Letter to Gabriel Mason, Oct. 9, 1935; Norma Baxt, Letter to Chipkin, Oct. 21, 1935.

25. New members included Harry H. Liebovitz, president of the JEA; Gabriel Hamburger, president of Ivriah; and James Waterman Wise, Rabbi Wise's son and communist and Zionist author. AJHS, SSW Papers, Wise, Letter to Julius Fischbach, Dec. 23, 1936; Chipkin, Letters to Wise, Dec. 22, 1936, May 26, 1937; Chipkin, Letter to Joseph Klein, Feb. 18, 1937; Wise, Letter to Mark Eisner, Mar. 23, 1937.

26. AJHS, BJE, Box 1, Folder 2, "Hebrew in the Public Schools," *Jewish Education to the Fore: Facts and Figures of the Work of the Jewish Education Association, NY*. New York: JEA, 1937, 16–17; JSO, "Learn Hebrew," *The Young Judaean*, Apr. 8, 1937, 10; "Learn Hebrew," *The Young Judaean*, Oct. 2, 1937, 10; Edward Horowitz, "Hebrew in the New York High Schools," *The Young Judaean*, Feb. 1938, 4, 14; Lapson 1945, 11.

27. AJHS, JSO, "Further Progress in High School Study of Hebrew Language," *The Young Judaean*, Apr. 2, 1939, 3; BJE, Box 1, Folder 2, *President's Report for Year Ending April 30, 1938, Annual Report of Jewish Education Association, Submitted by Harry H. Liebovitz, President*, 14–15; BoE, Series 755, Box 79, Folder 409, *Enrollment in the Different Foreign Languages in Senior High Schools as of March 1, 1939*; Box 74, Folder VF 409 NYC, 1933–1952; Benjamin Veit, Letter and Junior High School Division Circular No. 42, 1935–36, Apr. 24, 1936. By 1951, the majority of these colleges included Hebrew curriculum in their catalogs.

28. AJHS, BJE, Box 3, Folder 33, Judah Lapson, *Hebrew in the High Schools and Colleges*, n.d.; *NY Times*, June 22, 1942, 13, Aug. 26, 1947, 28; June 24, 1948, 27, July 29, 1948, 18.

29. *NY Times*, June 19, 1948, 17. Zimmermann (2002a) finds the road to inclusion for other European ethnic groups easier to travel than for Jews in NYC. However, upon its inclusion, these groups often found enrollment lacking, similar to Hebrew.

30. See Woodson (1990 [1933]) and his columns in the *Age* and *Amsterdam News* between 1930 and 1934, and Goggin (1997).

31. *Amsterdam News*, Jan. 12, 1946, 1, Feb 2, 1946, 1, Feb. 9, 1946, 10.

32. *Amsterdam News*, Feb. 15, 1947, 5.

33. *Age*, Feb. 9, 1946, 5; *Amsterdam News*, Feb. 9, 1946, 5, Mar. 9, 1946, 5, 8.

34. *Age*, Jan. 12, 1946, 5, Feb. 14, 1948, 5, Mar. 6, 1948, 5; *Amsterdam News*, Jan. 5, 1946, 2, Jan. 10, 1948, 8, Feb. 7, 1948, 1, Feb. 14, 1948, 5, Mar. 6, 1948, 5, Feb. 12, 1949, 31, Feb. 19, 1949, 17, May 7, 1955, 1

35. *Age*, Jan. 30, 1954, 10; *Amsterdam News*, Feb. 18, 1950, 14.

36. *Age*, Feb. 8, 1947, 81, Mar. 6, 1948, 5; *Amsterdam News*, Feb. 15, 1947, 25, Mar. 1, 1947, 4, Feb. 7, 1948, 1, 25, Feb. 12, 1949, 31, Feb. 19, 1949, 17.

37. *Age*, Mar. 9, 1946, 5; *Amsterdam News*, May 4, 1946, 5, Oct. 11, 1947, 7, Feb. 26, 1949, 1, 11, 23.

38. Created in 1935, the Harlem Committee of the Teachers Union provided teachers with African American history material. A special office contained books and bibliographies for children and adults and articles, pamphlets, posters, scripts for plays, skits, radio programs, and assembly ideas (Zitron 1968: 102); examples cited from the TU's pamphlet appeared in: Glen Moon, *Story of Our Land and People* (New York: Holt, 1944); Herbert Townsend, *Our America* (Boston: Allyn & Bacon, 1944).

39. NYCMA, BoE, Series 562, Box 4, Folder 32, "Texts on the 1950–1951 Board of Education Approved Textbook List Containing Objectionable Material against Minority Groups," June 1, 1951, 1–2.

40. *Age*, June 2, 1951, 2; *Amsterdam News*, Feb. 3, 1951, 5.

41. *Amsterdam News*, May 5, 1956, 6.

42. *Age*, Mar. 25, 1950, 15; *Amsterdam News*, Mar. 18, 1950, B1–9.

43. *Amsterdam News*, Jan. 21, 1950, 1.

44. *Amsterdam News*, Jan. 26, 1952, 6, Mar. 14, 1953, 16, Mar. 28, 1953, 18.

45. *Amsterdam News*, May 11, 1957, 36.

46. *Distant Lands*, 229 cited in ibid.; *Age*, May 25, 1957, 26.

47. *Age*, Oct. 5, 1946, 2; *Amsterdam News*, Feb. 15, 1947, 21, Oct. 26, 1963, 21.

48. *Amsterdam News*, Oct. 26, 1963, 21.

49. *Amsterdam News*, July 12, 1947, 1, Mar. 25, 1950, 15.

50. *Amsterdam News*, Mar. 4, 1961, 16, Oct. 10, 1959, 38.

51. *Age*, Jan. 17, 1959, 3, Jan. 31, 1959, 4; *Amsterdam News*, May 2, 1959, 2, June 13, 1959, 19, July 4, 1959, 2; *NY Times*, Jan. 13, 1959, 14.

52. *Amsterdam News*, Aug. 3, 1963, 8; CORE Papers, *Negro History Guide for Teachers* (New York: Interborough Negro History Committee, 1963).

53. *Amsterdam News*, Mar. 5, 1960, 12, Feb. 18, 1961, 7, Mar. 4, 1961, 6, 18.

54. *Amsterdam News*, Mar. 4, 1961, 16, June 10, 1961, 37; Dec. 23, 1961, 26, 34.

55. *Amsterdam News*, Feb. 11, 1961, 19, May 13, 1961, 21; CORE Papers, *A Report on the Treatment of Minorities in Elementary School Text Books* (New York: Brooklyn, May 1961), 2.

56. *Amsterdam News*, Nov. 18, 1961, 1, Feb. 17, 1962, 8, Jan. 13, 1962, 10, June 8, 1963, 10.

57. *Amsterdam News*, Oct. 26, 1963, 21, Mar. 14, 1964, 10; Zimmerman 2002b, 115.

58. *Amsterdam News*, Apr. 25, 1959, 1; *NY Times*, Apr. 19, 1959, E11; NYCMA, BoE, Series 755; Vertical File 261, Folder 48, "Policy Statement in Re: The Inclusion of representation of Non-White Individuals in Textbook Illustrations," Apr. 14, 1959.

59. *Amsterdam News*, Oct. 27, 1962, 23, Mar 23, 1963, 29; *NY Times*, Oct. 18, 1962, 41.

60. *Amsterdam News*, Sept. 25, 1960, 25, Nov. 20, 1960, 33, Jan. 7, 1961, 27, Apr. 1, 1961, 18, Apr. 29, 1961, 20, May 6, 1961, 24, Dec. 16, 1961, 30, July 6, 1963, 42, Apr. 25, 1964, 29.

61. *Amsterdam News*, Jan. 27, 1962, 40, June 22, 1963, 35, Oct. 12, 1963, 37, Oct. 19, 1963, 35.

62. *Amsterdam News*, Feb. 9, 1963, 28, Mar. 9, 1963, 29, Mar. 23, 1963, 29.

63. *Amsterdam News*, Feb. 3, 1962, 19, Feb. 22, 1964, 25.

64. *Amsterdam News*, May 17, 1958, 8, Dec. 20, 1958, 44.

65. *Amsterdam News*, Feb. 8, 1958, 25, Aug. 24, 1963, 1, Dec. 12, 1964, 34; *NY Times*, June 19, 1963, 21.

66. NYCMA, BoE, Series 565, Box 5, Folder 1, "Report on the Conference on Integration in the New York City Public Schools," May 3, 1963.

67. SCRBC, HANA, Box 6, Folder 8, "Memo to Committee Chairman, and Members of Steering Committee from Co-Chairman re: Follow-Up of General Meeting on 11 Nov. 1963," Nov. 12, 1963, "Pace Newsletter," Dec. 1963, "Statement on the Board of Education's Interim report on School Integration, Prepared and Delivered by Parents

Action Committee for Equality, Presented by Lemoine P. Callendar, Co-Chairman of PACE," Jan. 13, 1964.

68. *Amsterdam News*, Dec. 12, 1959, 1, Dec. 19, 1964, 41.

69. *Amsterdam News*, Jan. 25, 1964, 6, Feb. 1, 1964, 29, Feb. 8, 1964, 7, 23, 42.

70. *Amsterdam News*, June 30, 1964, 12, Oct. 17, 1964, 21; *NY Times*, Oct. 4, 1964, E9.

71. *Amsterdam News*, Oct. 17, 1964, 33, Nov. 14, 1964, 35.

72. *NY Times*, Dec. 27, 1964, 64.

73. SCRBC, Council on Interracial Books for Children, Directors Record, Finding Aid Folder, Description of Organization, undated.

74. See McAdam, Tarrow and Tilly (2001) for transgressive contentious politics and social movement mechanisms.

75. Aminzade & McAdam (2001), Gould (2003). Jasper (1998), and Goodwin, Jasper & Polletta's edited volume (2001) highlight the central role of emotions during social movements. See McCarthy and Zald (1973) and Tarrow (1998) for mobilizing structures' impact on protest generation.

76. See Tarrow (1998) for changing dynamics and tactical innovations during protest cycles.

77. See Calhoun (1994) for potential problems activists encounter during social movements featuring identity politics.

78. Schools often see parents as non-experts with regard to their children's education (Binder 1999; Stern 1997; Weiner 2009).

79. Champagne (1993) describes the importance of historical context to movement trajectories and outcomes.

80. See Gaventa (1982) for targets' use of acquiescence to stem protest and inhibit change.

CHAPTER 5   MULTICULTURAL CURRICULUM, REPRESENTATION, AND GROUP IDENTITIES

1. Fitzgerald (1979), Katz (1970), Loewen (1996), and Zimmerman (2002) address textbooks' obscuration of minorities' role in American history through inaccuracy and absence. For curriculum's role in maintaining racial meanings see Giroux (1997, 1992, 1985), Giroux & McLaren (1986), Hall (1995), McCarthy (1998), and Pinar (1993).

2. Taylor (1992) and Young (1990) argue that withholding recognition is central to oppression.

3. See Cook & Cook (1954), DuBois (1984), McGee Banks (1996), Montalto (1982), Taba, Brady & Robinson (1952), and Taba & Wilson (1946) for historical, and Banks (1996) for contemporary, minority efforts to align school-based ideologies with their own cultures. For contemporary minorities' parallel institutions, see Dove (1994), Gibson (1988), and Schecter, Sharkin-Taboada & Bayley (1979).

4. See Brumberg (1986), Greer (1972), Nasaw (1979), and Tyack (1974) for the schools' assimilatory Americanization efforts. Difference is socially constructed by populations in opposition to something considered to be "normal" and is therefore "always a product of history, culture, power, and ideology" (McLaren 1994: 53; also Bhabha 1992; Mercer 1992; Mohanty 1991; Zavarzadeh & Morton 1990). McLaren (1994) describes distinctions between critical, and other forms of, multiculturalism and this curriculum's potential to promote social justice. Kymlicka (1995) argues that preservation of societal culture is a central goal of multiculturalism.

5. These theoretical discussions of multiculturalism are guided by Kymlicka (1995), Modood (2007), Taylor (1994), and Young (1990).

6. Cultural citizenship is "the right to maintain cultures and languages differing from the dominant ones without losing civil or political rights or membership in the national community" (Glenn 2002: 54). See Binder (1999: 229, 243) and Raz (1994) for contemporary multicultural efforts.

7. AJHS, SSW, Stephen S. Wise, Letter to George M. Wiley, Jan. 10, 1933; "Memorandum Concerning the Reinstatement of Hebrew by the New York State Board of Examinations," Nov. 27, 1933; "Minutes of Conference Held at the Office of Dr. George M. Wiley of the State Department of Education at Albany, N.Y. on Monday Afternoon, January 16th, at 2:15 p.m.," Jan. 16, 1933; Israel S. Chipkin, Letter to Stephen S. Wise, Jan. 9, 1933; NYCMA, BoE, Series 755, Vertical File 409.1, Folder 74, "Junior High School Division Circular No. 42, 1935–36," Apr. 24, 1936.

8. AJHS, BJE, Box 3, Folder 33, Judah Lapson, *Hebrew in New York High Schools and Colleges*, n.d.; SSW, "Memorandum Concerning the Reinstatement of Hebrew by the New York State Board of Examinations," Nov. 27, 1933; "Memorandum I: Objections to the Study of Hebrew in the Public Schools," Mar. 5, 1930, JSO, Box 49, Folder "Young Judaean," *Young Judaean*, Feb. 1938, 4; JTS, RG12, Series 1, Box 1, Folder 14, Chipkin, "Hebrew in the Public High Schools," n.d. Courtesy of The Joseph and Miriam Ratner Center for the Study of Conservative Judaism, The Library of The Jewish Theological Seminary; *AH*, June 9, 1930, 962; *NY Times*, June 22, 1942, 13, June 24, 1948, 27.

9. YIVO, Judah Pilch Papers, Record Group 1145, Box 1, Folder 1, *Avukah Annual of 1928*, 11–12; AJHS, BJE, Box 2, Folder 18, *Jewish Education News*, No. 9, June 1935, 2; SSW, "Memorandum Concerning the Reinstatement of Hebrew by the New York State Board of Examinations," Nov. 27, 1933, 3; BJE, Box 1, Folder 2, Jewish Education Association, *Jewish Education to the Fore: Facts and Figures of the Work of the Jewish Education Association, NY*, 1937; Box 2, Folder 18, "Further Progress in High School Study of Hebrew Language," *Jewish Education News*, Vol. 4, No. 2, Apr. 1939, 3; untitled list of oppositions to Hebrew, June 5, 1935; "Minutes of Conference Held at the Office of Dr. George M. Wiley of the State Department of Education at Albany, N.Y. on Monday Afternoon, January 16th, at 2:15 p.m.," Jan. 16, 1933; Chipkin, Letter to Wise, May 29, 1934; JTS, RG12, Series 1, Box 1, Folder 14, Chipkin, "Hebrew in the Public High Schools," n.d. Courtesy of The Joseph and Miriam Ratner Center for the Study of Conservative Judaism, The Library of The Jewish Theological Seminary; *American Hebrew*, July 9, 1932, 225.

10. AJHS, SSW, untitled list of oppositions to Hebrew, June 5, 1935; YIVO, Judah Pilch Papers, Record Group 1145, Box 1, Folder 1, *Avukah Annual of 1928*, 11–12.

11. *Amsterdam News*, Feb. 9, 1946, 10, Mar. 22, 1952, 16. See Zimmerman (2004) for positive effects of multiethnic texts.

12. *Amsterdam News*, Jan. 13, 1962, 10, Nov. 18, 1961, 1, emphasis added.

13. *Age*, June 2, 1951, 2, *Amsterdam News*, May 24, 1947, 10, Jan. 21, 1950, 1, Feb. 18, 1950, 14.

14. *Age*, Oct. 5, 1946, 2, Oct. 31, 1959, 8; *Amsterdam News*, Mar. 14, 1953, 15, 16, Mar. 28, 1953, 18.

15. *Amsterdam News*, May 24, 1947, 10, June 21, 1958, 19, Feb. 11, 1961, 19, May 13, 1961, 21; CORE Papers, *The Treatment of Minorities in Elementary School Text Books*, May 1961.

16. *Amsterdam News*, Feb. 18, 1950, 14.

17. For links between recognition of identity and resource inequality see Blum (1998), Fraser (1998), Hobson (2003), Kymlicka & Norman (2000), and Young (1990, 1998).

18. AJHS, SSW, "Memorandum Concerning the Reinstatement of Hebrew by the New

York State Board of Examinations," Nov. 27, 1933, 3; Gabriel R. Mason, Letter to Avery Skinner, Nov. 21, 1935; JTS, RG12, Series 1, Box 1, Folder 14, "Hebrew in the Public Schools," n.d. Courtesy of The Joseph and Miriam Ratner Center for the Study of Conservative Judaism, The Library of The Jewish Theological Seminary; *AH*, June 9, 1930, 962.

19. *Amsterdam News*, May 24, 1947, 10; *Age*, Jan. 30, 1954, 10.

20. *Amsterdam News,* Jan. 26, 1952, 6, Feb. 8, 1958, 25.

21. *Amsterdam News*, June 8. 1963, 10.

22. JTS, RG12, Series 1, Box 1, Folder 14, Chipkin, "Hebrew in the Public High Schools," n.d. Courtesy of The Joseph and Miriam Ratner Center for the Study of Conservative Judaism, The Library of The Jewish Theological Seminary; CORE Papers, *The Treatment of Minorities in Elementary School Text Books*, May 1961, 2.

23. YIVO, Judah Pilch Papers, Record Group 1145, Box 1, Folder 1, *Avukah Annual of 1928*, 11–12; AJHS, BJE, Box 2, Folder 18, *Jewish Education News*, No. 9, June 1935, 2; SSW, Samson Benderly, Letter to Wise, May 4, 1933. See Johnson (2000), Malakof & Hakuta (1990), Molesky (1988), and Williams (1992) for language's centrality to cultural maintenance.

24. AJHS, SSW, Chipkin, Letter to Wise, June 27, 1932; YIVO, Judah Pilch Papers, Record Group 1145, Box 1, Folder 1, *Avukah Annual of 1928*, 11–12. A speech community is "characterized by regular and frequent interaction by means of a shared body of verbal signs and set off from similar [groups] by significant differences in language use" (Gumperz 1972: 219). See also Alba (1990), Anzaldúa (1987), Johnson (2000), Saville-Troike (1989), and Rabinowitz (1992) for Jewish education and cultural longevity.

25. AJHS, JSO, Box 48, Folder Young Judaean, 1930, *The Young Judaean*, May 1930, Vol. 20, No. 5, 1, 14; SSW, Harold G. Campbell, Letter to George M. Wiley, Dec. 1, 1933, *JDB*, May 7, 1929, 2.

26. *Amsterdam News*, Feb. 18, 1950, 14, Mar. 22, 1952, 16, Jan. 2, 1954, 12.

27. *Age*, Jan. 31, 1959, 4; *Amsterdam News*, Dec. 20, 1958, 44, Dec. 19, 1964, 41, emphasis added.

28. For negative connotations of "Negro" see Moore (1992). *Amsterdam News*, Nov. 10, 1959, 38, Sept. 23, 1961, 13.

29. YIVO, Judah Pilch Papers, Record Group 1145, Box 1, Folder 1, *Avukah Annual of 1928*, 11–12; AJHS, SSW, "Memorandum Concerning the Reinstatement of Hebrew by the New York State Board of Examinations," Nov. 27, 1933, 3; Wise, Letter to John Dewey, Mar. 27, 1936.

30. *Amsterdam News*, June 11, 1957, 36.

31. For critical multiculturalism, particularly Afrocentric curriculum, see Banks (1994), Binder (1999, 2002), Cross, Baker & Stiles (1977), Grant (1992), Nieto (1992), and Sleeter (1991). CORE Papers, *The Treatment of Minorities in Elementary School Text Books*, May 1961.

32. AJHS, SSW, "Excerpt from Mark Eisner's Speech Delivered at the Theater Rally, in the Forty-Eighth Street Theater on Monday Afternoon, February 29th, under the Auspices of Ivriah, the Women's Division of the Jewish Education Association," Feb. 29, 1932; W. F. Albright, Letter to Wise, Apr. 4, 1936.

33. *Jewish Daily Bulletin*, Jan. 11, 1929, 3; YIVO, Judah Pilch Papers, Record Group 1145, Box 1, Folder 1, *Avukah Annual of 1928*, 11–12; AJHS, BJE, Box 2, Folder 18, "Further Progress in High School Study of Hebrew Language," *Jewish Education News*, Vol. 4, No. 2, Apr. 1939, 3; SSW, "Excerpt from Mark Eisner's Speech," Feb. 29, 1932; Wise, Letter to Frank P. Graves, Dec. 6, 1934, Letter to John Dewey, Mar. 27, 1936; NYCMA, BoE,

Series 755, Vertical File 409.1, Folder 74, "Junior High School Division Circular No. 42, 1935–36," Apr. 24, 1936.

34. AJHS, BJE, Box 2, Folder 18, Otto Rosalsky, "The Mission of Jewish Education," *Jewish Education News*, Vol. 2, No. 3, May 1936, 5; Box 3, Folder 33, Judah Lapson, *Hebrew in New York High Schools and Colleges*, n.d; SSW, "Minutes of Conference Held at the Office of Dr. George M. Wiley," Jan. 16, 1933; JTS, RG12, Series 1, Box 1, Folder 12; Chipkin, Letter to Joshua Bloch, Apr. 29, 1936, Courtesy of The Joseph and Miriam Ratner Center for the Study of Conservative Judaism, The Library of The Jewish Theological Seminary.

35. *Amsterdam News*, Jan. 10, 1948, 8, Apr. 29, 1961, 10.

36. *Age* Sept. 12, 1959, 1; *Amsterdam News*, Feb. 8, 1958, 25, July 6, 1963, 42.

37. *Age*, Jan. 31, 1959, 4, Jan. 17, 1959, 3; *Amsterdam News*, June 21, 1958, 16; Aug. 3, 1963, 8.

38. *Amsterdam News*, Oct. 17, 1964, 21, 51; *NY Times*, Oct. 4, 1964, E9, Oct. 25, 1964, E9.

39. Henson acted as Robert E. Peary's servant on his 1909 expedition to the North Pole. Although contemporary works list Henson as a co-discoverer of the North Pole, books in the 1950s depicted him as a traditional manservant.

40. *Amsterdam News*, Oct. 17, 1964, 33.

41. See Akbar (1982), Anzaldua (1990), Apple (1990), Apple & Christian-Smith (1991), Bush (1999), Shujaa (1994), Solorzano (1997, 1998) for transformative knowledge's importance for subverting the dominant status quo.

42. AJHS, JSO, Box 48, Folder "Young Judean, 1937," "Learn Hebrew," *The Young Judaean*, Vol. 25, No. 8, Apr. 1937, 6, 10; *NY Times*, June 22, 1942, 13.

43. YIVO, Judah Pilch papers, Record Group 1145, Box 1, Folder 1, *Avukah Annual of 1928*, 11; AJHS, SSW, "Memorandum Concerning the Reinstatement of Hebrew by the New York State Board of Examinations," Nov. 27, 1933, 2; Robert B. Brodie, Letter to Wise, May 5, 1933; untitled list of oppositions to Hebrew, June 5, 1935.

44. AJHS, JSO, Box 49, Folder: Young Judaean, 1938–1939, Edward Horowitz, "Hebrew in the New York High Schools," *The Young Judaean*, Feb. 1938, 4, 14.

45. AJHS, BJE, Box 2, Folder 18, *Jewish Education News*, Vol. 2, No. 4, Sept. 1936, 3; Box 3, Folder 33, Judah Lapson, *Hebrew in New York High Schools and Colleges*, New York: Jewish Education Committee, n.d.; JSO, Box 49, Folder: Young Judaean, 1938–1939, Edward Horowitz, "Hebrew in the New York High Schools," *The Young Judaean*, Feb. 1938, 4, 14; Lapson 1941.

46. Du Bois's (the "Father of Pan-Africanism") Pan-African Conferences in the early 1900s featured Africans who later become leaders of newly independent countries (Du Bois 1933; Gbadegesin 1996; Marable 1991, 1996; Von Eschen 1997).

47. *Amsterdam News*, Jan. 7, 1961, 27; Apr. 1, 1961, 18, Apr. 29, 1961, 20.

48. *Amsterdam News*, May 6, 1961, 24, Dec. 16, 1961, 30.

49. *Amsterdam News*, June 22, 1963, 35, Oct. 12, 1963, 37.

50. *Amsterdam News*, Oct. 19, 1963, 35.

51. *Amsterdam News*, Oct. 12, 1963, 37.

52. *Amsterdam News*, Oct. 26, 1963, 21.

53. Hebrew Schools in NYC ranged from *chederim*, similar to those in the Russian Pale, to large synagogue centers in modern brick buildings with swimming pools, basketball courts, and movie theatres. To enhance attendance, volunteers scoured Jewish neighborhoods, encouraging parents to enroll their children in classes or, at minimum, send their children to the centers for recreation (Goren 1970, 1986; Moore 1981; Rischin 1978). See Abramson (1971), Gordon (1964) Johnson (1985), and Waters (1990) for cultural retention and Dove (1994), Gibson (1988), Schecter, Sharkin-

Taboada & Bayley (1979), and Zhou & Bankston (1998) for parallel institutions' role in doing so. *Boston Globe*, June 12, 2008, 1.

54. Brotherhood Week, a weeklong program in the schools, usually coinciding with Negro History Week in February, encouraged, but did not require, teachers to explore different group cultures to improve intergroup relations. *Age*, Jan. 30, 1954, 10, *Amsterdam News*, Jan. 25, 1958, 4, Feb. 8, 1958, 25, June 17, 1958, 8.

55. *Age*, Sept. 12, 1959, 1; *Amsterdam News*, Feb. 8, 1964, 7, 42.

56. *Amsterdam News*, Mar. 4, 1961, 16, May 13, 1961, 10, Oct. 20, 1962, 42, Feb. 23, 1963, 27, Feb. 1, 1964, 29.

57. *Amsterdam News*, Dec. 20, 1958, 44, Nov. 20, 1960, 33, Sept. 24, 1960, 25. See Brookfield (1991), Coben (1998), Kincheloe (1998), Mayo (1999) and Von Eschen (1997) for contemporary discourse of Africa.

58. Hall (1996) and Omi & Winant (1994) describe differences between wars of maneuver, which occur inside social institutions, and wars of position, which occur outside institutions, to promote racial justice. See Outlaw (1998) for monoculture in education.

59. See especially Binder (1999) and Moya (2002) for contemporary efforts to rearticulate racial (and religious) identities in public schools. Postpositivist theories of identity highlight the importance of epistemic privilege in constructing disparaged identities (Anzaldúa 1987; Mohanty 1997; Moraga 1983; Moya 2002). See Banks (1989) and Sleeter and Grant (1987) for essential components of multicultural education.

CHAPTER 6   RACISM, RESISTANCE, AND RACIAL FORMATION

1. For schools' impact on racial identities see Lewis (2003), McCarthy & Crichlow (1993), Perry (2002), Van Ausdale & Feagin (2001), and Watkins, Lewis & Chou (2001). For schools' replication of social class, see Apple (1993, 1995), Bourdieu (1977), Bourdieu & Passeron (1977), Bowles & Gintis (1976), Giroux & McLaren (1989), Nasaw (1979), and Willis (1981). Omi & Winant (1994) describe America's historic denial of education to African American constructed the "American" identity "as white, a negation of racialized otherness" which "took shape in both law and customs, in public institutions and forms of cultural representation" (66) as the schools inscribed upon the white identity civility, rationality, and intellect. Lacking the intellectual tools necessary to participate fully in American society, and perceived as unfit for citizenship, African Americans stagnated on the lowest rung of the social (and racial) ladder. Like African Americans, successive generations of immigrants encountered educational systems that trained them for lower-class positions in American society while degrading their cultures (Tyack 1974).

2. See Glazer (1997), Kymlicka (1995), Shapiro & Kymlicka (1997), and Taylor (1994) for multicultural citizenship. McCarthy (1998) describes minority groups who "emphasized a variety of transformative themes, insisting that curriculum and education policy address the vital questions of the distribution of power and representation in the schools and the status of minority cultural identities in curriculum organization and arrangements" (110).

3. Identity is at the core of the recognition paradigm explicating the connections between and the mutually reinforcing effects of, resource inequality and devalued identities (Fraser 1998; Hobson 2003; Honneth 1995; Taylor 1994; Young 1998; Yuval-Davis 1997). Gutmann (1999) provides a thorough outline of democratic education.

4. As Gerstle (2001), Mills (1997), Takaki (2000), and van den Berghe (1967) argue,

whiteness and American citizenship have long been tied together such that only whites received privileges affiliated with full membership in American society. Whiteness exists as an identity and a structural condition that confers privilege to members while simultaneously oppressing out-groups. As an identity, whiteness has been accessible to Europeans who claimed this identity to acquire resources, such as jobs, housing and the franchise (Roediger 1999). As a structural concept, whiteness constrains racialized groups' upward mobility through social practices denying them rights and resources and preserving their own privileged status (Morrison 1993; Rodriguez 1998).

5. See Wacquant (1997) and Winant (2001) for global applications of race theory and Bonilla-Silva (1997) for processes of racialization. Goldberg (1993), Gramsci (1971), and Hall (1996) describe the importance of "common sense" understandings of difference to maintain inequality.

6. Sleeter (1993) describes white teachers' construction of race and racial difference.

7. See Kincheloe & Steinberg (2000) for whiteness deployed in schools. Curricular conferences co-sponsored by Jews and African Americans reveal stereotyped depictions of Jews (cf. *Amsterdam News,* Mar. 14, 1953, 16; *Age,* June 2, 1951, 2).

8. Cultural approaches to race highlight the simultaneous fluidity and constraint of racial meanings as they reside in both the culture and politics of the time (Jacobson 1998). Racial constraints are contingent upon interactions with gender or class (Collins 2000; Kelley 1994), but cannot be completely explained away by other factors (Feagin 2001; Goldberg 1993; Omi & Winant 1994).

9. These findings conform to those of critical education scholars (Apple 1979, 1995; Bourdieu 1977; Carnoy 1974, Freire 2000; Giroux 1980, 1988; Morrow & Torres 1995; Popkewitz & Fendler 1999) who describe schools as integral to perpetuating social inequality.

10. When efforts to include African American history began, the first African American member of the Board of Education had not yet been appointed. Rev. Coleman was appointed in June of 1948. Adam Clayton Powell Jr. was a congressional representative, Benjamin Davis was a Harlem city councilman. Jewish politicians included Meyer London, a state representative during the Gary Plan, and Samuel M. Levy, Manhattan borough president during Hebrew efforts.

11. For example, the Supreme Court used scientific racism pronouncing white superiority to institutionalize racist practices in *Dred Scott v. John F.A. Sandford* (1857) and *Plessey v. Ferguson* (1896).

12. For the ubiquity and effects of racist media images on attitudes and policies see Dates & Barlow (1993), Dennis & Pease (1997), Gabriel (1998), Gilens (1999), McCarthy (1998), and Oliver & Armstrong (1998).

13. See Pride (2002) for racial narratives and Somers & Gibson (1994) and McIntosh (1997) for white privilege.

14. Although often discussed alongside race, ethnicity lacks the hierarchical power implications, and therefore constraints, of racial identities. Broad conceptual overviews of the term can be found in Cornell and Hartmann (2007) and Nagel (1994). Conzen et al (1992) and Sollors (1989) describe ethnicity's perpetual reconstruction in America. Gans (1962) and Waldinger (1996) describe ethnicity's role in promoting mobility resulting in a declining adherence to ethnic traditions and symbolic ethnicity (Gans 1979, 1994; Hunter 1974; Steinberg 1989; Waters 1990). However, Alba (1990), Handlin (1941), Thomas & Znaniecki (1918), Vecoli (1964), Whyte (1993), and

Zunz (1985) document persistent ethnic traditions and identities among European immigrants as they assimilate to the dominant culture.

15. See Goren (1970), Moore (1981), and Soyer (1997) for Jewish cultures. Drawing on Du Bois (1995 [1903], 1992 [1935]), Blassingame (1979) and Genovese (1976) document the persistence of African culture through the Middle Passage and American slavery.

16. Religion shapes how people act and interact and has increased salience when linked with ethnic cultures (Marty 1976; Orsi 1988). As an aspect of culture, religion provides agents with resources, values, guidelines for actions and ideas, shaping the narratives people tell about the group and the religion, which then shapes how they act and think in daily life. As Tarrow (1998) notes, "religion provides ready-made symbols, rituals, and solidarities that can be accessed and appropriated by movement leaders" (112). See Foner (1988), Harris (2001), Levine (1977), and Morris (1984) for religious narratives embedded in African American master narratives. Kosak (2000) describes Jewish synagogues' role in generating activism while Howe (1976) and Rischin (1978) document the persistent influence of Jewish values among secular Jews.

17. See Stryker (1968) for identity salience during social movements.

18. Young (1998) argues cultural recognition is a means to social justice. Schwalbe & Mason-Schrock (1996) and Snow & Anderson (1987) describe identity work during social movements.

19. See Alexander (2003) for discussions of cultural trauma. Discourses are "relatively bounded set of arguments organized around a specific diagnosis of and solution to some social problem . . . situated within a field of debate wherein speakers struggle with one another to establish meaning, earn legitimacy, and mobilize consensus on belief and action" (Taylor & Whittier 1992: 107). For subordinated groups' deployment of, and the complexities inherent in, masking strategies see Bhabha (2002), Du Bois (1995 [1903]), Fanon (1967), Kelley (1996), and Kosak (2000), and Scott (1990) for hidden transcripts.

20. See Gamson (1992), Kubal (1998), Scott (1990), and Snow & Benford (1992) for activists' shifting use of culturally resonant collective action frames and subsequent effects on mobilization trajectories. Alexander (2001) addresses differences between publicly versus privately enacted identities.

21. See Bernstein (1997) for celebration and suppression of identities during social movements.

22. While Kallen (1924) optimistically tied natal cultures and Americanness together, Du Bois highlighted African Americans' struggle with dual identities. Kallen described a hyphenated identity existing within immigrant communities, based on their inability to choose between being solely American or a member of an ethnic group, as "a fact which permeates all levels of life. A man is at once . . . one in an ethnic and social group and the citizen of a nation . . . it is absurd to lose sight of the truth that the hyphen unites very much more than it separates" (Kallen 1924, 62–63). African descendants, since their arrival in America, struggled with dual identities through a state in which he "ever feels his twoness,—an American, a Negro; two souls, two thoughts, two unreconciled strivings; two warring ideals in one dark body" (Du Bois 1995 [1903]: 45). In this framework, Du Bois highlights African Americans' desires to be free of systemic racism and discrimination while maintaining their cultural identities. All new immigrants experience racialization upon arrival such that they either access privileges of whiteness or encounter oppressive structures inhibiting

nonwhites (Alba 1999; Alba & Nee 1997; Massey 1995; Portes & Zhou 1993; Rumbaut 1994, 1997a, b).

CHAPTER 7   THE FORESEEABLE SPLIT

1. See Katznelson (2006) and Lipsitz (2006) for the government's extension of privileges of whiteness to Jews and other white ethnics in the post–World War II era.
2. See Goldstein (2006) for Jews' changing conceptions of their racial identity vis-à-vis whiteness.
3. *Amsterdam News*, Sept. 9, 1961, 34.
4. *Amsterdam News*, Jan. 20, 1962, 1, Feb. 10, 1962, 18.
5. *Amsterdam News*, Aug. 10, 1962, 2, 3 Aug. 3, 1963, 1, 2.
6. *NY Times*, Mar. 10, 1987, B6.
7. Taylor (1997: 102) directly attributes these tactics to the Harlem 9 in his book describing the movement and its leader, Milton Galamison.
8. See especially V. P. Franklin et al. (1998), Hentoff (1969), and Salzman and West (1997) for Jewish–African American conflict and collaboration.
9. Podair (2002) offers the best treatment of the strike.
10. Blalock (1967), Blumer (1958), Bobo (1990), and Bobo & Hutchings (1996) find that minorities competing for scarce resources experience perceived and real group threats and exhibit higher rates of antagonistic sentiment.
11. For contemporary Jewish–African American relations see Greenberg (2006), Lee (2002), and Lerner & West (2006). King and Weiner (2007) argue that African American anti-Semitism cannot be reduced to anti-whiteness.
12. See www.adl.org/combating_hate/HCSA_10year.asp for hate crime statistics between 1997 and 2007.

CONCLUSION

1. See Kao & Thompson (2003) for contemporary minority educational attainment and Rumbaut (2005) for immigrants' downward educational assimilation. Hao (2007) and Larsen (2004) document differences in wealth and employment among immigrants.
2. See Ahmad & Szpara (2003) for schools' treatment of Muslim students and Alavi (2001) for parents' efforts to include multicultural curriculum and develop parallel institutions. Amara (2006), Bowen (2004), and Werbner (2005) address debates over in-school displays of religiosity in European nations.
3. Cullen (2005) finds lower educational attainment among students unable to transfer out of schools under school choice programs. Gill et al. (2008) argue that even students transferring to better schools do not benefit. Archbald (2004), Bettinger (2005), Schemo (2004), and Robelen (2008) describe negative effects of charter schools on academic performance. Some charter schools, particularly those run using the KIPP Model, promote academic achievement (Dillon 2008). Herszenhorn (2004) and http://schoolsmatter.blogspot.com/2008/03/charter-school-corruption-summary.html document failings in charter schools nationally.
4. Funding allocations appear in HR1: The American Recovery and Investment Act of 2009.
5. See Metzger (1971) for a critique of scholarship about African Americans and academic perceptions that they sought to cast off their cultural identities. Stepick

et al. (2001) describe the mobility-limiting effects of acculturation to lower-class norms for Haitians in Miami but do not consider potential cultural resources they might engage to transcend the racist system.

6. Incorporation is quite different from assimilation, by which is often meant Anglo-conformity, but includes a variety of components (Gordon 1964). New immigration history scholars emphasize ethnics' longstanding desires for cultural retention. Sociologists debate (Barkan 1995, Brubaker 2001, Gans 1997, Glazer 1993) and reconfigure assimilation theory, rooted largely in Park's (1950) race relations cycle and Warner & Srole's (1945) straight-line theory, to capture the complex, often bumpy (Gans 1992), position in which new immigrants and their descendants find themselves with regard to cultural maintenance and desires to fit into their new homeland.

7. Cornell & Hartmann (2004) suggest that forthcoming research must address these overlapping concepts. Archer (1996) and Giddens (1979) outline the dialectical concepts of structure and agency.

METHODOLOGICAL APPENDIX

1. Connolly and Troyna's (1998), Parker, Deyle and Villenas's (1999), and Zuberi & Bonilla-Silva's (2008) edited volumes offer essential methodologies for scholars seeking to accurately represent minority groups. These feminist-influenced methods examining manifestations of gender in the structure of daily life (Harding 1991, Naples 2003, Smith 1990) are especially advocated by African American feminists (Collins 2000). I expand this framework's focus to include other disadvantaged groups whose voices rarely appear in social science research.

2. The Bureau of Jewish Education (BJE) absorbed the Jewish Education Association (JEA) in 1920 resulting in citations of the JEA in the BJE collection. The BJE became the Jewish Education Committee in 1940.

3. Stryker (1998) and Abbott (2001), Franzosi (1998), and Haydu (1998) describe the strategic narrative and comparative/case narrative approaches, respectively. See Clemens & Hughes (2002), Dibble (1963), Ellingson (1995), Fine (1995), Johnston (1995, 2002), and Steinberg (1999) for narrative and discourse analysis and Aminzade (1992), Quadagno & Knapp (1992), and Tilly (1984) for sequentiality in protest cases.

4. Narratives, the "stories that social actors use to make sense of—indeed, in order to act in—their lives . . . to define who [they] *are*" (Somers 1992: 603; Taylor & Whittier 1992) aid "in constructing shared meaning and group cohesion" (Fine 1995: 133).

BIBLIOGRAPHY

ARCHIVAL DOCUMENTS

Manuscript Collections

American Jewish Historical Society (AJHS), New York, NY
    Bureau of Jewish Education Papers (BJE)
    Educational Alliance Papers
    Jewish Student Organizations Papers (JSO)
    Kehillah Papers
    Stephen S. Wise Papers (SSW)
    Brandeis University
    Stephen S. Wise Papers (SSW)
Jewish Theological Seminary, New York, NY
    Record Group 12: Teachers Institute—Seminary College of Jewish Studies
Library of Congress
    Congress of Racial Equality (CORE) Papers
    John Purroy Mitchel Papers
New York City Municipal Archives
    Board of Education Records (BoE)
    Fiorello H. LaGuardia Papers
    James Walker Papers
    John F. Hylan Papers
    John L. O'Brien Papers
    John Purroy Mitchel Papers
    Robert F. Wagner Papers
    Vincent Impelliteri Papers
    William O'Dywer Papers
New York City Public Library
    Joseph Barondess Papers
New York State Supreme Court
Schlesinger Library at Radcliff College
    Justice Justine Wise Polier Papers
Schomburg Center for Research in Black Culture (SCRBC), The New York Public Library,
    Astor, Lenox, and Tilden Foundations
    Council on Interracial Books for Children Records (MG 438)
    Ella Baker Papers (MG 630)
    Harlem Neighborhoods Association Papers (MG 364) (HANA)
YIVO Institute for Jewish Research
    Judah Pilch Papers

Newspapers

American Hebrew (AH)
Brooklyn Daily Eagle (BDE)
Jewish Tribune and Hebrew Standard (HS)
Jewish Daily Bulletin
New York Times (NY Times)
New York Globe & Commercial Advertiser (Globe)
New York Amsterdam News (Amsterdam News)
New York Age (Age)

PUBLISHED SOURCES

Ahmad, Iftikhar, & Michelle Szpara. 2003. "Muslim Children in Urban America: The New York City Schools Experience." *Journal of Muslim Minority Affairs* 23(2):295–301.

Alavi, Gulafshan. 2001. "Muslim Parents' Activism in the Multicultural Education (MCE) Curriculum." *American Journal of Islamic Social Sciences* 18(3):51–89.

Alba, Richard D. 1999. "Immigration and the American Realities of Assimilation and Multiculturalism." *Sociological Forum* 14(1):3–25.

———. 1990. *Ethnic Identity: The Transformation of White America*. New Haven: Yale University Press.

Alba, Richard, & Victor Nee. 1997. "Rethinking Assimilation for a New Era of Immigration." *International Migration Review* 31(4):826–874.

Alexander, Jeffrey C. 2003. *The Meanings of Social Life: A Cultural Sociology*. New York: Oxford University Press.

———. 2001. "Theorizing the 'Modes of Incorporation': Assimilation, Hyphenation, and Multiculturalism as Varieties of Civil Participation." *Sociological Theory* 19(3):237–249.

Allport, Gordon. 1954. *The Nature of Prejudice*. Cambridge, MA: Addison-Wesley.

Amara, Fadela. 2006. *Breaking the Silence: French Women's Voices from the Ghetto*. Berkeley: University of California Press.

Aminzade, Ron, & Doug McAdam. 2001. "Emotions and Contentious Politics." In *Silence and Voice in the Study of Contentious Politics*, edited by Ronald R. Aminzade, Jack A. Goldstone, Doug McAdam, Elizabeth J. Parry, William H. Sewell, Jr., Sidney Tarrow, & Charles Tilly. New York: Cambridge University Press.

Andalzúa, Gloria. 1987. *Borderlands/La Frontera: The New Mestiza*. San Francisco: Spinsters/Aunt Lute.

Anderson, Benedict. 1991. *Imagined Communities: Reflections on the Origin and Spread of Nationalism*. Rev. ed. New York: Verso.

Anderson, James D. 1988. *The Education of Blacks in the South, 1860–1935*. Chapel Hill: University of North Carolina Press.

Ansell, Christopher K. 1997. "Symbolic Networks: The Realignment of the French Working Class, 1887–1894." *American Journal of Sociology* 103(2):359–390.

Apple, Michael W. 1995. *Education and Power*. New York: Routledge.

———. 1979. *Ideology and Curriculum*. London: Routledge and Kegan Paul.

Archer, Margaret S. 1996. *Culture and Agency: The Place of Culture in Social Theory*. Rev. Ed. New York: Cambridge University Press.

Baldwin, James. 1967. "Negroes are Anti-Semitic Because They're Anti-White." *New York Times Magazine*, Apr. 9, 26–7, 135–139.

Banfield, Beryl. 1998. "Commitment to Change: The Council on Interracial Books for Children and the World of Children's Books." *African American Review* 32(1):17–22.

Banks, James A. 2002. "Race, Knowledge Construction, and Education in the USA: Lessons from History." *Race, Ethnicity and Education* 5(1):7–27

Barkan, Elliott R. 1995. "Race, Religion, and Nationality in American Society: A Model of Ethnicity—From Contact to Assimilation." *Journal of American Ethnic History* 14(2):38–75.

Barnhouse Walters, Pamela. 1999. "Education and Advancement: Exploring the Hopes and Dreams of Blacks and Whites at the Turn of the Century." In *The Cultural Territories of Race: Black and White Boundaries*, edited by Michèle Lamont. Chicago: University of Chicago Press and Russell Sage.

Barnhouse Walters, Pamela, David James, &Holly McCammon. 1997. "Citizenship and Public Schools: Accounting for Racial Inequality in Education in the Pre- and Post-Disfranchisement South." *American Sociological Review* 62(1):34–52

Barrett, James R., & David Roediger. 1997. "In-Between Peoples: Race, Nationality and the 'New Immigrant' Working Class." *Journal of American Ethnic History* 16(3):3–44.

Bernstein, Mary. 1997. "Celebration and Suppression: The Strategic Uses of Identity by the Lesbian and Gay Movement." *American Journal of Sociology* 103(3):531–565.

Berrol, Selma C. 1976. "Education and Economic Mobility: The Jewish Experience in New York City, 1880–1920." *American Jewish Historical Quarterly* 65(1–4):257–271.

Bhabha, Homi. 2002. "Of Mimicry and Man: The Ambivalence of Colonial Discourse." In *Race Critical Theories*, edited by Philomena Essed& David Theo Goldberg. Malden, MA: Blackwell.

Binder, Amy. 2002. *Contentious Curricula: Afrocentrism and Creationism in American Public Schools*. Princeton, NJ: Princeton University Press.

———. 1999. "Friend and Foe: Boundary Work and Collective Identity in the Afrocentric and Multicultural Curriculum Movements in American Public Education." In *The Cultural Territories of Race: Black and White Boundaries*, edited by Michéle Lamont. Chicago and New York: University of Chicago Press and the Russell Sage Foundation.

Biondi, Martha. 2006. *To Stand and Fight: The Struggle for Civil Rights in Postwar New York City*. Cambridge, MA: Harvard University Press.

Blalock, Hubert M. 1967. *Toward a Theory of Minority Group Relations*. New York: Wiley & Sons.

Blassingame, John W. 1979. *The Slave Community: Plantation Life in the Antebellum South*. New York: Oxford University Press.

Blau, Joseph L. 1976. *Judaism in America: From Curiosity to Third Faith*. Chicago: University of Chicago Press.

Blum, Lawrence. 1998. "Recognition, Value, and Equality: A Critique of Charles Taylor's and Nancy Fraser's Accounts of Multiculturalism." In *Theorizing Multiculturalism: A Guide to the Current Debate*, edited by Cynthia Willett. Malden, MA: Blackwell Publishers.

Blumer, Herbert. 1958. "Race Prejudice as a Sense of Group Position." *Pacific Sociological Review* 1(1):3–7.

Bobo, Lawrence. 1999. "Prejudice as Group Position: Microfoundations of a Sociological Approach to Racism and Race Relations." *Journal of Social Issues* 55(3):445–472.

Bobo, Lawrence, & Vincent L. Hutchings. 1996. "Perceptions of Racial Group Competition: Extending Blumer's Theory of Group Position to a Multiracial Social Context." *American Sociological Review* 61(6):951–972.

Bogardus, Emory S. 1968. "Comparing Racial Distance in Ethiopia, South Africa, and the United States." *Sociology and Social Research* 52:149–156.

Bonilla-Silva, Eduardo. 2006. *Racism without Racists: Color-Blind Racism and the Persistence of Racial Inequality in the United States*. New York: Rowman & Littlefield.

———. 1997. "Rethinking Racism: Toward a Structural Interpretation." *American Sociological Review* 62(3):465–480.

Bonner, Marianne Walsh. 1978. "The Politics of the Introduction of the Gary Plan to the New York City School System." Ph.D. dissertation, Rutgers University.

Bourdieu, Pierre. 1977. "Cultural Reproduction and Social Reproduction." In *Power and Ideology in Education*, edited by Jerome Karabel & A. H. Halsey. New York: Oxford University Press.

Bourdieu, Pierre, & Jean Claude Passeron. 1977. *Reproduction in Education, Society, and Culture.* London: Sage.

Bourne, Randolph S. 1970. *The Gary Schools.* Cambridge, MA: M.I.T. Press.

Bowen, John R. 2004. *Why the French Don't Like Headscarves: Islam, the State, and Public Space.* Princeton, NJ: Princeton University Press.

Bowles, Samuel, & Herbert Gintis. 1976. *Schooling in Capitalist America: Education and the Contradictions of Economic Life.* New York: Basic Books.

Boykin, A. Wade. 2001. "The Challenges of Cultural Socialization in the Schooling of African American Elementary School Children: Exposing the Hidden Curriculum." In *Race and Education: The Roles of History and Society in Educating African American Students*, edited by William Watkins, James H. Lewis, & Victoria Chou. Boston: Allyn & Bacon.

Branch, Taylor. 1989. *Parting the Waters: America in the King Years, 1954–1963.* New York: Simon and Schuster.

Brandt, Nat. 1993. *Harlem at War: The Black Experience in WWII.* Syracuse, NY: Syracuse University Press.

Brubaker, Rogers. 2001. "The Return of Assimilation? Changing Perspectives on Immigration and Its Sequels in France, Germany, and the United States." *Ethnic and Racial Studies* 24(4):531–548.

Brumberg, Stephan F. 1986. *Going to America, Going to School: The Jewish Immigrant Public School Encounter in Turn-of-the-Century New York City.* Westport, CT: Praeger.

Buckingham, Burdette R. 1916. "Survey of the Gary and Prevocational Schools of New York City." *School and Society* 3:245–247.

Bush, Rod. 1999. *We Are Not What We Seem: Black Nationalism and Class Struggle in the American Century.* New York: New York University Press.

Calhoun, Craig. 1994. *Social Theory and the Politics of Identity.* Malden, MA: Blackwell Publishers.

———. 1993. "'New Social Movements' of the Early Nineteenth Century." *Social Science History* 17(3):385–427.

Callcott, Mary Stevenson. 1931. *Child Legislation in New York.* New York: Macmillan.

Capeci, Donald. 1977. *The Harlem Riot of 1943.* Philadelphia: Temple University Press.

Carnoy, Martin. 1974. *Education as Cultural Imperialism.* New York: Longman.

Cecelski, David S. 1994. *Along Freedom Road: Hyde County, North Carolina, and the Fate of Black Schools in the South.* Chapel Hill: University of North Carolina Press.

Champagne, Duane. 1993. "Toward a Multidimensional Historical Comparative Methodology: Context, Process, and Causality. In *Race and Ethnicity in Research Methods*, edited by John H. Stanfield, II & Rutledge M. Dennis. Thousand Oaks, CA: Sage Publications.

Chipkin, Israel S. 1937. *Twenty-five Years of Jewish Education in the United States.* New York: Jewish Education Association of New York City.

Clark, Kenneth B. 1989. *Dark Ghetto: Dilemmas of Social Power*, 2nd ed. Hanover, NH: Wesleyan University Press.

Cleaver, Eldridge. 1968. *Soul on Ice.* New York: McGraw-Hill.

Clift, Virgil A. 1966. "Educating the American Negro." In *The American Negro Reference Book*, edited by John P. Davis. Englewood Cliffs, NJ: Prentice-Hall.

Cohen, Naomi. 1984. *Encounter with Emancipation: The German Jews in the United States, 1930–1914*. Philadelphia: Jewish Publication Society of America.

Cohen, Rich. 1999. *Tough Jews: Fathers, Sons, and Gangster Dreams*. New York: Vintage.

Cohen, Ronald D. & Raymond A. Mohl. 1979. *The Paradox of Progressive Education: The Gary Plan and Urban Schooling*. Port Washington, NY: Kennikat Press.

Cohen, Sol. 1964. *Progressives and Urban School Reform: The Public Education Association of New York City, 1895–1954*. New York: Bureau of Publications, Teachers College.

Colclough, Glenna, & E. M. Beck. 1986. "The American Educational Structure and the Reproduction of Social Class." *Sociological Inquiry* 56(4):456–473.

Collier-Thomas, Bettye, & James Turner. 1994. "Race, Class, and Color: The African American Discourse on Identity." *Journal of American Ethnic History* 14(1):5–31.

Connolly, Paul. 1998. "Introduction." In *Researching Racism in Education: Politics, Theory and Practice*, edited by Paul Connolly & Barry Troyna. Philadelphia: Open University Press.

Connolly, Paul, & Barry Troyna, eds. 1998. *Researching Racism in Education: Politics, Theory, and Practice*. Philadelphia: Open University Press.

Conzen, Kathleen Niels, David A. Gerber, Ewa Morawska, George E. Pozzetta, & Rudoph J. Vecoli. 1992. "The Invention of Ethnicity: A Perspective from the U.S.A." *Journal of American Ethnic History* 12(1):3–41.

Cornbleth, Catherine. 1984. "Beyond the Hidden Curriculum." *Journal of Curriculum Studies* 16(1):29–36.

Cornell, Stephen E., & Douglas Hartmann. 2006. *Ethnicity and Race: Making Identities in a Changing World*. Thousand Oaks, CA: Pine Forge Press.

Cornell, Stephen E., & Douglas Hartmann. 2004. "Conceptual Confusions and Divides: Race, Ethnicity, and the Study of Immigration." In *Not Just Black and White: Immigration, Race, and Ethnicity, Then to Now*, edited by Nancy Foner & George M. Fredrickson. New York: Russell Sage Foundation.

Crew, Spencer R. 1987. *Field to Factory: Afro-American Migration 1915–1940*. Washington, D.C.: National Museum of American History, Smithsonian Institute.

Cusick, Philip A. 1983. *The Egalitarian Ideal and the American High School: Studies of Three Schools*. New York: Longman.

Dalfiume, Richard M. 1968. "The 'Forgotten Years' of the Negro Revolution." *Journal of American History* 55(1):90–106.

Darling-Hammond, Linda. 2007. "Race, Inequality and Educational Accountability: The Irony of 'No Child Left Behind.'" *Race, Ethnicity, and Education* 10(3): 245–260.

Dewey, John. 1990. *The School and Society—The Child and the Curriculum*. Chicago: University of Chicago Press.

———. 1964. *Democracy and Education*. New York: Macmillan.

Dillon, Sam. 2008. "2 School Entrepreneurs Lead the Way on Change." *New York Times*, June 19, A16.

Diner, Hasia R. 2003. *A New Promised Land: A History of Jews in America*. New York: Oxford University Press.

———. 1998. "Drawn Together by Self-Interest: Jewish Representation of Race and Race Relations in the Early Twentieth Century." In *African Americans and Jews in the Twentieth Century: Studies in Convergence and Conflict*, edited by V. P. Franklin, Nancy L. Grant, Harold M. Kletnick, & Genna Rae McNeil. Columbia: University of Missouri Press.

Dinnerstein, Leonard. 1994. *Antisemitism in America*. New York: Oxford University Press.

Dougherty, Jack. 2004. *More Than One Struggle: The Evolution of Black School Reform in Milwaukee*. Chapel Hill: University of North Carolina Press.

Douglas, Davison. 2005. *Jim Crow Moves North: The Battle Over Northern School Segregation, 1965–1954*. New York: Cambridge University Press.

Dreeben, Robert. 1984. "First Grade Reading Groups: Their Formation and Change." In *The Social Context of Instruction: Group Organization and Group Process*, edited by Penelope L. Peterson, Louise Cherry Wilkerson, & Maureen A. Hallinan. New York: Academic.

Dubnow, Simon. 1916. *The History of the Jews in Russia and Poland: From the Earliest Times Until the Present Day*. Philadelphia: Jewish Publication Society of America.

Dubofsky, Melvyn. 1968. *When Workers Organize: New York City in the Progressive Era*. Amherst: University of Massachusetts Press.

Du Bois, W.E.B. 1995 (1903). *The Souls of Black Folk*. New York: Signet.

———. 1992 (1935). *Black Reconstruction in America*. New York: Atheneum.

———. 1973. *The Education of Black People: Ten Critiques, 1906–1960*, ed. Herbert Aptheker. New York: Monthly Review Press.

———. 1935. "Does the Negro Need Separate Schools?" *Journal of Negro Education* 4(3):328–335.

Duker, Abraham G. 1939. *Jews in the World War: A Brief Historical Sketch*. New York: American Jewish Committee.

Dunn, Frederick. 1993. "The Educational Philosophies of Washington, Du Bois, and Houston: Laying the Foundations for Afrocentrism and Multiculturalism." *Journal of Negro Education* 62(1):24–34.

Dushkin, Alexander M. 1918. *Jewish Education in New York City*. New York: Bureau of Jewish Education.

Dwork, Deborah. 1986. "Immigrant Jews on the Lower East Side of New York: 1881–1914." In *The American Jewish Experience*, 2nd ed., edited by Jonathan D. Sarna. New York: Holmes & Meier.

Ellingson, Stephen. 1995. "Understanding the Dialectic of Discourse and Collective Action: Public Debate and Rioting in Antebellum Cincinnati." *American Journal of Sociology* 101(1):100–144.

Ellison, Ralph. 1992. *Invisible Man*. New York: Modern Library.

Ensign, Forest C. 1921. *Compulsory School Attendance and Child Labor*. Iowa City, IA: Athens Press.

Erickson, Ralph. 1997. "The Laws of Ignorance Designed to Keep Slaves (Blacks) Illiterate and Powerless." *Education* 118(2):206–209, 220.

Evans, Sarah M., & Harry C. Boyte. 1992. *Free Spaces: The Sources of Democratic Change in America*. 2nd ed. Chicago: University of Chicago Press.

Ewen, Elizabeth. 1985. *Immigrant Women in the Land of Dollars: Life and Culture on the Lower East Side, 1890–1925*. New York: Monthly Review Press.

Fanon, Frantz. 1967. *Black Skin, White Masks*. New York: Grove Press

Fantasia, Rick. 1995. "From Class Consciousness to Culture, Action, and Social Organization." *Annual Review of Sociology* 21:269–287.

Feagin, Joe R. 2005. *Systemic Racism: A Theory of Oppression*. New York: Routledge.

———. 2001. *Racist America: Roots, Current Realities, and Future Reparations*. New York: Routledge.

Featherstone, H. 1987. "Organizing Classes by Ability." *Harvard Education Letter* 3(40):1–9.

Fennema, Elizabeth, & Gilar C. Leder, eds. 1990. *Mathematics and Gender*. New York: Teachers College Press.

Fitzgerald, Frances. 1979. *America Revised: History Schoolbooks in the Twentieth Century*. New York: Vintage.

Foner, Eric 1988. *Reconstruction: America's Unfinished Revolution, 1863–1877*. New York: Harper & Row.

Foote, Thelma Wills. 2004. *Black and White Manhattan: The History of Racial Formation in Colonial New York City*. New York: Oxford.

Foster, Michele. 1995. "African American Teachers and Culturally Relevant Pedagogy." In *Handbook of Multicultural Education*, edited by James A Banks & Cheryl A. Banks. New York: Macmillan.

———. 1994. "Educating for Competence in Community and Culture: Exploring the Views of Exemplary African-American Teachers." In *Too Much Schooling, Too Little Education: A Paradox of Black Life in White Societies*, edited by Mwalimu J. Shujaa. Trenton, NJ: Africa World Press.

Foucault, Michel. 1970. *The Order of Things: An Archaeology of the Human Sciences*. London: Tavistock.

Franklin, V. P., Nancy L. Grant, Harold M. Kletnick, & Glenna Rae McNeil, eds. 1998. *African Americans and Jews in the Twentieth Century: Studies in Convergence and Conflict*. Columbia: University of Missouri Press.

Franklin, John Hope, & Alfred A. Moss Jr. 1994. *From Slavery to Freedom: A History of African Americans,* 7th ed. New York: McGraw-Hill.

Fraser, Nancy. 1998. "From Redistribution to Recognition? Dilemmas of Justice in a 'Post-Socialist' Age." In *Theorizing Multiculturalism: A Guide to the Current Debate*, edited by Cynthia Willett. Malden, MA: Blackwell Publishers.

Fraser, Nancy, & Linda Gordon. 1994. "Civil Citizenship against Social Citizenship?" In *The Condition of Citizenship*, edited by Bart Van Seenburgen. Thousand Oaks, CA: Sage Publications.

Fredrickson, George M. 1971. *The Black Image in the White Mind: The Debate on Afro-American Character and Destiny, 1817–1914*. New York: Harper & Row.

Freire, Paulo. 2000. *Pedagogy of the Oppressed*. Harrisburg, PA: Continuum.

———. 1976. *Education: The Practice of Freedom*. London: Writers & Readers.

Friedlaender, Israel. 1961. *Past and Present: Selected Essays*. New York: Burning Bush Press.

Fuchs, Lawrence H. 1956. *The Political Behavior of American Jews*. Glencoe, IL: The Free Press.

Gabriel, John. 1998. *Whitewash: Racialized Politics and the Media*. New York: Routledge.

Galston, William A. 1991. *Liberal Purposes: Goods, Virtues, and Diversity in the Liberal State*. New York: Cambridge University Press.

Gamson, William A. 1992. "The Social Psychology of Collective Action." In *Frontiers of Social Movement Theory*, edited by Aldon D. Morris & Carol Mueller McClurg. New Haven: Yale University Press

Gans, Herbert J. 1997. "Toward a Reconciliation of 'Assimilation' and 'Pluralism': The Interplay of Acculturation and Ethnic Retention." *International Migration Review* 31(4):875–892.

———. 1994. "Symbolic Ethnicity and Symbolic Religiosity: Towards a Comparison of Ethnic and Religious Acculturation." *Ethnic and Racial Studies* 17(4):577–592.

———. 1992. "Comment: Ethnic Invention and Acculturation, A Bumpy-Line Approach." *Journal of American Ethnic History* 12(1):42–63.

———. 1979. "Symbolic Ethnicity: The Future of Ethnic Groups and Cultures in America." *Ethnic and Racial Studies* 2(1):1–20.

———. 1962. *The Urban Villagers: Group and Class in the Life of Italian Americans*. New York: Free Press.

Gaventa, John. 1982. *Power and Powerlessness: Quiescence and Rebellion in the Appalachian Valley.* Urbana: University of Illinois Press.

Genovese, Eugene. 1976. *Roll, Jordon, Roll: The World The Slaves Made.* New York: Vintage.

Gerstle, Gary. 2001. *American Crucible: Race and Nation in the Twentieth Century.* Princeton, NJ: Princeton University Press.

Giddens, Anthony. 1979. *Central Problems in Social Theory: Action, Structure, and Contradictions in Social Analysis.* Berkeley and Los Angeles: University of California Press.

Gilens, Martin. 1999. *Why Americans Hate Welfare: Race, Media, and the Politics of Antipoverty Policy.* Chicago: University of Chicago Press.

Gilkes, Cheryl Townsend. 1983. "From Slavery to Social Welfare: Racism and the Control of Black Women." In *Class, Race and Sex: The Dynamics of Control*, edited by Amy Swerdlow & Hanna Lessinger. Boston: G. K. Hall.

———. 1980. "'Holding Back the Ocean with a Broom': Black Women and Community Work." In *The Black Woman*, edited by La Frances Rodgers-Rose. Beverly Hills, CA: Sage.

Gillborn, David. 1992. "Citizenship, 'Race,' and the Hidden Curriculum." *International Studies in Sociology of Education* 2(1):57–73.

Giroux, Henry. 1988. *Teachers as Educators: Toward a Critical Pedagogy of Learning.* Westport, CT: Bergin & Garvey.

———. 1980. "Beyond Correspondence Theory: Notes on the Dynamics of Educational Reproduction and Transformation." *Curriculum Inquiry* 10(3):225–247.

Giroux, Henry A., & Peter McLaren. 1989. *Critical Education, the State, and Cultural Struggle.* Albany: State University of New York Press.

Glazer, Nathan. 1997. *We Are All Multiculturalists Now.* Cambridge, MA: Harvard University Press.

———. 1993. "Is Assimilation Dead?" *Annals of the American Academy of Political and Social Science* 530:122–136.

Glazer, Nathan, & Daniel Patrick Moynihan. 1963. *Beyond the Melting Pot: The Negroes, Puerto Ricans, Jews, Italians, and Irish of New York City.* Cambridge, MA: M.I.T. Press.

Glenn, Evelyn Nakano. 2002. *Unequal Freedom: How Race and Gender Shaped American Citizenship and Labor.* Cambridge, MA: Harvard University Press.

Goggin, Jacqueline Anne. 1997. *Carter G. Woodson: A Life in Black History.* Baton Rouge: Louisiana State University Press.

Goldaber, Irving. 1965. "The Treatment by the New York City Board of Education of Problems Affecting the Negro, 1954–1963." Ph.D dissertation, New York University.

Goldberg, David Theo. 1993. *Racist Culture: Philosophy and the Politics of Meanings.* Cambridge, MA: Blackwell.

Goldstein, Eric L. 2006. *The Price of Whiteness: Jews, Race, and American Identity.* Princeton, NJ: Princeton University Press.

Goodwin, Jeff, James M. Jasper, & Francesca Polletta. 2001. *Passionate Politics: Emotions and Social Movements.* Chicago: University of Chicago Press.

Gordon, Milton M. 1964. *Assimilation in American Life: The Role of Race, Religion, and National Origins.* New York: Oxford University Press.

Gorelick, Sherry. 1981. *City College and the Jewish Poor: Education in New York, 1880–1924.* New Brunswick, NJ: Rutgers University Press.

———. 1975. "Social Control, Social Mobility, and the Eastern European Jews: An Analysis of Public Education in New York City, 1880–1924." Ph.D. dissertation, Columbia University.

Goren, Arthur A. 1999. *The Politics of Public Culture of American Jews.* Bloomington: University of Indiana Press.

————. 1987. "The Jewish Press." In *The Ethnic Press in the United States: A Historical Analysis and Handbook*, edited by Sally M. Miller. New York: Greenwood Press.

————. 1970. *New York Jews and the Quest for Community: The Kehillah Experiment 1908–1922*. New York: Columbia University Press.

————. 1969. "A Portrait of Ethnic Politics: The Socialists and the 1980 and 1920 Congressional Elections on the East Side." In *The Jewish Experience in America*, Volume 4: *At Home in America*, edited by Abraham J. Karp. Waltham, MA: American Jewish Historical Society.

Gould, Deborah B. 2003. "Passionate Political Processes: Bringing Emotions Back into the Study of Social Movements." In *Rethinking Social Movements: Structure Meaning and Emotion*, edited by Jeff Goodwin & James M. Jasper. New York: Rowman & Littlefield.

Gould, Stephen Jay. 1996. *The Mismeasure of Man*, Rev. ed. New York: W. W. Norton.

Gramsci, Antonio. 1971. *Selections from the Prison Notebooks*, Quintin Hoare & Geoffrey Nowell-Smith, eds. and trans. London: Lawrence and Wishart.

Greenberg, Cheryl Lynn. 1991. *Or Does It Explode? Black Harlem in the Great Depression*. New York: Oxford University Press.

Greer, Colin. 1972. *The Great School Legend: A Revisionist Interpretation of American Public Education*. New York: Viking Press.

Grinstein, Hyman B. 1947. *The Rise of the Jewish Community of New York, 1654–1860*. Philadelphia: Jewish Publication Society of America.

Gronowicz, Anthony. 1998. *Race and Class Politics in New York City before the Civil War*. Boston: Northeastern University Press.

Glazer, Nathan. 1997. *We Are All Multiculturalists Now*. Cambridge, MA: Harvard University Press.

Hale, Janice E. 2001. "Culturally Appropriate Pedagogy." In *Race and Education: The Roles of History and Society in Educating African American Students*, edited by William Watkins, James H. Lewis, & Victoria Chou. Boston: Allyn & Bacon.

Hall, Stuart. 1996. "Gramsci's Relevance for the Study of Race and Ethnicity." In *Stuart Hall: Critical Dialogues in Cultural Studies*, edited by David Morley & Kuan-Hsing Chen. London and New York: Routledge.

Handlin, Oscar. 1941. *Boston's Immigrants, 1790–1865: A Study in Acculturation*. Cambridge, MA: Harvard University Press.

Hao, Lingxin. 2007. *Color Lines, Country Lines: Race, Immigration, and Wealth Stratification in America*. New York: Russell Sage.

Harper, Pat, Alicia Fabbre, & Diane Rado. 2009. "Private Schools Caught in an Economic Storm." *Chicago Tribune*, Feb. 26.

Harris, Frederick C. 2001. "Religious Resources in an Oppositional Civic Culture." In *Oppositional Consciousness: The Subjective Roots of Social Protest*, edited by Jane Mansbridge & Aldon Morris. Chicago: University of Chicago Press.

Harris, Leslie M. 2003. *In the Shadow of Slavery: African Americans in New York City, 1626–1863*. Chicago: University of Chicago Press.

Hartmann, Douglas R. 2000. "Rethinking the Relationships between Sport and Race in American Culture: Golden Ghettos and Contested Terrain." *Sociology of Sport Journal* 17(3):229–253.

Hatcher, Richard, & Barry Troyna. 1993. "Racialization and Children." In *Race, Identity, and Representation in Education*, edited by Cameron McCarthy & Warren Chrichlow. New York: Routledge.

Hentoff, Nat, ed. 1969. *Black Anti-Semitism and Jewish Racism*. New York: Richard W. Baron.

Hercus, Cheryl. 1999. "Identity, Emotion, and Feminist Collective Action." *Gender & Society* 13(1):34–55.

Herszenhorn, David M. 2004. "Report Faults New York's First 3 Charter Schools." *New York Times*, January 13, A1.

Higham, John. 1969. "Social Discrimination Against Jews in America, 1830–1930." In *The Jewish Experience in America*, Volume 4: *At Home in America*, edited by Abraham J. Karp. Waltham, MA: American Jewish Historical Society.

Hill Collins, Patricia. 2000. *Black Feminist Thought: Knowledge, Consciousness, and the Politics of Power*. 2nd ed. New York: Routledge.

Hobson, Barbara. 2003. "Introduction." In *Recognition Struggles and Social Movements: Contested Identities, Agency and Power*, edited by Barbara Hobson. New York: Cambridge University Press.

———. 1999. "Women's Collective Agency, Power Resources, and the Framing of Citizenship Rights." In *Extending Citizenship, Configuring States*, edited by Michael Hanagan & Charles Tilly. Lanham, MD: Rowman & Littlefield.

Hodges, Graham Russell. 1999. *Root and Branch: African Americans in New York and East Jersey, 1613–1863*. Chapel Hill: University of North Carolina Press.

Honneth, Axel. 1995. *The Struggle for Recognition: The Moral Grammar of Social Conflicts*. Cambridge, UK: Polity Press.

hooks, bell. 1994. *Teaching to Transgress: Education as the Practice of Freedom*. New York: Routledge.

Howe, Irving. 1976. *World of Our Fathers: The Journey of the East European Jews to America and the Life They Found and Made*. New York: Simon & Schuster.

Hunter, Albert. 1974. *Symbolic Communities: The Persistence and Change of Chicago's Local Communities*. Chicago: University of Chicago Press.

Hyman, Paula. 1980. "Immigrant Women and Consumer Protest: The New York City Kosher Meat Boycott of 1902." *American Jewish History* 70:91–105.

Jacobson, Matthew Frye. 2002. *Special Sorrows: The Diasporic Imagination of Irish, Polish, and Jewish Immigrants in the United States*. Berkeley: University of California Press.

———. 1998. *Whiteness of a Different Color: European Immigrants and the Alchemy of Race*. Cambridge, MA: Harvard University Press.

Jasper, James M. 1998. *The Art of Moral Protest: Culture, Biography, and Creativity in Social Movements*. Chicago: University of Chicago Press.

Johnson, James Weldon. 1991. *Black Manhattan*. New York: De Capo Press.

Joselit, Jenna Weissman. 1994. *The Wonders of America: Reinventing Jewish Culture 1880–1950*. New York: Hill and Wang.

Kallen, Horace M. 1924. *Culture and Democracy in the United States: Studies in Group Psychology of the American Peoples*. New York: Boni and Liveright.

Kao, Grace, & Jennifer S. Thompson. 2003. "Racial and Ethnic Stratification in Educational Achievement and Attainment." *Annual Review of Sociology* 29:417–442. Karp, Abraham.1977. *The Golden Door to America: The Jewish Immigrant Experience*. New York: Viking Books.

Katznelson, Ira. 2005. *When Affirmative Action Was White: An Untold History of Racial Inequality in Twentieth-Century America*. New York: W. W. Norton

Kazal, Russell A. 1995. "Revisiting Assimilation: The Rise, Fall, and Reappraisal of a Concept in American Ethnic History." *American Historical Review* 100(2):427–471.

Keating, AnaLouise. 1996. *Women Reading Women Writing: Self-Invention in Paula Gunn Allen, Gloria Anzaldúa, and Audre Lorde*. Philadelphia: Temple University Press.

Kelley, Robin D. G. 1996. *Race Rebels: Culture, Politics, and the Black Working Class.* New York: Free Press.

Kersten, Andrew E. 2002. "African Americans and World War II." *Magazine of History* 16(3):13–17.

Kincheloe, Joe L., & Shirley R. Steinberg. 1998. "Addressing the Crisis of Whiteness: Reconfiguring White Identity in a Pedagogy of Whiteness." In *White Reign: Deploying Whiteness in America*, edited by Joe L. Kincheloe, Shirley R. Steinberg, Nelson M. Rodriguez, & Ronald E. Chennault. New York: St. Martin's Press.

King, Joyce E. 1995. "Culture-Centered Knowledge: Black Studies, Curriculum Transformation, and Social Action." In *The Handbook of Research on Multicultural Education*, edited by James A. Banks & Cherry A. Banks. New York: Macmillan.

———. 1991. "Black Student Alienation and Black Teachers' Emancipatory Pedagogy." In *Readings on Equal Education*, Volume 11: *Qualitative Investigations into Schools and Schooling*, edited by Michele Foster. New York: AMS Press.

King, Ryan D., & Melissa F. Weiner. 2007. "Group Position, Collective Threat, and American Anti-Semitism." *Social Problems* 54(1):47–77.

Klandermans, Bert, Jojanneke van der Toorn, & Jacquelien van Stekelenburg. 2008. "Immigrant Embeddedness and Identity: How Immigrants Turn Grievances Into Action." *American Sociological Review* 73(6):992–1012.

Kluger, Richard. 1977. *Simple Justice: The History of Brown v. Board of Education and Black America's Struggle for Equality.* New York: Knopf.

Kosak, Hadassa. 2000. *Cultures of Opposition: Jewish Immigrant Workers, New York City, 1881–1905.* Albany: State University of New York Press.

Kubal, Timothy J. 1998. "The Presentation of Political Self: Cultural Resonance and the Construction of Collective Action Frames." *Sociological Quarterly* 39(4):539–554.

Kymlicka, Will. 1995. *Multicultural Citizenship: A Liberal Theory of Minority Rights.* Oxford: Clarendon Press.

Kymlicka, Will, & Wayne Norman, eds. 2000. *Citizenship in Diverse Societies.* New York: Oxford University Press.

Ladson-Billings, Gloria. 1994. *The Dreamkeepers: Successful Teachers of African American Children.* New York: Routledge & Kegan Paul.

———. 1992. "Liberatory Consequences of Literacy: A Case of Culturally Relevant Instruction for African American Students." *Journal of Negro Education* 61(3):378–391.

Ladson-Billings, Gloria, & William F. Tate. 1995. "Towards a Critical Race Theory of Education." *Teachers College Record* 97:47–68.

Lapson, Judah. 1945. *Hebrew in New York High Schools and Colleges.* New York: Bureau of Jewish Education.

———. 1941. "A Decade of Hebrew in the High Schools of New York City." *Journal of Jewish Education* 13(1):34–45.

Larsen, Luke J. 2004. *The Foreign-Born Population in the United States: 2003.* Washington, D.C.: U.S. Census.

Lerner, Michael, & Cornel West. 1996. *Jews & Blacks: A Dialogue on Race, Religion, and Culture in America.* New York: Plume.

Levine, Lawrence W. 1977. *Black Culture and Black Consciousness: Afro-American Folk Thought from Slavery to Freedom.* New York: Oxford University Press.

Lewis, David Levering. 1997. *When Harlem Was in Vogue.* New York: Penguin Books.

Lewisohn, Edwin R. 1965. *John Purroy Mitchel: The Boy Mayor of New York.* New York: Astra Books.

Lieberman, Joshua. n.d. *A New Approach to the Education of American Jewish Children.* New York: Jewish Education Committee of New York.

Lipsitz, George. 1998. *The Possessive Investment in Whiteness: How White People Profit from Identity Politics.* Philadelphia: Temple University Press.

Loewen, James. 2006. *Sundown Towns: A Hidden Dimension of American Racism.* New York: New Press.

Lukes, Steven. 1974. *Power: A Radical View.* Hampshire, UK: Palgrave.

Mahoney, James. 2000. "Path Dependence in Historical Sociology." *Theory and Society* 29(4):507–548.

Mansbridge, Jane, & Aldon Morris. 2001. *Oppositional Consciousness: The Subjective Roots of Social Protest.* Chicago: University of Chicago Press.

Markowitz, Gerald, & David Rosner. 1996. *Children, Race, and Power: Kenneth and Mamie Clark's Northside Center.* Charlottesville: University of Virginia Press.

Marshall, T. H. 1992. *Citizenship and Social Class.* Concord, MA: Pluto Press.

Martin, Waldo E. Jr. 2005. *No Coward Soldiers: Black Cultural Politics in Post-War America.* Cambridge, MA: Harvard University.

Marty, Martin E. 1976. *A Nation of Behaviors.* Chicago: University of Chicago Press.

Marx, Gary T. 1967. *Protest and Prejudice: A Study of Belief in the Black Community.* New York: Harper & Row.

Massey, Douglas S. 1995. "The New Immigration and Ethnicity in America." *Population and Development Review* 21(3):631–652.

Massey, Douglas S., & Nancy Denton. 1993. *American Apartheid: Segregation and the Making of the Underclass.* Cambridge, MA: Harvard University Press.

McAdam, Doug. 1999. *Political Process and the Development of Black Insurgency, 1930–1970.* 2nd ed. Chicago: University of Chicago Press.

———. 1983. "Tactical Innovation and the Pace of Insurgency." *American Sociological Review* 48(6):735–54.

McAdam, Doug, Sidney Tarrow, & Charles Tilly. 2001. *Dynamics of Contention.* New York: Cambridge University Press.

McCarthy, Cameron. 1998. *The Uses of Culture: Education and the Limits of Ethnic Affiliation.* New York: Routledge.

McCarthy, John D., & Meyer N. Zald. 1973. *The Trend of Social Movements in America: Professionalization and Resource Mobilization.* Morristown, NJ: General Learning Press.

McDowell, Winston C. 1984. "Race and Ethnicity in the Harlem Jobs Campaign, 1932–1935." *Journal of Negro History* 69(3/4):34–46.

McIntosh, Peggy. 1997. "White Privilege and Male Privilege: A Personal Account of Coming to See Correspondences through Work in Women's Studies." In *Critical White Studies: Looking Behind the Mirror*, edited by Richard Delgado & Jean Stefancic. Philadelphia: Temple University Press.

McKay, Claude. 1940. *Harlem—Negro Metropolis.* New York: E. P. Dutton.

Meier, August, & Elliott Rudwick. 1976. *From Plantation to Ghetto.* 3rd ed. New York: Hill & Wang.

Metzger, L. Paul. 1971. "American Sociology and Black Assimilation: Conflicting Perspectives." *American Journal of Sociology* 76(4):627–647.

Mills, Charles W. 1997. *The Racial Contract.* Ithaca, NY: Cornell University Press.

Modood, Tariq. 2007. *Multiculturalism.* Boston: Polity Press.

Mohanty, Chandra Talpade. 1991. "Introduction. Cartographies of Struggle: Third World Women and the Politics of Feminism." In *Third World Women and the Politics of Femi-*

nism, edited by Chandra Talpade Mohanty, Ann Russo, & Lourdes Torres. Bloomington: Indiana University Press.

Mohl, Raymond A. 1974. "Schools, Politics, and Riots: The Gary Plan in New York City, 1914–1917." *Paedagogica Historica* 15(1):39–72.

Moore, Deborah Dash. 1981. *At Home in America: Second Generation New York Jews.* New York: Columbia University Press.

———. 1976. "Jewish Ethnicity and Acculturation in the 1920s: Public Education in New York City." *Jewish Journal of Sociology* 18(2):96–104.

Moore, Richard B. 1992. *The Name "Negro": Its Origin and Evil Use.* Baltimore: Black Classic Press.

Moreau, Joseph. 2003. *School Book Nation: Conflicts over American History Textbooks from the Civil War to the Present.* Ann Arbor: University of Michigan Press.

Morris, Aldon, B. 1984. *The Origins of the Civil Rights Movement: Black Communities Organizing for Change.* New York: Macmillan/FreePress.

Morris, Aldon B., & Jane Mansbridge, eds. 2001. *Oppositional Consciousness: The Subjective Roots of Social Protest.* Chicago: University of Chicago Press.

Morris, Vivian Gunn, & Curtis L. Morris. 2002. *The Price They Paid: Desegregation in an African American Community.* New York: Teachers College Press.

Morrison, Toni. 1993. *Playing in the Dark: Whiteness and the Literary Imagination.* New York: Vintage.

Morrow, Raymond Allen, & Carlos Alberto Torres. 1995. *Social Theory and Education: A Critique of Theories of Social and Cultural Reproduction.* Albany: State University of New York Press.

Motley, Mary Penick. 1987. *The Invisible Soldiers: The Experience of the Black Soldier in World War II.* Detroit: Wayne State University Press.

Moya, Paula M. 2002. *Learning from Experience: Minority Identity, Multicultural Struggles.* Berkeley: University of California Press.

Myrdal, Gunnar. 1944. *An American Dilemma.* New York: Harper and Bros.

Nagel, Joane. 1994. "Constructing Ethnicity: Creating and Recreating Ethnic Identity and Culture." *Social Problems* 41(1):152–168.

Naison, Mark. 1983. *Communists in Harlem during the Depression.* Urbana: University of Illinois Press.

Naples, Nancy A. 2003. *Feminism and Method: Ethnography, Discourse Analysis, and Activist Research.* New York: Routledge.

———. 1996. "Activist Mothering: Cross-Generational Continuity in the Community Work of Low-Income Urban Neighborhoods." In *Race, Class and Gender: Common Bonds, Different Voices,* edited by Esther Ngan-Chow, Doris Wilkinson, & Maxine Baca Zinn. Thousand Oaks, CA: Sage.

Nasaw, David. 1979. *Schooled to Order: A Social History of Public Schooling in the United States.* New York: Oxford University Press.

Oakes, Jeannie. 2005. *Keeping Track: How Schools Structure Inequality.* 2nd ed. New Haven: Yale University Press.

Oliver, Mary Beth, & G. Blake Armstrong. 1998. "The Color of Crime: Perceptions of Caucasians' and African-Americans' Involvement in Crime." In *Entertaining Crime: Television Reality Programs,* edited by Mark Fishman & Gray Cavender. New York: Aldine de Gruyter.

Omi, Michael, & Howard Winant. 1994. *Racial Formation in the United States from the 1960s to the 1990s.* 2nd ed. New York: Routledge.

Orsi, Robert A. 1988. *The Madonna of 115th Street: Faith and Community in Italian Harlem, 1880–1950*. New Haven: Yale University Press.

Osofsky, Gilbert. 1996. *Harlem: The Making of a Negro Ghetto, Negro New York, 1890–1930*. Chicago: Ivan R. Dee.

Ottley, Roi. 1943. *New World A-Coming: Inside Black America*. Boston: Houghton-Mifflin.

Ottley, Roi, & William J. Weatherby. 1967. *The Negro in New York: An Informal Social History, 1626–1940*. New York: New York Public Library.

Outlaw, Lucius Jr. 1998. "'Multiculturalism,' Citizenship, Education, and American Liberal Democracy." In *Theorizing Multiculturalism: A Guide to the Current Debate*, edited by Cynthia Willet. Malden, MA: Blackwell Publishers.

Page, Reba. 1987. "Lower-Track Classes at a College-Preparatory High School: A Caricature of Educational Encounters." In *Interpretive Ethnography of Education at Home and Abroad*, edited by George D. Spindler & Louise Spindler. Hillsdale, NJ: Lawrence Erlbaum.

Palmer, A. Emerson. 1905. *The New York Public School*. New York: Macmillan.

Park, Robert E. 1950. *Race and Culture*. Glencoe, IL: The Free Press.

Parker, Laurence, Donna Deyle, & Sofia Villenas, eds. 1999. *Race Is . . . Race Isn't: Critical Race Theory and Qualitative Studies in Education*. Boulder, CO: Westview Press.

Paul, Shuva, Sarah J. Mahler, & Michael Schwartz. 1997. "Mass Action and Social Structure." *Political Power and Social Theory* 11:45–99.

Piven, Francis Fox, & Richard A. Cloward. 1977. *Poor People's Movements: Why They Succeed, How They Fail*. New York: Vintage.

Podair, Jerald E. 2003. *The Strike That Changed New York: Blacks, Whites, and the Ocean Hill–Brownsville Crisis*. New Haven: Yale University Press.

Popkewitz, Thomas S., & Lynn Fendler, eds. 1999. *Critical Theories in Education: Changing Terrains of Knowledge and Politics*. New York: Routledge.

Portes, Alejandro, & Min Zhou. 1993. "The New Second Generation: Segmented Assimilation and Its Variants." *Annals of the American Academy of Political and Social Science* 530:74–96.

Prell, Riv-Ellen. 1999. *Fighting to Become Americans: Jews, Gender, and the Anxiety of Assimilation*. Boston: Beacon Press.

Pride, Richard A. 2002. *The Political Use of Racial Narratives: School Desegregation in Mobile, Alabama, 1954–97*. Urbana: University of Illinois Press.

Pritchett, Wendell E. 2002. *Brownsville, Brooklyn: Jews, Blacks, and the Changing Face of the Ghetto*. Chicago: University of Chicago Press.

Public Education Association. 1955. *The Status of the Public School Education of Negro and Puerto Rican Children in New York City*. New York: New York University Research Center for Human Relations.

Rasler, Karen. 1996. "Concessions, Repression, and Political Protest in the Iranian Revolution." *American Sociological Review* 61(1):132–152.

Ravitch, Diane. 1968. *The Great School Wars: A History of the New York City Public Schools*. Baltimore: Johns Hopkins University Press.

Reid, Ira De A. 1927. "Mirrors of Harlem—Investigations and Problems of American's Largest Colored Community." *Social Forces* 5(4):628–634.

Rieder, Jonathan. 1985. *Canarsie: The Jews and Italians of Brooklyn Against Liberalism*. Cambridge, MA: Harvard University Press.

Rischin, Moses. 1986. "Germans versus Russians." In *The American Jewish Experience*. 2nd ed, edited by Jonathan D. Sarna. New York: Holmes & Meier.

———. 1978. *The Promised City, New York's Jews, 1870–1914*. Cambridge, MA: Harvard University Press.

Rist, Ray C. 1970. "Student Social Class and Teacher Expectations: The Self-Fulfilling Prophecy in Ghetto Education." *Harvard Educational Review* 40(3):411–451.

Rizvi, Fazal. 1993. "Children and the Grammar of Popular Racism." In *Race, Identity and Representation in Education*, edited by Cameron McCarthy & Warren Chrichlow. New York: Routledge.

Robelen, Erik W. 2008. "NAEP Gap Continuing for Charters: Sector's Scores Lag in Three Out of Four Main Categories." *Education Week*, May 21.

Robinson, Cedric. 1983. *Black Marxism: The Making of Black Radical Tradition*. London: Zed Press.

———. 1997. *Black Movements in America*. New York: Routledge

Rodriguez, Nelson M. 1998. "Emptying the Content of Whiteness: Toward an Understanding of the Relation between Whiteness and Pedagogy." In *White Reign: Deploying Whiteness in America*, edited by Joe L. Kincheloe, Shirley R. Steinberg, Nelson M. Rodriguez, & Donald E. Chennault. New York: St. Martin's Press.

Roediger, David R. 1999. *The Wages of Whiteness: Race and the Making of the American Working Class*. Rev. ed. London and New York: Verso Books.

Rogers, David. 1968. *110 Livingston Street: Politics and Bureaucracy in the New York City Schools*. New York: Random House.

Rohrbacher, Stefan. 1997. "From Württemberg to America: A Nineteenth-Century German-Jewish Village on Its Way to the New World." In *The American Jewish Experience*. 2nd ed., edited by Jonathan Sarna. New York: Holmes & Meier.

Rosenwaike, Ira. 1972. "Estimates of the Jewish Old Population in the United States." *Research on Aging* 14(1):92–109.

Rubinow, I. M. 1907. *Economic Conditions of the Jews in Russia*. New York: Arno Press.

Rumbaut, Rubén G. 2005. "Turning Points in the Transition to Adulthood: Determinants of Educational Attainment, Incarceration, and Early Childbearing among Children of Immigrants." *Ethnic and Racial Studies* 28(6):1041–1086.

———1997. "Assimilation and Its Discontents: Between Rhetoric and Reality." *International Migration Review* 31(4): 923–60.

———1994. "The Crucible Within: Ethnic Identity, Self-Esteem, and Segmented Assimilation among Children of Immigrants." *International Migration Review* 28(1): 748–94.

Salzman, Jack, & Cornell West, eds. 1997. *Struggles in the Promised Land: Toward a History of Jewish-Black Relations in the United States*. New York: Oxford University Press.

Sarna, Jonathan D. 1997. *The American Jewish Experience*. 2nd ed. New York: Holmes & Meier.

Scheiner, Seth M. 1965. *Negro Mecca: A History of the Negro in New York City, 1885–1920*. New York: New York University Press.

Schemo, Diana Jean. 2004. "Charter Schools Trail in Results, U.S. Data Reveals." *New York Times*, August 17, A1.

Schwalbe, Michael L., & Douglas Mason-Schrock. 1996. "Identity Work as Group Process." *Advances in Group Processes* 13:113–147.

Scott, James C. 1990. *Domination and the Arts of Resistance: Hidden Transcripts*. New Haven: Yale University Press.

Sewell, William H. Jr. 1996. "Historical Events as Transformations of Structures: Inventing Revolution at the Bastille." *Theory and Society* 25(6):841–881.

Shandler, Jeffrey. 2000. "Beyond the Mother Tongue: Learning the Meaning of Yiddish in America." *Jewish Social Studies* 6(3):97–123.

Shapiro, Ian, & Will Kymlicka, eds. 1997. *Ethnicity and Group Rights.* New York: New York University Press.

Shujaa, Mwalimu J., ed. 1994. *Too Much Schooling, Too Little Education: A Paradox of Black Life in White Societies.* Trenton, NJ: Africa World Press.

Silvera, John D. 1969. *The Negro in World War II.* New York: Arno Press.

Sinkoff, Nancy. 1990. "Socialist and Community Yiddish Schools." In *The Encyclopedia of the American Left,* edited by Mari Jo Buhle, Paul Buhle, & Dan Georgakas. New York: Oxford University Press.

Smith, Dorothy E. 1990. *The Conceptual Practices of Power: A Feminist Sociology of Knowledge.* Toronto: University of Toronto Press.

Smith, Rogers M. 1993. "Beyond Tocqueville, Myrdal, and Hartz: The Multiple Traditions in America." *American Political Science Review* 87 (3): 549–566.

Snow, David A., & Leon Anderson. 1987. "Identity Work among the Homeless: The Verbal Construction and Avowal of Personal Identities." *American Journal of Sociology* 92(6):1336–1371.

Snow, David A., & Robert D. Benford. 1992. "Master Frames and Cycles of Protest." In *Frontiers of Social Movement Theory,* edited by Aldon D. Morris & Carol Mueller McClurg. New Haven: Yale University Press.

———. 1988. "Ideology, Frame Resonance, and Participant Mobilization." *International Social Movement Research* 1:197–217.

Sollors, Werner. 1989. *The Invention of Ethnicity.* New York: Oxford University Press.

Somers, Margaret R. 1995. "What's Political or Cultural about Political Culture in the Public Sphere? Toward an Historical Sociology of Concept Formation." *Sociological Theory* 13(2):113–144.

———. 1994. "The Narrative Constitution of Identity: A Relational and Network Approach." *Theory and Society* 23(5):605–649.

———. 1992. "Narrativity, Narrative Identity, and Social Action: Rethinking English Working-Class Formation." *Social Science History* 16(4):591–630.

Somers, Margaret R., & Gloria D. Gibson. 1994. "Reclaiming the Epistemological 'Other': Narrative and the Social Constitution of Identity." In *Social Theory and the Politics of Identity,* edited by Craig Calhoun. Malden, MA: Blackwell Publishers.

Soyer, Daniel. 1997. *Jewish Immigrant Associations and American Identity in New York, 1880–1939: Jewish Landsmanshaftn in American Culture.* Detroit: Wayne State University Press.

State Education Commissioner's Advisory Committee on Human Relations and Community Tensions. 1964. *Desegregating the Public Schools of New York City.* New York: Institute of Urban Studies, Teachers College, Columbia University.

Steinberg, Stephen. 2007. *Race Relations: A Critique.* Stanford, CA: Stanford University Press.

———. 1989. *The Ethnic Myth: Race, Ethnicity, and Class in America,* 2nd ed. Boston: Beacon Press.

Sterba, Christopher M. 2003. *Good Americans: Italian and Jewish Immigrants during the First World War.* New York: Oxford University Press.

Stern, Susan Parkinson. 1997. "Conversation, Research, and Struggles over Schooling in an African American Community." In *Community Activism and Feminist Politics: Organizing Across Race, Class, and Gender,* edited by Nancy Naples. New York: Routledge.

Stevens, Hope R. 1971. "Aspects of the Economic Structure of the Harlem Community." In *Harlem, U.S.A,* edited by John Henrik Clarke. New York: Collier.

Stryker, Sheldon. 1968. "Identity Salience and Role Performance." *Journal of Marriage and the Family* 30(4):558–564.

Szajkowski, Zosa. 1972. *The Attitude of American Jews to World War I, the Russian Revolutions of 1917, and Communism (1914–1945)*. New York: Ktav.

Takaki, Ronald. 2000. *Iron Cages: Race and Culture in 19th-Century America*. Rev. ed. New York: Oxford.

Tarrow, Sidney. 1998. *Power in Movement: Social Movements and Contentious Politics*. 2nd ed. New York: Cambridge University Press.

——. 1992. "Mentalities, Political Cultures, and Collective Action Frames: Constructing Meanings through Action." In *Frontiers in Social Movement Theory*, edited by Aldon D. Morris & Carol McClurg Mueller. New Haven: Yale University Press.

Taylor, Charles. 1994. *Multiculturalism: Examining the Politics of Recognition*. Princeton, NJ: Princeton University Press.

Taylor, Clarence. 1997. *Knocking at Our Own Door: Milton Galamison and the Struggle to Integrate New York City Schools*. New York: Columbia University Press.

Taylor, Verta, & Nancy E. Whittier. 1992. "Collective Identity in Social Movement Communities: Lesbian Feminist Mobilization." In *Frontiers of Social Movement Theory*, edited by Aldon D. Morris & Carol Mueller McClurg. New Haven: Yale University Press.

Thomas, William I., & Florian Znaniecki. 1918. *The Polish Peasant in Europe and America*. Boston: Richard G. Badger.

Tilly, Charles. 2002. *Stories, Identities, and Political Change*. Lanham, MD: Rowman & Littlefield.

——. 1978. *From Mobilization to Revolution*. Reading, MA: Addison-Wesley.

Trend, David. 1995. *The Crisis of Meaning in Culture and Education*. Minneapolis: University of Minnesota Press.

Trotter, Joe W. Jr. 2000. "From a Raw Deal to a New Deal? 1929–1945." In *To Make Our World Anew: A History of African Americans*, edited by Robin D. G. Kelley & Earl Lewis. New York: Oxford University Press.

——. 1991. *The Great Migration in Historical Perspective: New Dimensions of Race, Class, and Gender*. Bloomington: University of Indiana Press.

Tyack, David. 1974. *The One Best System: A History of American Urban Education*. Cambridge, MA: Harvard University Press.

Vallance, Elizabeth. 1974. "Hiding the Hidden Curriculum: An Interpretation of the Language of Justification in Nineteenth-Century Educational Reform." *Curriculum Theory Network* 4(1):5–21.

Van Ausdale, Debra, & Joe R. Feagin. 2001. *The First R: How Children Learn Race and Racism*. Lanham, MD: Rowman & Littlefield.

van den Berghe, Pierre. 1967. *Race and Racism: A Comparative Perspective*. New York: Wiley.

Van Denburg, Joseph K. 1912. *Causes of the Elimination of Students in Public Secondary Schools of New York City*. New York: Teachers College, Columbia University.

Vecoli, Rudolph. 1964. "Contadini in Chicago: A Critique of the 'Uprooted.'" *Journal of American History* 51(3):404–416.

Von Eschen, Penny M. 1997. *Race Against Empire: Black Americans and Anticolonialism, 1937–1957*. Ithaca, NY: Cornell University Press.

Wacquant, Loïc J. D. 1997. "For an Analytic of Racial Domination." *Political Power and Social Theory* 11:221–234.

Waldinger, Roger. 1996. *Still the Promised City? African-Americans and New Immigrants in Post-Industrial New York*. Cambridge, MA: Harvard University Press.

Walker, Vanessa S. 2000. "Valued Segregated Schools for African American Children in the South, 1935–1969: A Review of Common Themes and Characteristics." *Review of Educational Research* 70(3):253–285.

———. 1996. *Their Highest Potential: An African American School Community in the Segregated South.* Chapel Hill: University of North Carolina Press.

Warner, W.L., & L. Srole. 1945. *The Social Systems of American Ethnic Groups.* New Haven: Yale University Press.

Waters, Mary C. 1990. *Ethnic Options: Choosing Identities in America.* Berkeley: University of California Press.

Watkins, William H. 2001. *The White Architects of Black Education: Ideology and Power in America, 1865–1954.* New York: Teachers College Press.

Watkins, William H., James H. Lewis, & Victoria Chou, eds. 2001. *Race and Education: The Roles of History and Society in Educating African American Students.* Boston: Allyn & Bacon.

Weiner, Melissa F. 2008. "Integration and Educational Welfare: Black Activists' Preferences for the New York City Public Schools, 1950–1960." *The Sociological Quarterly* 50(1):89–119.

Weiner, Melissa F., & Bedelia Richards. 2008. "Bridging the Theoretical Gap: The Diasporized Hybrid in Sociological Theory." In *Hybrid Identities: Theoretical and Empirical Examinations*, edited by Keri E. Iyall Smith & Patricia Leavy. Boston: Brill.

Wenger, Beth. 1996. *New York Jews and the Great Depression: Uncertain Promise.* New Haven: Yale University Press.

Werbner, Pnina. 2005. "Honor, Shame, and the Politics of Sexual Embodiment among South Asian Muslims in Britain and Beyond: An Analysis of Debates in the Public Sphere." *International Social Science Review* 6(1):25–47.

West, Cornel. 2002. "A Genealogy of Modern Racism." In *Race Critical Theories*, edited by Philomena Essed & David Theo Goldberg. Malden, MA: Blackwell.

Whitebrook, Maureen. 2001. *Identity, Narrative, and Politics.* London and New York: Routledge.

Whyte, William F. 1993. *Street Corner Society: The Social Structure of an Italian Slum.* 4th ed. Chicago: University of Chicago Press.

Wilder, Craig Steven. 2001. *A Covenant with Color: Race and Social Power in Brooklyn.* New York: Columbia University Press.

Wilkerson, Isabel. 1989. "'African-American' Favored by Many of America's Blacks." *New York Times*, Jan. 31, A1, A14.

Willis, Paul E. 1981. *Learning to Labour: How Working Class Kids Get Working Class Jobs.* New York: Columbia University Press.

Wilson, Charles E. 1971. "Education in Harlem—I.S. 201 in Perspective." In *Harlem, U.S.A.*, edited by John Henrik Clarke. New York: Collier.

Winant, Howard. 1994. *Racial Conditions: Politics, Theory, Comparisons.* Minneapolis: University of Minnesota Press.

———. 2001. *The World Is a Ghetto: Race and Democracy Since World War II.* New York: Basic Books.

Winter, Nicholas J. G. 2008. *Dangerous Frames: How Ideas about Race and Gender Shape Public Opinion.* Chicago: University of Chicago Press.

Wirt, William. 1916. *The Official Wirt Reports to the Board of Education of New York City.* New York: Public Education Association.

Woodson, Carter G. 2000 (1933). *The Mis-Education of the Negro.* Chicago: African American Images.

Wynn, Neil A. 1993. *The Afro-American and the Second World War*. New York: Holmes & Meier.

Yan, Holly. 2009. "Weak Economy Takes its Toll on Dallas-Area Private Schools." *Dallas Morning News*, Feb. 26.

Young, Iris Marion. 1998. "Unruly Categories: A Critique of Nancy Fraser's Dual Systems Theory." In *Theorizing Multiculturalism: A Guide to the Current Debate*, edited by Cynthia Willett. Malden, MA: Blackwell Publishers.

———. 1990. *Justice and the Politics of Difference*. Princeton, NJ: Princeton University Press.

Yuval-Davis, Nira. 1997. *Gender and Nation*. London: Sage.

Zimmerman, Jonathan. 2002a. "Ethnics Against Ethnicity: European Immigrants and Foreign-Language Instruction, 1890–1940." *Journal of American History* 88(4):1383–1404.

———. 2002b. *Whose America? Culture Wars in the Public Schools*. Cambridge, MA: Harvard University Press.

Zitron, Celia Lewis. 1968. *The New York City Teachers Union, 1916–1964: A Story of Educational and Social Commitment*. New York: Humanities Press.

Zuberi, Tukufu, & Eduardo Bonilla-Silva, eds. 2008. *White Logic, White Methods: Racism and Methodology*. Lanham, MD: Rowman and Littlefield.

Zunz, Olivier. 1985. "American History and the Changing Meaning of Assimilation." *American Journal of Ethnic History* 4(2):53–73.

INDEX

ABOUT THE AUTHOR

MELISSA F. WEINER is an assistant professor of sociology at Quinnipiac University. She was born in a suburb of Boston but has been deeply influenced by her family's history in New York City. She completed her Ph.D. in sociology at the University of Minnesota in 2006. Her research and teaching areas include race/ethnicity, education, social movements, and popular culture.